Working With Emotion
in Psychodynamic,
Cognitive Behavior, and
Emotion-Focused
Psychotherapy

Working With Emotion

in Psychodynamic, Cognitive Behavior, and Emotion-Focused Psychotherapy

Leslie S. Greenberg, Norka T. Malberg, and Michael A. Tompkins

AMERICAN PSYCHOLOGICAL ASSOCIATION
Washington, DC

Published by
American Psychological Association
750 First Street, NE
Washington, DC 20002
www.apa.org

APA Order Department
P.O. Box 92984
Washington, DC 20090-2984
Phone: (800) 374-2721; Direct: (202) 336-5510
Fax: (202) 336-5502; TDD/TTY: (202) 336-6123
Online: http://www.apa.org/pubs/books
E-mail: order@apa.org

In the U.K., Europe, Africa, and the Middle East, copies may be ordered from
Eurospan Group
c/o Turpin Distribution
Pegasus Drive
Stratton Business Park
Biggleswade, Bedfordshire
SG18 8TQ United Kingdom
Phone: +44 (0) 1767 604972
Fax: +44 (0) 1767 601640
Online: https://www.eurospanbookstore.com/apa
E-mail: eurospan@turpin-distribution.com

Typeset in Goudy by Circle Graphics, Inc., Reisterstown, MD

Printer: Sheridan Books, Chelsea, MI
Cover Designer: Beth Schlenoff, Bethesda, MD

Library of Congress Cataloging-in-Publication Data
Names: Greenberg, Leslie S., author. | Malberg, Norka T., author. | Tompkins, Michael A., author.
Title: Working with emotion in psychodynamic, cognitive behavior, and emotion-focused psychotherapy / by Leslie S. Greenberg, Norka T. Malberg, and Michael A. Tompkins.
Description: Washington, DC : American Psychological Association, [2019] | Includes bibliographical references and index.
Identifiers: LCCN 2018045156 (print) | LCCN 2018046508 (ebook) | ISBN 9781433830792 (eBook) | ISBN 1433830795 (eBook) | ISBN 9781433830341 (pbk.) | ISBN 1433830345 (pbk.)
Subjects: | MESH: Emotions | Psychotherapy--methods | Psychotherapy, Psychodynamic | Emotion-Focused Therapy | Cognitive Therapy
Classification: LCC RC480.5 (ebook) | LCC RC480.5 (print) | NLM WM 420 | DDC 616.89/14--dc23
LC record available at https://lccn.loc.gov/2018045156

British Library Cataloguing-in-Publication Data
A CIP record is available from the British Library.

Printed in the United States of America

http://dx.doi.org/10.1037/0000130-000

10 9 8 7 6 5 4 3 2 1

CONTENTS

Working With Emotion
in Psychodynamic,
Cognitive Behavior, and
Emotion-Focused
Psychotherapy

1

INTRODUCTION

LESLIE S. GREENBERG, NORKA T. MALBERG,
AND MICHAEL A. TOMPKINS

Emotion is central to being human. It has been the focus of study in one way or another for thousands of years; however, after some early attention in psychology (James, 1890; McDougall, 1926), it largely was ignored by early therapeutic pioneers (e.g., Freud, 1896/1961; Skinner, 1974). Art and literature have repeatedly made use of emotion: For example, poetry and music evoke strong emotion and increase our appreciation of emotion as central to the human experience (Frost, 1934; Juslin & Sloboda, 2013). In the past decades, a sea change has occurred within the sciences—from affective neuroscience, to biology, to social and cultural studies—as investigators have tried to understand emotion (Damasio, 1999; Greco & Stenner, 2008; LeDoux, 1996, 2012; Panksepp, 1998). Psychotherapeutic approaches now are increasingly incorporating findings from the fields of psychology of emotion, from advances in physiological psychology, and from elsewhere. These influences have contributed to our collaboration in writing this book—an

http://dx.doi.org/10.1037/0000130-001
Working With Emotion in Psychodynamic, Cognitive Behavior, and Emotion-Focused Psychotherapy,
by L. S. Greenberg, N. T. Malberg, and M. A. Tompkins

3

example, we hope, of the value of psychotherapy integration and widening interdisciplinary collaboration.

The process of using language to label and identify different intensities of emotion can be a complex and even risky enterprise. Using language to make sense of what we feel was evolutionarily adaptive but, over time, also came to limit what we experience. People often create verbal narratives that may not capture the felt sense or intensity of their experience. In addition, emotion is not singular; rather, it presents in many colors and layers. Because emotion is dynamic and constantly shifting, it is difficult to capture in static categories.

Although researchers can study emotion in the laboratory, psychotherapy is a much more ecologically valid relational laboratory. In psychotherapy, we can observe the type of emotional experience and emotion processes that more closely capture lived emotion—that is, in a manner and at an intensity that occur as emotion actually affects lives (Greenberg, 2017; Whelton, 2004). As we discuss in this book, the challenge in psychotherapy is to surmount the restrictions made by both conceptual language and the findings of laboratory-based psychological science so that we may examine how psychotherapists actually understand and work with emotion in psychotherapy itself (Panksepp, Lane, Solms, & Smith, 2017).

Although different models of psychotherapy conceptualize and work with emotion in distinct ways, a primary goal of all psychotherapy approaches is to help people alleviate emotional suffering; psychotherapy approaches also strive to understand emotion and its contribution to the day-to-day experience of being human. Many features of the different models are similar; however, they often are viewed as more different than perhaps they really are. Perhaps one day, through collaborations such as ours, these models will merge to form a coherent view of emotion and an agreed on approach that will help people who suffer with emotional problems.

THREE VIEWS OF EMOTION IN PSYCHOTHERAPY

This section briefly summarizes the theoretical and practical understanding and the role of emotion in psychodynamic, cognitive behavior, and emotion-focused therapies. In subsequent chapters, we elaborate on these quick snapshots.

The Psychodynamic View of Emotion

All throughout its history, psychoanalysis has considered emotions as gateways to meaning in the context of the therapeutic relationship between a client—who usually arrives with a set of concerns, problems, or ways in which he or she feels stuck—and a therapist—who bring his or her own emotional history to the relationship. Typically, some level of psychic and emotional pain constitutes the initial motivation to seek therapy. The therapist's initial posture of empathy and curiosity is an invitation to the client to find the motivation to work toward increased self-observation and to explore difficult thoughts and feelings while the therapist is fully present by supporting and "being with" the client. Psychoanalysis sees emotion emerging in the context of a therapeutic relationship built on basic trust and genuine curiosity. The hope is that such exploration will deepen the understanding and management of emotions in the context of emotions emerging in the here and now of the transference. The transference is used as a sort of relational pretend space in which therapist and client can explore those emotions. In this context, emotion is taught as an experiential process, a way to explore the client's internal world with all the representations of self and other that the client historically had constructed in the context of significant relationships.

A client's attachment behavioral patterns are activated in the context of the therapeutic relationship. This sets the scene for the client to begin exploring his or her emotions in a potentially stressful situation and use his or her usual coping strategies alongside the emotions they produce. In the context of this relational matrix, the psychodynamic clinician looks for opportunities for exploration and manifestation of emotions. The main goal is to increase the sense of safety and personal freedom. In this way, psychoanalysis makes use of emotions as gateways to the client's psyche and functioning by inviting the client to revisit, reexperience, and process emotions. Emotions become a bridge to memories of the past that the client can experience again in the here and now of the therapeutic relationship. The psychoanalytic psychotherapist no longer is a blank slate, as traditionally described; instead, the therapist presents himself or herself as a person with his or her own feelings and thoughts who is inviting the client to explore the emotional dialogue in the room while the therapist listens to his or her own emotional experience in the context of an intersubjective environment created by two psychologies. Psychoanalysis seeks to offer a new developmental experience—one in which emotions can be expressed safely and responded to in a different way with somebody who is genuinely trying to mentalize the client's experience while supporting strategies for affect regulation. All psychodynamic interventions work with emotion while keeping the unconscious processes in mind. At the core of psychodynamic work is the belief that ownership of emotions and integration of both positive and negative feelings result in an increased sense of self and overall feeling of agency in relationships.

The Cognitive Behavior View of Emotion

According to the cognitive model, which is the theoretical model that underpins cognitive behavior therapy (CBT), thoughts or cognitions, emotions, and behaviors are interconnected. The goal of CBT is to teach clients skills and strategies to manage effectively the problems that they bring to therapy, particularly strategies that enable clients to alter or shift the unhelpful thoughts and beliefs that influence their emotional responses to internal and external events. Furthermore, emotional change is in the service of behavioral change. Often, these strategies include devising opportunities for clients to change their behaviors to gather new and more helpful information. This new information then inhibits or counters unhelpful or maladaptive thoughts and beliefs. For example, individuals who are afraid to ride elevators but who ride elevators nonetheless, will, with time, become less fearful because they learn that elevators are not as dangerous as they perceive.

CBT includes a number of strategies, regardless of the problem, that use emotion to achieve the overarching goal of assisting clients to live fully and effectively. Psychoeducation plays an important role in assisting psychological change. Cognitive behavior therapists assist clients to understand emotion and its role in the problems that bring them to therapy. In the early phase of CBT, the primary goal is to enhance the client's emotional intelligence. Often, clients are perplexed by what they are feeling and may not even have the language to describe it. Psychoeducation includes not only education about emotions themselves but introduces clients to the cognitive model and how this model maintains psychological problems.

An important goal of CBT is to teach clients skills to manage their emotions and behaviors in the service of resolving the problems that brought them to therapy. Unsurprisingly, those skills include cognitive, behavioral, and somatic skills to manage the physical features of intense emotion. However, in CBT, it is not sufficient to teach a skill to clients; rather, it is essential that clients gain confidence so they can use those skills in the presence of strong emotion. To that end, cognitive behavior therapists use a host of strategies, such as role plays or imagery, that bring emotion into the therapeutic moment so that clients can practice the skills they have learned when feeling anxious, angry, or depressed. Cognitive behavior therapists view emotion as the pathway to deep and durable new learning. The deepest learning occurs in the presence of the emotional state in which the old problematic learning occurred. Therapists then use a variety of experiential strategies to trigger the emotional experiences of clients so that clients learn something new that is accurate and helpful. Those strategies—many of them borrowed from other therapies—that cognitive behavior therapists use to generate emotion in therapy reflect the comprehensive and integrative nature of this psychological treatment approach.

The Emotion-Focused View of Emotion

Emotion-focused therapy (EFT) is an experiential approach based on both emotion theory and affective neuroscience views of emotion. EFT suggests that emotions are fundamentally adaptive; it adds clinical differentiations about different types of emotion to aid clinical work. Thus, emotions can be seen as healthy (i.e., adaptive) or unhealthy (i.e., maladaptive), and as primary, secondary, or instrumental. *Primary emotions* are the first emotions people have—their gut feelings. *Secondary emotions* are more self-protective or defensive, and they generally obscure primary emotions. *Instrumental emotions* are emotions expressed to achieve an aim and often are more manipulative in nature. Primary emotions can be adaptive, in which case they give us good information. They also can be maladaptive as a function, perhaps, of past trauma or attachment problems. In the present, they can become a reaction to the past and, thus, are no longer helpful in attaining need satisfaction.

In addition, emotion schematic memory structures, or emotion schemes, are of central importance in EFT. An *emotion scheme* is an internal mental structure formed from lived emotional experience (Greenberg, 2011). Emotion schemes are action and experience that produce structure, as opposed to a *cognitive schema*, which produces a belief in language. When a child comes into the world, we do not teach that child how to be angry or sad—that is hardwired. However, what the child becomes angry at or sad about is a function of learning and is formed into, and later activated through, an emotion scheme. The emotion scheme produces experience and is the target of therapy. Lack of awareness of adaptive emotions and arousal of painful emotions by activation of maladaptive schemes are the source of many psychological difficulties.

According to EFT, feeling is the master, and cognition is the servant. In situations of great personal significance, what people feel influences what they think, much more than vice versa. In EFT, cognition is brought to emotion to make sense of it, thus transforming the client from a passive recipient of emotion into an active agent who understands and can influence the emotion.

EFT therapists help people to effectively process their emotions by getting them to approach, accept, express, regulate and tolerate, understand

and reflect on, and, perhaps most important, to transform their emotions. All are different processes, and each is a basis for intervention. To help process emotion in that way, EFT therapists offer a facilitative relationship in which the therapist is present in the moment, is empathically attuned to affect moment by moment, and creates a collaborative alliance. This is a strongly process-oriented approach. Therapists keep their finger on the client's emotional pulse, reading the client's and their own bodily felt sense and action tendencies moment by moment and responding to the client's momentary shifting states. Through a client's body posture, pitch rise in voice, disconnected eye gaze, or tight facial expression, a therapist may sense that the client is not feeling safe—and that the therapist may have said something that has led the client to not feel heard. The therapist then adjusts accordingly and subsequently intervenes to try to correct any misattunement. The therapist then watches to see if his or her responses cause the client's facial expression to soften or the client to breathe more deeply, and to see if the client again feels safe in the relationship or that a tear in the alliance has been repaired.

In EFT, therapists help people stay in touch with their feelings and allow feelings to serve their adaptive purpose. However, they also activate old, core, and painful maladaptive feelings and change them by activating new feelings. A key process is changing emotion with emotion. For example, the withdrawal tendencies of shame can be changed by activating the approach tendency of assertive anger, whereas the tendency to run away in fear can be changed by experiencing the tendency to reach out to seek comfort in sadness. Old emotional memories can be activated in the session and introduced to new in-session experience. This helps people change their emotional memories by a process of memory reconsolidation (Lane, Ryan, Nadel, & Greenberg, 2015; Nadel & Bohbot, 2001; Nader, Schafe, & LeDoux, 2000). Thus, the therapists activate emotion schematic memories in therapy to produce emotional experiences and then activate new emotions to change old ones (Greenberg, 2011, 2017).

EFT therapists facilitate acceptance of emotion by helping people sit with the feelings in a session. If the client is expressing an emotion, the therapist responds by compassionately empathizing with the painful aspect of the experience and helps the client articulate the meaning of the emotion. The therapist pays attention to the client's moment-by-moment experience and helps the client to not judge his or her emotions but genuinely accept them. EFT therapists help clients symbolize and put the emotion into words because putting feeling into words in and of itself has adaptive and regulating value (Kircanski, Lieberman, & Craske, 2012). Moreover, therapists help clients experience new emotions to change old ones (Fredrickson, Mancuso, Branigan, & Tugade, 2000; Lane et al., 2015).

ORGANIZATION OF THE BOOK

Each of the next three chapters describes a different therapeutic model and the role of emotion in maintaining psychological problems within the respective model. In addition, each chapter describes the key role that emotion plays in the process of psychological change. Each chapter includes strategies that psychotherapists use to evoke emotion in the service of emotional change, such as those to enhance the awareness of emotion, symbolize emotion in words, encourage acceptance of emotion, and improve the capacity to regulate and express emotion, when doing so would be helpful. The overarching goal of all psychotherapies, including the three presented in this book, is to alleviate emotional suffering and to enhance the emotional competence of clients so that they can live more meaningful and fulfilling lives.

We have organized each chapter relative to several broad themes that cross the respective theoretical and psychotherapeutic approaches, such as emotion in development and learning, and the relationship between emotion and motivation. The authors present the emotion process in their respective approaches and the methods used to evoke and work with emotion. They also discuss the value and role of emotion in improving interpersonal relationships in the process of psychological change. Furthermore, they describe the role of emotion in the therapeutic relationship and how to work with emotion to develop and maintain an effective therapeutic alliance.

Chapter 2 looks at psychoanalytic and psychodynamic therapies. It examines the conceptualization of emotion particular to psychodynamic approaches and offers mentalization-based therapy as an example of a contemporary modification of psychodynamic technique based on the empirical findings of attachment and neurobiology. *Mentalization-based therapy* focuses on working with emotions and guiding the scaffolding of the treatment based on the intensity and frequency of emotional dysregulation in the client and the mentalization failures that result from them. In that context, the process of identifying the current feeling between client and therapist is seen as central. Furthermore, that chapter examines the process of psychodynamic therapy and the use of essential technical tools in the process of working with emotions: the therapeutic alliance, interpretation of defenses, work in the transference, and the therapist's countertransference. Case materials throughout the chapter help the reader to trace the evolution of psychoanalytic theory and technique in the context of emotion.

Chapter 3 begins with a description of CBT and explains the cognitive behavior conceptualization of emotion and its relationship to cognition. The chapter presents several strategies in Beckian and other CBT approaches that cognitive behavior therapists use to evoke and work with emotion.

Chapter 4 briefly describes the third approach and explains EFT's conceptualization of emotion and the strategies it brings to working with emotion. The chapter discusses different types of intervention from empathic attunement to affect, to focusing on a bodily felt sense to aid symbolization of emotion, to the psychodramatic use of empty chair dialogues and imagery to stimulate emotion. Case vignettes illustrate different processes.

Chapter 5 compares and contrasts the three psychotherapeutic models and their approaches to working with emotion. In this final chapter, the authors identify a number of common themes among the three approaches. For example, they all view the appearance of emotion arousal as a clinically relevant event, recognize the importance of identifying the origins of emotion and what that means for treatment, value working with emotion in session, and emphasize the vital role of the therapeutic relationship in working with emotion in and across sessions.

In all chapters, materials have been disguised to protect client confidentiality.

Audience

This book is appropriate for graduate-level courses and for psychotherapy practitioners of all orientations who wish to learn different approaches to working with emotion. In addition, it will be helpful in a general way for people in the helping professions, such as nurses, doctors, and teachers to help them understand different approaches to dealing with emotion.

Accompanying Video Series

The three authors of this book have contributed to a series of American Psychological Association videos titled the *Emotion in Psychotherapy Video Series*. The video series includes four programs. Three of them, one for each psychotherapy approach, include the authors as guest experts who describe their particular psychotherapy model and approach, and present video segments to illustrate how their approach works with emotion. In the fourth and final program, the three authors discuss the different video segments that each had selected. Although the video series and this book are standalone products, this book complements the video series because it continues and elaborates our conversations regarding the important role of emotion in our psychotherapeutic work. The videos are available online (see http://www.apa.org/pubs/videos/browse.aspx?query=series:Emotion+in+Psychotherapy).

REFERENCES

Damasio, A. R. (1999). *The feeling of what happens: Body and emotion in the making of consciousness*. New York, NY: Harcourt Brace.

Fredrickson, B. L., Mancuso, R. A., Branigan, C., & Tugade, M. M. (2000). The undoing effect of positive emotions. *Motivation and Emotion, 24*, 237–258. http://dx.doi.org/10.1023/A:1010796329158

Freud, S. (1961). The aetiology of hysteria. In J. Strachey (Ed. and Trans.), *The standard edition of the complete psychological works of Sigmund Freud* (Vol. 3, pp. 189–224). London, England: Hogarth Press. (Original work published 1896; addendum originally published 1924)

Frost, R. (1934). *Selected poems* (3rd edition). New York, NY: Holt.

Greco, M., & Stenner, P. (Eds.). (2008). *Emotions: A social science reader*. New York, NY: Routledge.

Greenberg, L. S. (2011). *Emotion-focused therapy*. Washington, DC: American Psychological Association.

Greenberg, L. S. (2017). *Emotion-focused therapy* (Rev. ed.). Washington, DC: American Psychological Association.

James, W. (1890). *Principles of psychology* (Vol. 1). New York, NY. Holt.

Juslin, P. N., & Sloboda, J. A. (2013). Music and emotion. In D. Deutsch (Ed.), *The psychology of music* (3rd ed., pp. 583–645). New York, NY: Academic Press. http://dx.doi.org/10.1016/B978-0-12-381460-9.00015-8

Kircanski, K., Lieberman, M. D., & Craske, M. G. (2012). Feelings into words: Contributions of language to exposure therapy. *Psychological Science, 23*, 1086–1091. http://dx.doi.org/10.1177%2F0956797612443830

Lane, R. D., Ryan, L., Nadel, L., & Greenberg, L. (2015). Memory reconsolidation, emotional arousal, and the process of change in psychotherapy: New insights from brain science. *Behavioral and Brain Sciences, 38*, e1. http://dx.doi.org/10.1017/S0140525X14000041

LeDoux, J. (1996). *The emotional brain: The mysterious underpinnings of emotional life*. New York, NY: Simon and Schuster.

LeDoux, J. (2012). Rethinking the emotional brain. *Neuron, 73*, 653–676. http://dx.doi.org/10.1016/j.neuron.2012.02.004

McDougall, W. (1926). The derived emotions [Supplementary Chapter 2]. In W. McDougall, *An introduction to social psychology* (Rev. ed.). Boston, MA: Luce.

Nadel, L., & Bohbot, V. (2001). Consolidation of memory. *Hippocampus, 11*, 56–60. http://dx.doi.org/10.1002/1098-1063(2001)11:1<56::AID-HIPO1020>3.0.CO;2-O

Nader, K., Schafe, G. E., & LeDoux, J. E. (2000). Fear memories require protein synthesis in the amygdala for reconsolidation after retrieval. *Nature, 406*, 722–726. http://dx.doi.org/10.1038/35021052

Panksepp, J. (1998). *Affective neuroscience: The foundations of human and animal emotions*. New York, NY: Oxford University Press.

Panksepp, J., Lane, R. D., Solms, M., & Smith, R. (2017). Reconciling cognitive and affective neuroscience perspectives on the brain basis of emotional experience. *Neuroscience and Biobehavioral Reviews, 76*, 187–215. http://dx.doi.org/10.1016/j.neubiorev.2016.09.010

Skinner, B. F. (1974). *About behaviorism*. New York, NY: Knopf.

Whelton, W. J. (2004). Emotional processes in psychotherapy: Evidence across therapeutic modalities. *Clinical Psychology & Psychotherapy, 11*, 58–71. http://dx.doi.org/10.1002/cpp.392

2

PSYCHODYNAMIC PSYCHOTHERAPY AND EMOTION

NORKA T. MALBERG

> One of our greatest difficulties as a species concerns our ability to experience emotions, a difficulty caused by defects in our mental development. The experiencing of emotions depends on a great deal of constant work, which in turn presupposes the integrity of the apparatus that allows them to be assimilated, managed and contained. (Ferro, 2007, p. 1)

A theory of emotions is essential to an understanding of human thought and behavior. In 1930, Sigmund Freud (1930/1961a) pointed out that "it is not easy to deal scientifically with feelings" (p. 65). With that statement, he recognized the inherently ambiguous and complex nature of emotions.

Freud did not leave a single theory of emotions but, rather, a series of theories difficult to reconcile with one another. After his death in 1939, psychoanalysts returned to the topic of emotions in an effort to devise a theory that would be conceptually viable and meet their theoretical and practical needs. A survey of psychoanalytic literature demonstrates that the

http://dx.doi.org/10.1037/0000130-002
Working With Emotion in Psychodynamic, Cognitive Behavior, and Emotion-Focused Psychotherapy,
by L. S. Greenberg, N. T. Malberg, and M. A. Tompkins

concepts of instinct or drive did not provide a foundation on which a theory of emotion could be built successfully. However, the shift in the contemporary psychoanalytic landscape toward a *two-person psychology*, that is, a focus on the interaction of two subjectivities in the consulting room—namely, the client's and the therapist's—ideally results in a therapeutic exchange marked by the coconstruction of meaning around the emerging emotions in the room.

Furthermore, as this chapter seeks to illustrate, this new state of affairs allows for a bridge between the drive (i.e., the internal experience) and object relations (i.e., the relationships between an individual and others). This interactive model of emotion between internal and external experiences has influenced psychodynamic theory and practice regarding the understanding and the ways of working with emotion in the consulting room and outreach settings.

Contemporary psychodynamic practice comprises a kaleidoscope of schools of thought and practice, all of which work with emotion. One of the challenges one encounters when trying to summarize the evolution of a concept in psychoanalysis is that each school of psychoanalytic thought presents with a different explanatory language and different metaphors and versions of development.

In this chapter, I offer a brief survey of the evolution of the theory of affects in psychoanalysis followed by the implications of the theoretical evolution to the clinical practice of psychodynamic psychotherapy. The chapter starts with a look at Freud's thinking about affects in the context of theoretical evolution to connect it to clinical practice, a case study is introduced and considered through the different lenses of Freud's three models of the mind. Next is an exploration of the contributions of contemporary psychoanalysts to the theory of affects and the impact on contemporary clinical practice. Clinical cases (all of which are fictional but not far removed from what happens in therapy) are included to illustrate the technical impact of such theoretical formulations. Two sections describe the ways in which change and motivation are conceptualized in psychodynamic psychotherapy. A final section explores how psychodynamic thinking and clinical practice conceptualize and work with emotion in the clinical realm. Technical constructs, such as transference, are examined with a focus on emotion.

PSYCHOANALYTIC THEORY OF EMOTION IN FREUD'S THREE MODELS OF THE MIND

Freud's thinking regarding affects can be traced in the context of the development of his overall psychoanalytic theory (i.e., metapsychology) and practice. In my study of psychoanalysis, I have found that the evolution of

Freudian thinking is best understood by structuring one's learning around his three models of the mind: the affect-trauma, topographical, and structural models (Sandler, Holder, Dare, & Dreher, 1997).

Initially, the term *affect* encompassed the whole descriptive field of emotions. Freud himself did not define clear terminological boundaries, and it was only at a later stage that it became necessary to establish the difference between *affect, emotion,* and *feeling.*

According to British psychoanalyst Graham Music (2001), the concepts feeling, emotion, and affect have similar meanings in psychoanalysis. Psychoanalytic and ordinary dictionaries tend to define one in relation to the others. *Affect* is a less widely used concept and is seen mainly in the domains of academic psychology and theoretical psychoanalytic literature. It tends to have a more objective feel of something that can be observed rather than experienced. *Feeling,* on the other hand, denotes an internal state, someone's private experience. One cannot observe a feeling, but one can observe the effect of a feeling or see signs of someone's feelings. For psychoanalysts, *emotion* is the ordinary language equivalent of *affect* having a more objective quality than *feelings.* We talk about observing an emotional response in someone, and some have argued that the site of an emotion is the body, whereas the site of a feeling is the mind.

In this chapter, I adhere to these definitions and mostly speak of affect because it is the predominant word used in the psychoanalytic literature. Given the well-known complexity of the psychoanalytic lexicon, I have chosen to use clinical material to look at through the different lenses of Freud's models of the mind and the theory of affects in each of them.

Accompanying us through the evolution of Freud's thinking about affect is one of my clients, "Linda," a 16-year-old young woman referred due to repeated episodes of bodily self-harm (i.e., cutting) and panic attacks both at home and school characterized by freezing and uncontrolled vomiting (see Exhibit 2.1). Let's look at Linda's case from Freud's theoretical multiple lenses regarding affect.

Affect in the Affect-Trauma Model of the Mind

Psychoanalysis originated in Freud's study with Josef Breuer of the etiology and treatment of hysteria. Breuer and Freud (1895/1955) devised a model of the mind based on their findings from working clinically with hysteria. This model came to be known as the *affect-trauma model.* Affect, they held, was principally aroused by traumatic experiences via perceptions and ideas. Once aroused, the affect constituted an increase in the normally prevailing excitation in the nervous system to attempt to relieve this excess of excitation in some fashion to return to an optimal level (i.e., homeostasis).

EXHIBIT 2.1
Case Study: 'Linda'

Sixteen-year-old Linda entered twice-weekly psychotherapy with the chapter author after being referred by her school counselor, who was concerned about her increasing school phobic behavior and overall social isolation. Linda's motivation to seek psychotherapy emanated mainly from a great deal of emotional pain. She described herself as lonely and always sad and frightened. She spoke of not finding a better way of talking about it. Indeed, our sessions were filled with silence and tears during the initial period of our work. At times, she was able to give a detailed description of her latest panic attack or describe the sense of guilt and shame she felt after a self-harming episode. However, Linda seemed stuck; in her own words: "Her body took over all the time," as if she was not in control of it. Linda was the only child of two older (mid-50s) parents. She described a close relationship with her father and a competitive and ambivalent relationship with her mother.

By the time she was 16, she had been under the care of nine au pairs/nannies. Her parents described Linda as stubborn and uncommunicative. She had slept in her parents' room until the age of 8 due to night terrors, a practice she resumed at 14 years old. She now slept on the floor of her parents' room most evenings. Linda began to exhibit scars due to self-harming (i.e., cutting) at the age of 14 after her favorite nanny left the family. Shortly thereafter, she began to suffer from unprovoked and unexpected vomiting that frequently would occur in the middle of the school day. Social situations exacerbated both symptoms. Linda's self-harming had come to the attention of the school after two other students reported having witnessed it at the school's bathroom. The cuts were deep and mostly on her thighs and upper torso near her breasts.

In contemporary terms, this could be thought of as the process from affect dysregulation to regulation. These attempts to return to homeostasis take place through movements; sounds; secretions, such as tears; and actions known as expression of the affects. Based on their clinical experience, Freud and Breuer determined that affect may occur in three forms:

1. Spontaneous reactions to an event (e.g., freezing after exposure to a traumatic exchange or situation)
2. A transformed reaction to an event (e.g., a phobia to certain events that triggers affective reactions in the person related to the original trauma)
3. An induced reaction from the outside that causes either a or b (e.g., the environment's reaction to qualities or actions of the person)

During this period in Freud's thinking, affects were thought of as energy, that is, as quantity and force. Accordingly, accumulated affect could be disposed of by direct, real action, such as crying or running away; by indirect, verbal action; or by cognitive elaboration, such as talking about the experience and transforming its meaning (i.e., comparing "affected" ideas with normal ideas—similar to the focus of contemporary cognitive behavior interventions).

Freud and Breuer's clinical interests regarding affects differed slightly. Initially, for Freud, the main aim of therapeutic work was catharsis—meaning getting the feelings out—preferably but not necessarily with the accompaniment of the verbalization of the events and experiences that had surrounded them. Breuer, on the other hand, thought of affects as being experienced through some meaningful event that lingers as a material "foreign body" that must be let out and drained away. Already at this time, we can witness in Freud's writings his belief that what makes the conflict poignant and personally significant is the *affect that is attached* to it. The affect-trauma model asserts that undigested affect, which is neither metabolized (i.e., thought about, understood while experienced) nor let out (i.e., through expression of emotion), generates symptoms or causes illness.

Affect, at this stage, was not differentiated from *cathexis*, the sum of excitation or feelings. It was used to denote the more durable moods (e.g., melancholia), as well as sensations of pleasure and "un-pleasure" (e.g., sadness). Parallel to that development, we can see eventually became Freud's definition of the drives both as a charge and discharge phenomenon. As a *discharge* phenomenon, affect is captured by the psyche and expressed in the body (e.g., panic attack). As a *charge* phenomenon, it is manifested through intensity and through the significance of the representational field (i.e., a feeling is attached to an idea and able to be represented verbally).

During that period, Freud's theory would have considered Linda's symptoms (see Exhibit 2.1) as possibly the result of an early traumatic experience. Her use of the body indicated difficulties with creating a coherent verbal narrative of the early trauma that now was being expressed through the body, in this case, via the vomiting (i.e., release). From this perspective, for Linda, both self-harming and vomiting seemed to serve as a way of seeking a feeling of internal balance through the use of the body. Her inability to metabolize, represent, or verbalize her affective experience rendered her prisoner of a series of repetitive actions to create the illusion of balance. What is missing in this model is the impact of the loss of multiple caregivers, what psychodynamic thinking calls *object loss*. Linda's wish to exorcise the painful feelings of longing and emptiness through action (i.e., self-harming) was not providing her the necessary means to achieve reconstruction of the narrative of her early trauma of loss or long-term relief. She felt helpless and caught in a vicious cycle.

The other aspect that would have been a focus of clinical formulation at that time in psychoanalytic theory would have been the close and somewhat seductive relationship Linda had with her father and, potentially, the traumatic effect that relationship would have had during the period of puberty.

In summary, from this perspective, the traumatic event and its emotional impact are stored and represented in the body via the hysteric symptom (i.e., panic attacks and vomiting). Because the focus was on the internal management of an external trauma, the impact of multiple losses on further relationships and on Linda's sense of agency and ability to understand, modulate, and change such harmful behaviors would have not been considered as a main therapeutic aim. That does not mean those factors would not have emerged in response to the therapeutic intervention. This model of the mind, however, did not focus yet on this aspect of the work; it simply allowed a safe environment in which reproduction of reenactments of memories could take place—seeing that as the main mutative therapeutic factor.

Affects in the Topographical Model of the Mind

In 1900, Freud published "The Interpretation of Dreams" (Freud, 1900/1953) and, with it, the *topographical model of the mind*, which later was revised twice. In that context, affects were no longer equated solely with the reproduction of reenactments of memories but were seen as also linked with fantasies and wishes through their postulated common source, the instinctual drives. Furthermore, affects were considered indicators of significant unconscious dream contents; they were considered significant meaning bearers or signifiers. Freud argued that affects were not distorted in dreams but were either suppressed or detached from their accompanying ideas. What Freud called *dream work* was defined as the agency that deals with affects in the dream, organizing according to the wishes of the dreamer. Freud considered affects absolutely necessary for understanding the dream experience; they are, more than any other dream element, he said, reliable indicators of what the dream is about. So, when someone recounts a dream in the context of a psychodynamic session, the cognitive associations are relevant, but the emotions that come from those associations and the feelings felt by the dreamer in the dream and at the time of awakening are central to the analysis of a dream. Affects in this context are considered a compass that guides us toward an understanding of the unconscious wishes and fantasies.

The 5 years after the publication of "The Interpretation of Dreams" were extremely productive for Freud. His thinking about affects and the lack of clear differentiation among affects, feelings, and emotions continued throughout that period. Freud struggled with reconciling his aim of creating a general psychology with the influence of his clinical observation on his theorizing.

In 1915, Freud finalized the discharge theory of affect that had been implicit in many aspects of his thinking to that point. Many areas of Freud's thinking were integrated into his "Papers on Metapsychology" (Freud,

1915/1957b), and the theory of affect was one. Those papers were followed by profound modifications in Freud's thinking. However, it was only in the area of affect that he could be said to have altered his basic beliefs entirely. By 1915, he did not seem to consider affect only in terms of quantity or a state of mind but as a *drive-derived phenomenon*. The paper on instincts (Freud, 1915/1957a) does not deal explicitly with affects, but Freud discussed the feelings of love and hate as springing from different sources rather than being the opposite of each other.

Also, in 1915, Freud (1915/1957c) wrote about *repression*, another important theoretical construct that influenced his thinking about affects. The concept of repression, as well as other transformations, leads to a *topography of the mind* (Sandler et al., 1997) in which there are unconscious, preconscious, and conscious systems and, with it, the possibility of unconscious affects too. This is an important shift from placing emphasis on the external (i.e., trauma) impact toward a focus on the internal world of the client and the processes through which we manage affects in ways of which we are both aware and unaware. At that time, from Freud's perspective, the true task of repression was to deal with the quota of affect, although the vanished affect came back as social or moral anxiety and self-reproach (Freud, 1915/1957c). We can see that during that period, quantitative (i.e., amount) and qualitative (i.e., how experienced) aspects of the instincts were given the name *affects*, thus adding to the conceptual confusion that one feels when studying the genesis of the concept of affects in Freudian theory.

During my second year of work with Linda (see Exhibit 2.1), she had begun to bring dreams to our work. Usually, she would sit in silence, a cascade of tears falling down her face—but no facial expression—followed by a comment, or in this occasion, the report of her first dream:

> I am walking in a meadow, and I see my mom. She smiles at me, so I feel like I want to hug her. Then I hear a song, is a familiar song, one that makes me feel happy but sad. . . . I recognize it. I look. My mom is nowhere to be found now, and I am feeling very angry. . . . The song is playing louder, and I wake up. . . .

I asked Linda about her emotional state when she woke up and also invited her to tell me the thoughts that came to mind while telling me the dream. In response, Linda talked about how much she loved that song when she was about 11, when her favorite nanny came. She spoke about the fun things she used to do with her nanny, and her seemingly "cold tears" became infused with feeling and painful facial expression. She said she felt sad and, oddly, quite angry.

From a topographical perspective, one could conceptualize Linda's dream as an expression of her wish for the lost nanny and the repressed feelings she felt toward her mother: Perhaps rather simultaneously, she wished her mom to be gone so she could get the love and peaceful song in her nanny's voice. Yet, she also longed for her mom's love and presence. Furthermore, one could understand Linda's self-harming behavior as a way of dealing with her repressed conflicting (i.e., love and hate) feelings toward her mother. Linda was an only child and, since a young age, had struggled in her relationships with peers, who described her as a bossy and difficult playmate. As a toddler, she had been left in the care of multiple caregivers who described her as a difficult and tantrum-prone child. As an adolescent, she was now faced with an overweight female body and significant difficulty in managing her aggressive behavior, especially in the context of her wish to be liked and loved. This perception of herself as an unlovable, powerful bully was a significant source of anxiety for Linda, one that manifested itself mostly via bodily expressions and inhibition of her social functioning. Nights were scary because she was alone with her aggression. Linda's anxiety was coming from both inside (her fear over what she thought of as destructive aggression) and the anxiety from the outside (the increasing pressure from the world of peers and her parents' incapacity to help her contain and metabolize distressing thoughts and feelings).

Affect in the Structural Model of the Mind

Within the topographical model of the mind, there is an assumption that instinctual drive energy connected with repressed ideas may be converted into anxiety. In Freud's (1895/1950) first theory of anxiety, affects are seen as entirely drive derivatives, and anxiety represents a transformation of the instinctual drive energy of repressed contents. The topographical model presented some difficulties in terms of conceptualizing issues, such as the role of aggression in mental life. Initially, Freud (1915/1957a) allocated aggression to the self-preservative or ego drives and regarded it nonlibidinal (i.e., not attached emotionally to someone) in nature. Freud's struggles to conceptualize the concept of aggression within the topographical model of the mind was among many of the difficulties he encountered when putting his conceptualizations to the test in the context of clinical manifestations. For instance, he observed that people tended to unconsciously repeat patterns of behavior and experience that might be painful or self-damaging. Those observations led him to conceptualize the death drive (i.e., Thanatos), which he contrasted with the life instinct (i.e., Eros). Motivated by these observations, Freud's reformulations of theory led to a shift away from an emphasis on the movement from the depths to the surface—characteristic of the topographical model—toward a theoretical model that began to acknowledge both the role of the external and internal worlds, and their interaction. That shift sets the foundation for the development of a structural model of the mind.

With the introduction of the structural theory in "The Ego and the Id" (Freud, 1923/1961b), we entered the period of Freud's third model of the mind. The possibility to conceive of an agency that could respond with anxiety to both external and internal danger situations emerged. Those responses might or might not reach consciousness. Freud (1923/1961b) stated that "the ego is the actual seat of anxiety" (p. 56). In that way, he defined the ego as the adaptive portion of the personality. The second chapter of "The Ego and the Id" (Freud, 1923/1961b) returned to the question of whether affects can be unconscious, drawing to a conclusion that moved away from his stance in 1915, when he spoke of affect only in terms of quantity and described it as quality-less energy (Freud, 1915/1957a). Dealing clinically with issues such as narcissism and mourning (in Linda's case [see Exhibit 2.1], being able to mourn the loss of her nanny) began to challenge such a stance; the role of the external and its impact on the quality of the affect became obvious to Freud clinically, thus challenging him theoretically.

In 1926, in "Inhibitions, Symptoms and Anxiety," Freud (1926/1959) put the second theory of anxiety forward. It reflected a significant shift in his thinking that clearly was influenced by the challenges presented to him by the increasing clinical data. He introduced the concept of *signal anxiety*, arising within the ego as the main motive for defensive action. Here, anxiety was assumed to signal danger (usually experienced in the body at first and sometimes further represented in unpleasurable and disrupting thoughts) and motivate subconscious defensive processes (e.g., momentary disavowal of reality, projection).

In the first theory of anxiety, defense leads to anxiety; in the second one, anxiety leads to defense. As a result, the concept of anxiety became radically more complex and multidimensional. Anxiety was seen as a psychologically more elaborate feeling, an experience with symbolic contents (i.e., meaning) rather than a mere sensation. Freud did not give up the idea that emotions are mobile, able to change the objects on which they are attached and to change themselves into different emotions, notably, into their opposites (e.g., love transformed into hate, gratitude into envy, fear into defiance) and into anxiety. Anxiety occupied a privileged position in psychoanalytic studies of emotion. Initially seen as an emotional waste product that offered an outlet for all poorly discharged emotions (including love and hate, anger and jealousy), anxiety came to be seen increasingly either as the psychological state to be defended against or as a signal that alerts the ego to the imminence of danger, thus setting off defensive mechanisms, such as repression (Freud, 1915/1957c).

The concept of *signal affect* implied anticipation and symbolization. Signal anxiety involved the transformation of traumatic anxiety to a thoughtlike communication within the psyche. The concept of signal anxiety introduced new regulatory and communicative dimensions of affect. It was a developmental skill acquired in the context of experience and maturation. (Blum, 1991). Furthermore, it comprised the unconscious status of the signal and introduced the emotional significance of situations for the person who experienced them. It also introduced the idea of those experiences, informing the way that we think of others internally—what psychoanalysis calls *internalized object relations* (i.e., the way we see ourselves in relationships and how we think others see us).

In Linda's case (see Exhibit 2.1), for example, her panic attacks signaled her desire to seek proximity to her mom out of anxious tension and helplessness. Linda was unaware that feeling angry with her mom motivated the proximity seeking. Looking at Linda's case from a structural lens, we are able to understand her symptomatology as the response to internal and external forces, the theoretical seeds for what is today's focus in psychoanalysis on the interaction between the intrapersonal and the interpersonal when trying to observe, understand, and work with emotion in the context of psychotherapy.

POST-FREUDIAN THEORY OF AFFECTS

Psychoanalytic theory after Freud's death in 1939 was in a state of fermenting diversity. Embedded in those efforts were various ways to conceptualize emotions and how to work with them. Eventually, two groups evolved to carry psychoanalytic theory further. In the United Kingdom, efforts were focused on reconciling the "dynamic" and "experiential" dimensions of psychic reality. Namely, they sought how to understand, conceptualize, and work the relationship with what happened inside (i.e., dynamically) in the context of the relationship with the external world and its demands for adaptation (i.e., experiential). In Vienna and the United States, there was a focus on developing a protobiological aspect of psychoanalytic theory, eventually known as *ego psychology*. The British group, represented by Balint, Winnicott, and Fairbairn, among others, laid greater stress on the experiential and the interpersonal. They focused on the importance of the first relationships in the lives of a person and how those relationships inform the person's personality development and the way in which he or she interacts with the world, thus departing from an internal set of experiences that inform who they see themselves to be in relationships.

In contrast, proponents of ego psychology began to develop a framework in which affect development and maturation were discussed mostly in terms of the ability to delay, to tolerate tension, or to bind energy (Rapaport, 1953). Affects were conceived in the framework of early ego psychology as energies that became increasingly structuralized, even tamed, in the context of development (Fenichel, 1945). Eventually, affects came to be seen either as experiences to be defended against or as cognitive and motivational tools of the ego, that is, providing information to the ego about psychic states. From this perspective, affects now were regarded partly as ego functions (i.e., defensive and adaptive) and partly as stimuli controlled by the ego (i.e., the agency-managing conflicts emerging from the interaction of the internal [i.e., id] and the external worlds [i.e., superego] of the client).

In contemporary psychodynamic theory and practice, we increasingly witness the integration of both of these schools of thought: object relations and ego psychology. As a result, there is a focus on the impact of relationships and on the impact on the internal conflicts and adaptations. As I hope to illustrate in the further pages of this chapter, thought integration has significant implications for the practice of psychodynamic psychotherapy and psychoanalysis in the context of emotions. To illustrate, I have chosen to review briefly the work of two post-Freudian psychoanalytic authors who explored further the role of emotion in psychoanalysis: Wilfred Bion and Joseph Sandler. Following that review, I introduce an example of contemporary developmental psychodynamic psychotherapy in the work of Peter Fonagy, a contemporary psychoanalytic psychologist and clinical researcher.

Wilfred Bion: The Containment and Metabolization of Emotion

Wilfred Bion expanded on the original work of Melanie Klein, a child and adult psychoanalyst. Bion's (1962) theoretical work is complex, but his clinical applications to working with emotion have proven invaluable to infusing awareness of the role of emotion into psychodynamic clinical practice. In Bion's theory, the term *emotions* is not given specific emphasis. However, his writings indicate a continual engagement with the complexities of emotional life. In 1970, Bion wrote, "What takes place in the consulting room is an emotional situation" (p. 118). For him, the unifying concept is that of the psyche and its functioning. The purpose of the psyche is to tame and contain thoughts and emotions; for example, to make tolerable the experience of "suffering" feelings.

For Freud, the question of pleasure or "un-pleasure" framed a fundamental first principle, and the management of anxiety occupied a central place in this theory of ego functioning and defense. For Bion (1962), the capacity or incapacity to bear frustration and its attendant emotions defines the dividing line between the psychotic and nonpsychotic parts of the personality. Whatever emotions are, Bion concluded that awareness of them is of the utmost importance: "There is a need for awareness of an emotional experience . . . because lack of such awareness implies deprivation of truth and truth seems essential for psychic health" (Bion, 1962, p. 56).

Bion's (1962) work invites both psychotherapist and client to be steeped in, to brood over, and to reflect on one's emotion to "know" oneself. He conceived of thinking as a result of the transformation of nonelaborated emotional experiences (Blum, 2000). One has to possess curiosity to arrive at authenticity and truthful knowledge. He emphasized the primacy of the potentially metabolizing and containing role of early relationships. Specifically, he postulated that an infant's arousal states that are communicated by bodily sensations and actions are transformed with the support of the caregiver into symbols that enable the infant to experience his or her capacity to communicate needs and feelings. From a Bionian perspective, every person is constantly struggling between the tendency to have consciousness and the wish to not have it, and between his or her capacity to tolerate consciousness and the inclination to avoid it because of the pain feelings it may bring. When consciousness is avoided, the alpha functioning does not operate.

Joseph Sandler: Feeling States, Well-Being, and Sense of Safety

Joseph Sandler's work represents a significant contribution to the efforts in the field toward adaptation and integration of psychoanalytic theory into clinical practice. He contributed greatly to understanding the role of affect expression and communication in psychodynamic work and in object relations. Sandler was a key catalyst in bringing about what Ogden (1992) called "the quiet revolution" (p. 624) in psychoanalytic theory. His competence in fusing empirical research skills with the highest order of understanding of psychoanalytic theory was visible in his achievements. As with Bion, I offer a brief summary of Sandler's contributions to hopefully add to the technical explorations that lay ahead in this chapter regarding the role of emotion in the practice of psychodynamic psychotherapy.

Sandler (1960) argued that a person defends not against causes of his feelings but against the feelings themselves, which are both the cause and the reaction to wishes. In general, Sandler preferred to speak of wishes rather than drives, and of the relations between feelings and wishes rather than between feelings and drives. The reason? According to him, drives were hypothetical constructs, whereas wishes entailed feelings, as well as self- and object representations. Sandler is known for his conceptualizations of feeling states, well-being, and safety, and how he understands them in the context of relationships (see Sandler, 1960).

Sandler (1960) described a *feeling of safety* as a feeling that is so much a part of us that we take it for granted as a background to our everyday experience. He stated that this feeling of safety is more than a simple absence of discomfort or anxiety; it is a definite feeling quality within the ego. From this perspective, we can further regard much of ordinary everyday behavior as being a means of maintaining a minimum level of safety feeling. Furthermore, average behavior and many clinical phenomena (e.g., certain types of psychotic behavior, addictions) can be more fully understood in terms of the ego's maladaptive attempts to preserve this level of safety. According to Sandler (1960), safety is not connected a priori with ego boundaries or with the consciousness of self but develops from an integral part of primary narcissistic experience (in early stages of life) and must exist in rudimentary form from the time of the earliest experiences of need satisfaction (i.e., infancy). Later, of course, it becomes attached to different ego activities and structures, and to mental content; we can postulate safety signals in the same way as we do signals of anxiety. These safety signals are related to such things as the awareness of being protected; for example, by the reassuring presence of the mother. Many safety signals come in implicit, nonverbal forms (Gergely, 2013).

Through his conceptualization of safety, Sandler revised psychoanalytic theory by placing feeling states rather than psychic energy at the center of the psychoanalytic theory of motivation. His emphasis on feeling states created a bridge between classical drive and object relations theories (Fonagy, 2005), a connection that was particularly important in the context of working with affects in psychodynamic psychotherapy because they are considered the holders of memory and gateways into the relational past. Furthermore, affects represent an opportunity for challenging both therapist and client to work new versions of them that are revived in the here and now of the therapeutic relationship.

Mentalization-Based Therapy: Toward a Developmental Understanding of Affect Regulation

Through a developmental psychoanalytic lens, the work of Fonagy and colleagues represents an integration of the work of psychoanalytic thinkers Bion, Winnicott, Klein, and Anna Freud, among others, under the theoretical umbrella of attachment theory and research. Based on such strong theoretical foundations, Fonagy and Bateman developed *mentalization-based therapy* (MBT; Bateman & Fonagy, 2016), a clinical modality initially designed for working with clients who present with a borderline personality organization (Lingiardi & McWilliams, 2017). MBT incorporates Wilfred Bion's (1970) ideas regarding the role of the caregiver as metabolizer and container of the experience in the context of the emergence of a child's sense of self. MBT has a strong focus on affect regulation in the context of relational trauma and its organizing role in the formation of personality.

What happens when the client has not had a "good enough" (Winnicott, 1953, p. 94) early caregiving experience in which he or she is the beneficiary of the curiosity of an adult mind about that client's mind? What happens when the transference may feel too scary or painful? Sometimes, a developmentally informed approach, such as MBT, is helpful to create a therapeutic environment in which such a developmental experience can be revisited, reconstructed, and repaired. MBT seeks to engage and motivate the client to observe his or her dysfunctional relational patterns in the context of the here and now of the emerging psychotherapeutic relationship.

Mentalization refers to the developmental capacity of being able to think about one's own thoughts and feelings from the outside and imagine other's thoughts and feelings from the inside (Allen, 2013). It lies on the spectrum between empathy and mindfulness, and between the focus on the other and the focus on one's experience. Mentalization needs curiosity and the capacity for flexibility. It also requires the capacity to differentiate between the self and the other, and between what is implicit and what is explicit.

In MBT, being *affect focused* means grasping the affect in the immediacy of the moment, not so much in its relation to the content of the session but primarily as it relates to what is currently happening between client and therapist. MBT believes that a brief intervention that identifies the current feeling between client and therapist is likely to propel a session forward more effectively than a focus on the detail of the content of the narrative (Bateman & Fonagy, 2016).

The mentalization-based therapist is constantly assessing the emotional temperature in the room by noticing and naming shifts in verbal and nonverbal affects. Moreover, empathy usually is the port of entry. The mentalization-based therapeutic stance is characterized by an inquisitive stance: an attitude of genuine curiosity in which the therapist shares his or her surprise, joy, confusion, and so on, as they emerged in the context of the therapeutic exchange. As the work progresses and a basic sense of safety is created, perhaps for the first time in the client's life, deeper exploration and the feelings that accompany them begin to emerge slowly in the safety of the therapy. When *affective storms*—sudden and unpredictable high levels of emotional expression that often seem unprovoked and during which the individual seems to lose agency over capacity to reflect and regulate—emerge, the mentalization-based therapist observes them and reflects aloud in a curious and genuine tone—in a way the therapist feels the client can access and take in so that the client can achieve containment and an increasing sense of agency over his or her thoughts and feelings (Bateman & Fonagy, 2004). Mentalizing begets mentalizing. MBT seeks to motivate the client to express emotions without fear and with increased self-observation.

Furthermore, MBT emphasizes the transformation from implicit to explicit emotional awareness in developing psychic structure. It requires careful attention of the therapist's own emotional reactions and the capacity to acknowledge mentalizing impasses that often are felt in the countertransference in the form of anger, boredom, rejection, and many other emotional experiences that inform what is going on in the therapeutic relationship.

LINDA'S CASE THROUGH THE CONTEMPORARY PSYCHODYNAMIC LENS

To illustrate this point further, let's return to Linda's case (see Exhibit 2.1), particularly to my countertransference as her psychotherapist: one of helplessness when presented with a quiet and tearful 16-year-old. I often felt the urge to speak and ask questions to make her speak. I often felt the wish to make her face have an expression. I often felt alone and surprisingly not empathic toward her. I was not able to mentalize, process her emotional experience, and provide what Fonagy, Gergely, Jurist, and Target (2002) described as *marked mirroring* of her affective states. According to their social biofeedback theory, the primary caregiver enables the infant to identify and become aware of distinct affect states, which forms the basis of psychological self-representation (i.e., Who am I in the world? Who do others see?)

In my work with Linda, I had to step back and recognize that my initial role as her therapist was to provide enough marked mirroring in the context of unbearable and unspeakable feelings. Eventually, this process led to Linda's ability to explore difficult feelings, first by self-observing the painful familiar ways in which she managed them and hurt herself (e.g., overeating, vomiting, cutting) while expressing emotions within a safe and predictable therapeutic relationship. Later, by making explicit attempts to mentalize her experience and that of the people important to her (e.g., parents, nannies, teachers, friends), I allowed for a more coherent and grounded internal image of her and others to emerge, and with it, a sense of agency and new ways of managing overwhelming affects.

My 3-year psychotherapeutic relationship with Linda resulted in an increase self-observation and awareness in the context of relationships, and in more adaptive defense mechanisms when dealing with the anxiety of difficult cognitions and the feelings they awakened. Linda developed a sense of safety alongside an increased capacity to verbalize and mentalize her experience and that of others. I believe my work as a contemporary psychoanalyst shows the integration of a focus on drive and object relations in the context of both an ego psychology and interpersonal theoretical framework.

The next pages of this chapter seek to illustrate contemporary psychodynamic thinking and practice regarding the role of emotion by reflecting on how we understand change, motivation, and the role of the therapeutic relationship.

EMOTION AND CHANGE IN PSYCHODYNAMIC PSYCHOTHERAPY

During the early period of psychoanalysis, the mechanism of change can be summed up this way: "Transform what is unconscious into what is conscious" (Freud, 1916/1963, p. 194). In general, psychoanalysts and psychoanalytic psychotherapists agree that therapeutic change is effected through analysis of resistances, defenses, conflicts, and transference, and entails insight plus affective involvement.

Contemporary psychoanalytic theory and practice continues to emphasize the goal of helping clients become aware of their emotional functioning and of developing a greater capacity to tolerate and manage a wider range of emotional experience. The following clinical vignette illustrates the work with a young mother in psychodynamic psychotherapy and the process leading to change:

"Mercedes," a 25-year-old Hispanic woman, called to ask for an appointment to explore the possibility of psychodynamic psychotherapy. At the age of 19, during her sophomore year at a prestigious college, she realized she had become pregnant by her old boyfriend during a visit home. He was attending a local university and offered to marry her, and she agreed. Mercedes had to drop out of her college, return home, and get a job locally. The marriage struggled under the usual stressors of parenting and financial distress, and 5 years later, it dissolved, leaving Mercedes with two children, ages 4 and 1, all of whom went to live with her parents. A year later, thanks to the support of her family, she was able to resume higher education. She left her parents' house to live independently with her daughters, and her mother moved in to support her for the first 6 months.

Mercedes was a well-spoken, assertive young woman who was seeking treatment to learn to cope with the stress and guilt over her perception that she had to sacrifice the quality of care of her daughters to satisfy her professional ambitions. Furthermore, she reported having a tough time coparenting with her mother and felt bad about being ungrateful and mean. She spoke of having small panic attacks and feeling concerned that the attacks might increase and affect her time management and her capacity to parent her children with patience. She spoke of having frequent fights with her oldest daughter and feeling very sad afterward. The fights were over the issue of self-reliance and independence. She believed her mother pampered her daughter too much, and her daughter in turn would refuse to follow up on Mercedes's basic requests to pick up her toys or take a bath. Mercedes felt trapped, exhausted, and full of rage. She often argued with friends and fellow students over "small issues" and described herself as being in a constant state of "irritation."

During our first session, it was my impression that Mercedes was somewhat anxious, as indicated by her uncomfortable-looking hunched body and her arms crossed across her chest as she looked around the room. I registered feeling a bit anxious as to how to begin our consultation.

> *Therapist:* You seemed very uncomfortable. I am wondering if coming for therapy feels uncomfortable, perhaps?
>
> *Mercedes:* I am just taking the room and you in for a minute. . . . It is all so nice. . . . (First speaks defensively, then begins to cry.) I just feel so embarrassed that it has come to this. I can't even manage my own feelings.
>
> *Therapist:* It is difficult to feel so out of control sometimes. Do you think you could tell me a bit more about your experience during those moments?
>
> *Mercedes* (speaks in between sobs): I really don't seem to have the words. It is a feeling that takes over; it becomes fuzzy in my head . . . so when I try to think about it later, I can't even remember why I was so angry.
>
> *Therapist:* The tears that you are sharing with me. . . . Do you think those are the only way you can tell me a bit of the story of what happens?
>
> *Mercedes:* I actually think so. . . . It is so embarrassing . . . like an infant.
>
> *Therapist:* Lots of shame . . . over feeling needy? Angry?
>
> *Mercedes* (nods in agreement): Lots of sadness. . . . I can't remember the last time I woke up feeling happy to be alive. (Long, tense silence follows.)
>
> *Therapist:* It's an awful way of living . . . but you keep waking up and living. . . . If I may, . . . I know we just met, but I am wondering if there is shame and fear perhaps . . . that someone like me in a nice room like this might judge you and remind you of all the mistakes you feel you have made.

Mercedes: I don't want to be afraid and sad anymore. Can you help?

Therapist: We can certainly try to figure it out together by talking and trying to make connections while following the rhythm of your feelings. From what I see today here, they are quite strong and take over as you describe. (Mercedes smiles shyly.)

Mercedes: We can make new music together. . . . That is what "our" people do [referring to our common cultural background]. (She laughs, and I laugh back.)

The emotional climate of the room has shifted from one of fear and shame to one of emerging safety. My client and I have found a new metaphor in our common cultural identity as Hispanic women, one that has made her feel understood and contained but potentially also could facilitate the exploration of the shame and guilt she felt. Furthermore, sharing that common identity has served to invite her, in an explicit manner, to observe her emotional shifts in response to a new relationship.

Although words matter and remain central in psychoanalytic practice, the contemporary psychodynamic psychotherapist also listens for and observes changes in tone of voice, use of the body, and speed and rhythm of speech. Informed by the findings in the field of infant mental health (Stern, 1985, 2010), psychodynamic psychologists also pay attention to the shifts in affects as expressed in words and actions, and how they help us weave the unfolding narrative in the context of the emerging therapeutic relationship.

Many wonder if psychoanalytic listening is guided by affects or by words. In a session, psychodynamic psychologists not only listen but also feel. Communication is not just verbal; it also is emotional. The Freudian attempt to neutralize the analyst's emotional response was not successful. Affect slipped through, and since Heimann's seminal work in the 1950s (Heimann, 1950), countertransference has been theorized once again as the analyst's emotional response. For example, when listening to Mercedes tell me her story, I was not only paying attention to her words but also to her facial and body expressions, and the impact it all had on my own feelings, thoughts, and bodily reactions. In that context, coming from a curious and unknowing therapeutic stance, I was able to invite Mercedes to think about her inside and outside realities in the context of her expressed emotions. Emotions are memory, and so her tears, I wondered, were her way of letting me know many things about her past, including the shame she had experienced as a young mother in her community, as well as about her present feelings of fear, rage, and loneliness.

Expression of emotions is the gateway to future construction of meaning around the narrative psychodynamic psychotherapists help our clients construct. They do this one way by offering a hypothesis to clients about the way in which they cope with difficult feelings and thoughts by using defense mechanisms that help people to keep feelings, such as anxiety, at bay or under control. Once the psychotherapists have given the hypothesis, they check for the emotional reaction in the client—verbally and nonverbally; consciously and unconsciously are even more relevant. A psychodynamic approach seeks change from surface to depth, concentrating on content and process simultaneously.

Psychoanalytic-oriented psychotherapy focuses on the movement from the discharge of impulses to the symbolization of affective experience (Bateman & Fonagy, 2016). For instance, helping Mercedes to express, understand, and modulate what she felt was her unjustified rage toward her mother was an important motivation for change for her. Why? Feeling that her mother did not deserve her anger, she often would find herself unusually impatient with her children and in what she thought were irrational battles about fairness with people in her academic department. Mercedes seemed to be expressing and displacing her conflicted emotions toward her mother onto other relationships, thus impacting her functioning as a parent and jeopardizing her professional future. Change for Mercedes would come in the way of being able to recognize the feeling, mentalize it (i.e., look at it from the outside and imagine how others might be receiving it from the inside), contain it, own it, and experience it not as something that is happening to her but, rather, as something she is allowing herself to experience and process.

Mercedes's panic attacks were a message to her and also to me as her therapist regarding the resentment and jealousy she felt toward her daughter, and how dangerous and forbidden those feelings felt. Some emotional responses can be a sign whose coded language we may be lucky enough to decipher. Other feelings awake in us a sense of otherness, of feelings being out of character. For Mercedes, becoming aware of her forbidden feelings in the context of a safe therapeutic relationship freed her to become aware of them and manage and contain them. Accepting her loving self as a mother and also the side of her who envied her daughters brought her not only a sense of safety and freedom but also a change in the way she understood and contained her feelings and those of others close to her. Change in this context meant increased insight and self-observation, plus affective involvement without fear and avoidance.

Central to the psychodynamic process leading to change is the relational matrix and the transference/countertransference that emerges in the room and creates an "as-if" quality to the relationship. In this context, fears and forbidden desires can be reexperienced, expressed, contained, and owned. Resentment, envy, and jealousy are examples of emotions that many of us wish we did not feel, and so they fit the description of the unacceptable feelings, urges, drives, and emotions that Freud spoke about. Such feelings can be taken as signs to be read—a form of communication from one part of the self to another.

EMOTION AND MOTIVATION IN
PSYCHODYNAMIC PSYCHOTHERAPY

> Psychoanalytic investigation suggests that people are motivated or driven in order to gain a sense of a meaningful life and manage threatening conscious and [unconscious] affects and beliefs to create or interpret external experiences in ways that resonate with internal experiences, preoccupations, fantasies and senses of self-other relationships. (Chodorow, 1999, p. 14)

From a structural model of the mind, the psychoanalytic task is to help alter the structures (i.e., ego, id, and superego) that have been deformed and inadequately energized in the course of development. Transference became central to psychoanalytic theory and practice when clinical experience showed that it was the transference that provided the motivation for the clients' efforts to change. In contemporary psychodynamic thinking and practice, the analytic encounter is mutually constructed and contingent on the transference rather than intrapsychically orchestrated by one person. The psychotherapist's thoughts and feelings influence those of the client, and vice versa.

"Rick," a 20-year-old who had dropped out of high school and had been working in a local restaurant since he was 17 had decided he needed to find new ways of managing his social anxiety so he could pursue a technical education as a plumber. A year ago, he began dating Mary, a stable and hardworking 19-year-old in her sophomore year at a local community college. He feared that he would lose her if he did not learn to manage his anxiety and his tendency to isolate socially, which was the main reason he had left high school (i.e., school phobia). He had tried more cognitive-based approaches in the past and medications too, but after talking to Mary, they had decided he needed to look at the trauma of losing his mother at the age of 8 and how it affected him. Rick felt lost and a bit worried because Mary was his first girlfriend. He could not concentrate at work; he found himself feeling insecure and easily frustrated, and often felt competitive with Mary. He felt he had lost control of his thoughts and feelings. He could not sleep because of feeling worried all the time.

Rick had been attending psychodynamic psychotherapy sessions for about 5 months; he attended regularly and worked hard at reflecting on his concerns and accessing his feelings. He often was articulate and controlled in his responses to my interventions. However, the following is an excerpt from a session with Rick in which his usual style seemed to fail and resulted in the expression of affect in the transference.

Rick: I am not sure that you value the effort I make to pay for these sessions.

Therapist: Is there something I have said or done that makes you feel that or indicates this to you?

Rick: Well. . . . I saw you looking at the clock twice in the past 30 minutes. . . . Do you have a better place to be?

Therapist: There are many reasons why I might be looking at the clock, but you seem to know with some certainty that it is because I don't value your effort? . . . That most make you feel quite ignored, mistreated?

Rick: Don't try to use your PhD with me, Dr. M. . . . I know you must be tired of this stupid jerk who does not seem to be able to do anything but lament and go in circles. . . .

Therapist: So, let me get this right. I find you boring, stupid, and inferior, so I can't wait to get rid of you? (Rick looks down and then laughs in a weird and somewhat sinister fashion.)

Rick: Tell me that is not the truth. Look me in the eye and tell me that is not the truth. . . .

Therapist: Do I have any chance of you believing me?

Rick: Good point. . . .

Therapist: Is this a familiar place where you and I are right this minute?

Rick: Yes. . . . My father always thought I was a lazy, stupid, dyslexic jerk. . . . I suppose I think everyone else does. . . .

Therapist: You worry Mary will wake up one day and see you like that . . . the need to change—to be better—feels urgent . . . but change does not seem to come fast enough. . . . We are wasting each other's time and resources. . . . (Rick's body posture changes, and he cries in a controlled fashion.)

Rick: Sometimes when you help me see the shit I do to myself and you don't just dismiss it and get angry, you make me miss my mom. . . . She had patience. . . .

Therapist: You never mention her. . . . Too much sorrow?

Rick: Yes. . . . My dad always said the dead need to be left alone. . . . No sense in crying over them.

Rick's anger and accusations directed at me as an ineffective and uncaring psychotherapist were the first manifestations of his real motivation to seek psychotherapy: that of mourning the death of his mother and, with it, revisiting the anger and sense of betrayal a child feels when a parent dies. The fear of losing his girlfriend was driven by a past unresolved desire awakened by a new version of desire to merge and remain close, and by the knowledge and memory, both cognitively and emotionally, that it can end quite unexpectedly. Rick perceived himself as a loser not worthy of love and recognition. This state of affairs, I suspected, was linked to being left with a father who could not mourn and resented his child's survival.

Role of Motivation and Emotion in Clinical Practice

Let us return for a moment to the psychodynamic theoretical framework informing work with affects and also to the work of David Rapaport, a major representative of ego psychology considered for a long time as the psychoanalytic author who focused on affects. In 1950, he published his book *Emotions and Memory* (Rapaport, 1950), an exploration of the role of affects in psychoanalysis. He considered that what motivated a person was a lack of internal balance (i.e., energy unbalance) and not feelings states. Unfortunately, the result of that approach was an exclusion of the unique individual meaning all of us give to our experience in the context of relationships. For example, in the context of a session, how do client and therapist experience the same interpersonal exchange and attach different meanings to it? What does it mean to each of them? How does it create a space in which a dialogue about the impact of one on the other is experienced, contained, and metabolized by the therapeutic dyad?

Looking at further evolution of the role of emotion and motivation in the psychoanalytic literature, we find the pivotal work of Otto Kernberg (1982), who proposed a modification of drive theory in his paper "Self, Ego, Affects and Drives." This was an important shift that moved psychoanalytic thinking toward an awareness of the central importance of object relations and, with it, a reconsideration of the role of emotion in the context of relationships. Similar to Sandler, in Kernberg's work, affects become hierarchically more significant than the drives, bringing back the relationship between affects and the psychological manifestations of the drives. That is, how do we manage internal conflict and how it impacts our emotions? Kernberg's notion of affects as developing alongside the integration of the internal picture we have of relationships (i.e., internalized object relations) signals and monitors activated drives. This notion is especially true in the context of working with highly disturbed clients whose relational experiences have not allowed for such integration to take place. In the context of working with these clients, it becomes important when thinking about emotions as the holders of memory, both in the mind and body, and the developmental impact of early disturbed relationships with caregiving figures. For example, if the same caregiver who was supposed to make a person feel safe made that person feel scared in unpredictable fashion, the person would think of other relationships as potentially dangerous too and would organize his or her emotions and behavioral responses based on that belief.

Kernberg (1988) considered affect to be the indicator or psychic representation of the instinctual needs, which primary caregivers either have met or neglected during the early stages of life. According to him, maturity is indicated by the simultaneous awareness or integration of positive and negative emotions with regard to self and others, and an increasing ability to become aware of and to tolerate negative emotions. One can love and hate the same person, and one is aware that someone can feel rage toward him or her but also can keep strong loving feelings. In that way, Kernberg has retained the dual drive theory of Freud (i.e., Eros and Thanatos) discussed earlier. However, he has enveloped it in the relationship. Therefore, clinically what happens in the relationship between a therapist and a client in the transference allows for the revisiting, reexperiencing, and reorganizing of early emotional experience in the context of two: psychotherapist and client. In that context, the main goal of easing psychic pain and freeing the clients' capacity to mentalize could be conceptualized and formulated as a constant interchange and mutually influential process between client and therapist (Kernberg, 2009).

Emotion as Motivation for Exploration

In my work with Rick, as discussed earlier in the Emotion and Motivation in Psychodynamic Psychotherapy section, I was able to stay in the "as if" of the transference. Suddenly, it was my impression that I had become the judgmental father, the ineffective parent who can't appreciate and validate the efforts of the grieving child. Instead of highlighting, for instance, that his accusations had to do with a cognitive distortion, I began by keeping the conflict in the here and now of the transference and responded in a different way. I invited Rick to look at the strength of his feelings, namely, his aggression toward the ineffective and judgmental parent, while acknowledging and empathizing with his longing for the lost mother and the conflicting feelings of anger and helplessness that accompanied the experience. By evoking the memory of the "client" mother, Rick helped me understand that something good had been given early on, an experience that allowed Rick to work with me in the transference.

Clients who seek psychotherapeutic help are motivated by many reasons: Psychic pain as a result of difficulties in the realm of close relationships is a primary one. We all desire to feel loved and to be able to love others. It sounds so simple, yet we all know from personal experience that is it not at all simple. Using the motivation to connect that is innate in all humans since birth is what a psychodynamic psychotherapy approach is centered on. In the context of a therapeutic relationship, that approach uses motivation as a driving force to promote acceptance of an invitation to experience the emotions emerging in the here and now, and revisit those of the past. This exploration takes place with and without words; it is explicit and implicit in nature. The contemporary psychodynamic psychotherapist invites his or her clients to embark on an exploration of departing from a mutual stance of not knowing and of curiosity. In the context of that journey, the psychodynamic therapist listens and observes within a clinical framework, which invites the therapist to listen for transference and countertransference manifestations, projection, and other defensive moves. In that context, the therapeutic relationship becomes the container for all of these.

EMOTION AND THE THERAPEUTIC RELATIONSHIP IN PSYCHODYNAMIC PSYCHOTHERAPY

When two personalities meet, an emotional storm is created. If they make sufficient contact . . . an emotional state is produced by the conjunction of these two individuals. (Bion, 1979, p. 247)

As illustrated in previous sections in this chapter, today's psychodynamic psychotherapy and psychoanalysis have now turned to two centers: client and psychotherapist/psychoanalyst. When psychoanalysts speak of a *two-person psychology*, we are referring to two individuals interacting, influencing, and complementing each other in the safety of the as-if environment of the clinical situation. Transference and countertransference now are considered to be an artificial production of the analytic technique indispensable for the treatment's evolution and resolution (Baranger, 2012).

The Observing, Listening, and Feeling Psychodynamic Therapist in the Room

Much has been written in the psychoanalytic literature regarding the role of the therapeutic dyad and the intersubjective space that it creates. Thomas Ogden (1994), for example, developed the concept of the *intersubjective analytic third*. He considered the dialectic movement of *individual subjectivity* (i.e., therapist and client as separate people with separate unconscious lives) and of *intersubjectivity* (i.e., unconscious life created conjointly by the therapeutic couple) as central phenomena in psychoanalysis. That *third subjectivity*, acquiring a life of its own, is the result of the separate subjectivities of psychotherapist and client in the psychodynamic/psychoanalytic situation. Being aware of, observing, and listening for these processes become of technical importance, particularly in the context of affects and their manifestations in the room. As explored later in this chapter, this phenomenon impacts not only what to listen for but also how to listen for it and how to use it in the context of the role as psychodynamic psychotherapists and psychoanalysts.

The process of *psychic change* occurs in the context of the therapeutic relationship as client and psychotherapist together pay attention to the different feelings and emotional manifestations present in the room or that are evoked in the room from the recent or remote past. The psychoanalyst lends his or her "free-swinging attention" (Carlson, 2002, p. 726) to the client, who in turn chooses to come every week willing to explore sometimes painful and sometimes joyous emotions all motivated by the hope of relief, freedom, and self-awareness. According to Carlson (2002, p. 748), this free-swinging attention reminds psychodynamic psychotherapists and psychoanalysts of the following:

- We continually swing between focused and free-swinging attention.
- We are not a passive register.
- We must learn how to swing in rhythm with the client as we once learned to do with the child swinging next to us on the school playground.
- Like a child on a swing, we should be aware of constantly shifting perspectives on the scenery.
- Our attention is loving, but it is aggressive too in understanding differently what the client thinks he or she is conveying.
- A lack of tact or of accuracy can leave the client feeling like the object of a free-swinging assault.
- At any moment, we must be ready to let the material conduct a free-swinging assault on the client's preconceptions.
- Just as at the playground, if we are not experiencing part of the ride as effortless flight, we are missing part of the experience.
- People cannot swing without pleasant sensations—and, at times, a little fear.

As Carlson's (2002) wonderful metaphor conveys, working as a psychodynamic psychotherapist or psychoanalyst requires the capacity to be in touch with one's feelings, positive and negative, while attempting to be present and alive in a genuine way for clients and their own emotional experience expressed verbally and nonverbally. Many elements of a psychodynamic psychotherapist or psychoanalyst's technique come into play during a session and are organized around the ever emerging and transforming therapeutic relationship. As hopefully illustrated in this chapter so far, an important shift in psychodynamic thinking has been that the psychoanalyst is seen not only as an observer and investigator but as a full participant in the process (Bollas, 1979).

Treatment Alliance and Emotions: Ruptures and Repairs

Developmental research has stressed the importance of learning to regulate one's emotional life (Beebe, 2000; Mahler, Pine, & Bergman, 1975; Stern, 1985). That work has shown how the roots of this learning lie firmly in early childhood and in having a good experience of one's emotions being observed, regulated, and understood. One of the first links between a mother and a baby is an emotional one, from mind to mind, even if the fetus or infant does not yet have a mind discriminated from the body. The individual capabilities of awareness of, contention with, and understanding of the infant or fetus's own emotional experiences will evolve from these early emotional contacts, giving him or her the possibility of experiencing his or her feelings and to suffer and have pleasure emotionally (de Bianchedi, 2001).

Usually, pleasurable affects originally are associated with gratifying interactions with the primary caregiver and often are in relation to feeding and other drive experiences (e.g., sleeping, soothing). However, pleasure, interest, surprise, excitement, enthusiasm, delight, joy, and so on can quickly come to be experienced in relation to exploration, discovery, and mastery. Those positive emotions lead to a pleasurable sense of well-being and competence, gradually building a sense of agency. Eventually, if it all goes well, those affects function to ensure that a sense of competence and well-being remains relatively stable.

Regulation of positive and negative feelings depends on the capacity to develop a stable *signal function* of affect. That signal function (i.e., the capacity to discern between what behavior or emotion is threatening and what is not) emerges from the experience of caregiver–child reciprocity, which is characterized by a basic, two-way, meaningful communication process an *affective dialogue*. Once this affective dialogue becomes well established, the infant begins to participate in regulation interactions and develop some self-regulatory skills.

In his 1960 seminal paper "On the Therapeutic Action of Psycho-Analysis," Hans Loewald (1960) provided a coherent, inclusive account of the analytic therapeutic process. He introduced an interactional, object relational view of the psyche for understanding development and current psychic functioning. He thought that the therapeutic action of psychoanalysis depended on the new experience with the analyst that induced a resumption of development by permitting transference regression and by providing the client with a new opportunity for an appropriate parenting experience. That appropriate parenting included the therapist's modeling or communicating to the client as an integrated human with a past and an expected future. Loewald emphasized the humanity of the analyst and the humanistic terms of the transaction between analyst and client.

In the context described by Loewald (1960), the idea that people may have feelings inside that we need to get rid of is common and is based on a view of emotions as being like bodily substances that we need to discharge. This is a kind of "toxic waste model" of emotionality in which the bad feelings, if allowed to remain inside, will do us or someone else harm. From a psychodynamic perspective, the value of expressing feelings is not in just "getting them out" but expressing them to another person in the context of a predictable and safe therapeutic relationship in which they can be expressed, understood, and modulated. What is helpful is having someone else, or a part of the self, who can listen to one's emotional state and help manage it. A consistent, predictable psychodynamic psychotherapist seeks to provide an environment of safety in which expression, witnessing, and metabolizing of difficult emotion take place.

The contemporary psychoanalytic encounter pays attention to content and process. Working with emotions and their representational manifestations, what is defined as *affects*, occurs in the context of the therapeutic relationship. The therapist's interventions in this process are primarily informed by his or her evolving clinical formulation of the client but, most importantly, by the emerging coconstruction of meaning between client and therapist. However, the therapist also is guided in this joint quest by his or her understanding of the importance of the quality of the relationship as developed in the emerging therapeutic alliance; the application of clinical tools, such as interpretation of defenses (e.g., projection), the process of introjection, the work in the transference, and the importance of exploring the therapist's countertransference. The process of psychodynamic psychotherapy truly is a developmental process in which a scaffolding process takes place with the collaboration of client and therapist, and one in which the therapist attempts to meet the client where he or she is in terms of the client's capacity to express, explore, and modulate emotions.

I offer the following clinical example to illustrate the role of emotion in the context of the therapeutic relationship between a client and a psychodynamic psychotherapist. I highlight the value of the therapeutic alliance as a way of constructing a space for safety and creativity.

"Joseph" was a 50-year-old middle-aged man who had spent his life going from job to job. After two failed marriages, he decided that he needed to explore his difficulties in managing his "temper" with women. After 3 months in twice-weekly psychodynamic psychotherapy, Joseph walked into the consulting room, complaining that he thought the therapist was not doing anything helpful:

> *Joseph:* I come here, open my heart and soul to you, and you just listen and leave me hanging for the whole weekend with thoughts and feelings that just make me feel worse.
>
> [As I listen, I become aware of my feelings of guilt over having "left" Joseph for 4 days after a painful session in which he had relived the feelings of loss over the end of his second marriage and that he was 50 and had no children of his own.]
>
> *Therapist:* I might be wrong, but I think you are letting me know how painful it is to come here and be with someone who is inviting you to be vulnerable.
>
> [A long silence ensues; I can see the face of my client transform. I register a change in my own emotional state: I feel anxious.]
>
> *Joseph* (tone of voice rises as he looks at me with hatred):   I am feeling irritated by your smug face. . . . You came recommended, but I am starting to doubt your skill set. . . . I am feeling worse, not better. I guess this is meant to be my destiny: can't find a woman who does not aggravate me. . . . I just hate not knowing what you are thinking. And please, don't ask me what I imagine you are thinking because it is not my job! I have spent my whole life trying to figure out difficult people, particularly women. I don't understand why I set people off that way, why they think I am a jerk. I don't know why people don't think my jokes are funny. I don't know why people can't just see I just want some warmth and acceptance. . . . I feel I am doing all the work here. . . . I feel like I am going to implode!
>
> [I find myself feeling lost but also mindful of Joseph's history as a child of a depressed mother. I change my body posture and become more aware of my facial expression. I move slightly and lean toward him. Joseph seems to calm, and his body visibly relaxes.]
>
> *Therapist:* I can see and I can feel that I did or said something that is making you feel disappointed and angry with me. I am not asking you to change the way you feel, I am also not asking

you to do all the work alone, but I can see and hear that it is the first place you go to. . . . I wonder if we could look at what happened just now between us while paying attention and accepting how you feel right now. Nobody has to work alone. . . .

(Silence.)

Joseph: I feel a rush of blood in my head, and then I can't stop the anger. It is like—is like wanting a drink, just wanting revenge . . .

Therapist: On the ineffective and bad therapist. (Joseph smiles, and I smile back.)

Therapist: It seemed the stronger the feeling got, the scarier yet strangely satisfying it did too.

Joseph: Yes. . . . I wish I could say I am sorry, but I am not. I feel better. . . .

Therapist: I wonder if we could look at what just happened now that the emotional storm has passed?

Joseph: I think I can now. . . .

My work with Joseph does not only show the process of rupture and repair that resulted in a stronger therapeutic alliance (Safran, Muran, & Eubanks-Carter, 2011). It also illustrates the value of working on the here and now of the transference in the consulting room.

Transference

No single psychological process provides as sharp a testing ground for the transformation of emotions as transference. Transference is, in the first place, part of the complex emotional bond that develops between client and psychotherapist. The main characteristic of this situation, and the one that provides vital leverage for psychoanalytic interpretations, is the repetition of earlier emotional experiences. The client does not merely recollect these experiences but actually relives them emotionally, redirecting many feelings, such as love, hate, fear, anger, and envy, onto the person of the therapist. In this manner, emotions, qualities, and symbols that once held a powerful grip over an individual resurface in psychodynamic psychotherapy to provide strong evidence as to the origins of mental disturbances. The centrality of the mutative value of the therapeutic relationship and the belief in the unconscious remain central to all psychodynamic endeavors. Observing, acknowledging and working in the transference remain essential elements in the psychodynamic psychotherapist's toolbox.

Returning to the client vignette in the preceding section, it was my impression that Joseph's experience of an ineffective and unpredictable caregiving mind was being reexperienced in the safety of the therapeutic relationship. However, given that we had been working only for 3 months, I decided to weather the affective storm (Bateman & Fonagy, 2016) without offering any interpretation but staying at a level of being with, noticing, and wondering. That led us back to a safe place, where, after a period of focusing on his capacity to regulate his rage in a way in which we could still mentalize it and survive it together, we were able to eventually explore his strong emotions of fear, pain, and rage in the safety of the transference. A premature interpretation in that case would have resulted in Joseph's fleeing the therapy as he had done many times before with other therapists and with his two wives. A scaffolding process needed to take place with the foundation of trust that any emotion could be explored, contained, and metabolized in our relationship.

According to Loewald (1960), Freud used the transference in three ways:

- Transference refers to the transfer of relations with infantile object onto later objects (e.g., from a parent to a spouse).
- A second meaning involves the transfer of libido from ego to objects (i.e., from oneself to others).
- Transference refers to the way that unconscious ideas transfer their intensity to preconscious and ultimately to conscious ideas (e.g., unconscious guilt turns into feelings of rage against the source of the conflict causing the feeling of guilt).

Loewald (1960) claimed that transferences in all three senses is normal and desirable, but it is the third meaning that most concerns the psychoanalytic practitioner (Chodorow, 1999). Contemporary psychoanalysts have described transference not so much as bringing feelings about the person of the parent to the person of the analyst but within the context of the psychoanalytic situation as a whole (Joseph, 1985; Loewald, 1960). Psychoanalysts are no longer talking only about old versions of old relationships; rather, they talk about how the client expresses inner psychic reality in whatever he or she does, whether in talk about feelings, during a work event, at a party, in the family, or in silence. Psychoanalysts begin by investigating the analytic encounter but rapidly realize that transferences are found whenever feelings, fantasies, and emotional meaning are given to people and situations. In the contemporary view of transference, the analytic encounter is mutually constructed and contingent rather than intrapsychically orchestrated by one person (Chodorow, 1999).

Christopher Bollas (1979) described an intermediate zone between the subjectivities of client and analyst. According to Bollas, the analyst embodies a transformational role that imitates the transformational function of mother with baby. Therapy offers clients a space and a relationship that facilitate sharing a secret mother–baby culture. In this context, the safety of the relationship and benevolent attitude of the analyst foster a new capacity for an accepting and tolerant attitude toward one's unconscious infantile and current sexual, aggressive, and narcissistic wishes. From this perspective, the capacity of the analyst for self-care, for understanding his or her own feelings, and for reflecting on his or her own emotional lives will only develop, assuming that there are no organic problems, if one has thoughtfully reflected on one's emotions.

Countertransference

Contemporary psychoanalytic thinking and practice consider *countertransference* as the way in which the analyst perceives and processes, and listens to and learns from to the client. The psychotherapist's instrument of research is the countertransference as it was originally theorized in the British object relations school, which favored a restriction of what counts as countertransference to what the psychotherapist can tell from analyzing his or her own responses to the client. A broader definition of countertransference covers not only feelings of emotion but also behaviors, fantasies, and other responses to the client's unconscious communication, including what Sandler and Sandler (1978) described as "role responsiveness" (p. 289) of the therapist's behavior. That role responsiveness can be used by the therapist trained to a heightened form of ordinary reflective self-interpretation to orient him or her in his or her relationship with the client.

Psychodynamic psychotherapy emphasizes the importance of observing the therapist's emotional reactions, attitudes, values, and preferential interests not only in glaring but also in subtle verbal and nonverbal influences in the process of two psychologies' interacting in the consulting room (i.e., psychotherapists' character, temperament and style, age and gender; Anderson, Ogles, Patterson, Lambert, & Vermeersch, 2009; Lambert & Ogles, 2004). Every client–psychotherapist pair is different and has its own unique transference–countertransference.

Loewald (1986) formulated that both analyst and client have countertransference to each other's transference. However, the client's countertransference cannot be clearly separated from the client's transference. In that context, Loewald spoke of how clients' transference reacts to the analyst's countertransference.

Another perspective is that of child psychoanalyst Donald Winnicott (1949), who proposed that the therapist should work at clarifying and detoxifying the countertransference to maintain objectivity. As a corollary, he suggested that some disturbed clients evoke intense hatred so that the therapist should be able to hate the client objectively, which, in turn, would provide beneficial, realistic communication to the client concerning the client's provocation. What was Winnicott referring to? Let's return to Joseph's case.

I understood Joseph's accusations toward me as he reexperienced strong feelings, which scared him as our therapeutic relationship became closer and stronger. Would I turned out to be a depressed mother? Would I leave him too? On the other hand, as I registered my own feelings of being attacked and accused, I was able to use my emotional reactions to imagine my client's own experiences as a small child losing his mother, while allowing myself to recognize that I felt annoyed at his accusations. That process allowed me to provide marked mirroring (Fonagy et al., 2002), that is, the experience of someone's truly being curious about and receptive to another's feelings, followed by an attempt to genuinely respond in a way that makes the other person feel understood and, most important, recognized. In this way, working with one's countertransference allows one to create a safe therapeutic environment in which all emotions, positive or negative, are allowed, expressed, felt, and contained.

Projection

The process of disowning aspects of ourselves yet seeing those traits all too clearly in others in called *projection* (Klein, 1946). The angry person who feels he or she should not be angry quickly accuses others of being aggressive when he or she is stirred up. For Joseph, it was easier to see others as ineffective and smug than to face the amount of contempt and grievance he felt. People place feelings and emotional states that we cannot manage in ourselves out there in others so that we do not view and own them as belonging to us. This is sometimes purely a mental event—what psychoanalysis calls an intrapsychic process. Another version of projection is what psychoanalysts call *projective identification*: that occurs when a feeling is unbearable and is evacuated into someone else. This process, coined by Melanie Klein, describes how a person sees in the other parts of himself or herself that the person perceived as bad and dangerous. The other, the receiver, tends to feel those feelings, sometimes realizing they are not really his or hers because they feel foreign and uncomfortable, and usually are felt emotionally but also are accompanied by cognitions (i.e., ideas and thoughts). The process of projective identification often manifests itself in the context of unconscious fantasies, emerging in the "as if" of the therapeutic relationship. It is up to the therapist to recognize the foreign feelings and try to link them to what is going on in the here and now of the session and the therapeutic relationship.

Such ways of communicating can become ingrained and indeed can have their secondary rewards. For example, Joseph felt guilty about being verbally abusive to his wife but also began to enjoy the power and control he felt. The ability to manage one's own emotional states rather than having to discharge them into others is considered in psychoanalysis as a sign of maturity, and it is central to the improvement in affect regulation.

Interpretation and Exploration of Emotion

Laplanche and Pontalis (1973) defined *interpretation* in *The Language of Psycho-Analysis* as

A) Clarification, by means of analytical investigation, of the hidden meaning in the talk and behavior of a subject; B) During treatment, communication made to the client aiming to provide him with access to this hidden meaning, according to rules determined by the direction and the evolution of the treatment. (p. 227)

The meaning of the term *interpretation* as an intervention during psychoanalysis has gradually expanded to include Wolf's (1993) definition: "all those intentional activities of the analyst, that in their totality bring about a modification of the therapist's psyche" (p. 45).

The following example of my work with 25-year-old "Silvia" illustrates briefly the use of interpretation seeking to explore the use of emotion as a way of defending against a difficult feeling that emerges in the relationship with a therapist:

Silvia: I felt less alone during the break this time. I was able to deal with it. . . . I think I am making progress not getting all anxious when I am alone and bored.

Therapist: It is difficult when everyone is away during the spring break, even me.

Silvia: Well, yes . . . but not you exactly. I expect that you will be taking a break. Makes me happy to think you are taking care of yourself, really. . . . I can't feel angry at that. It would be stupid and it would be needy of me in a childish way. (Laughs.)

Therapist: I think you are reminding me about how forbidden it feels to need people and allow yourself to feel dropped and left behind. . . . It seems to feel like it is childish . . . embarrassing perhaps?

[Silvia is silent. Tension and a tone of defensiveness emerge in the room. I can see her hands moving more, her face getting red.]

Silvia:	Look, I think you are reading too much into it. I am feeling a bit judged . . .
Therapist:	It seems like you feel I crossed the line with my comment.
Silvia:	I don't like thinking about this . . . makes me feel pathetic. (Becomes tearful and somber.)
Therapist:	What is going on for you right now?
Silvia:	I wish you would have just stopped at believing that I am doing better. . . . . It is like nobody can ever believe me.

In that segment of a psychodynamic psychotherapy with a young adult woman who lost her mother at age of 14, the client defended against feelings of rage at having been left by her therapist for a weeklong break. The therapist's interpretation sought to acknowledge the difficulties Silvia had observing her sense of loss and experiencing safely the feelings of anger and sadness that come from them. The interpretation sought to invite the client to experience those feelings within the safety of the psychotherapeutic relationship in which the therapist responded differently than had other important attachment figures in the client's life.

Nacht (1962) stressed the importance of the analyst's personality in the analytic process: What the analyst says is less important than his or her attitude, which is "the main factor in the recovery, as it provides the client with the acceptance he did not receive during his childhood" (p. 209). Returning to the case vignette, working with Silvia in the context of emotion, my attitude remained genuine, humble, and curious by accepting and exploring the feelings that had emerged in the here and now of our therapeutic relationship. In that way, I offered my client the opportunity of greater self-observation and agency in the context of emotions often repressed and defended against. In the context of unresolved mourning and other deeply rooted traumatic experiences, and the painful emotions they bring about, the timing and tone of the interpretation becomes very important. There is the risk, as expressed by Donald Winnicott (1958), that an interpretation made too early may prevent the client from comprehending on his or her own, thus denying the client his or her only possible experience of competence and creativity. What does that mean? The process of working with emotion in psychodynamic psychotherapy is one of coconstruction and not that of an all-wise psychotherapist who tells the client how he or she feels.

Contemporary authors have observed that insight does not work with severely disturbed clients; what does work is that the message is carried by the relationship, with the message transmitted through the tone of voice and the feeling it conveys rather than its content. For example, Fonagy

(1991) explained the ineffectiveness of interpretation with borderline clients because of their deficit of mentalization, which prevents them from even understanding the content of the interpretations. Hence, from a contemporary perspective, the therapeutic action of interpretation no longer refers to the insight it conveys but is sought within the relationship, from which it arises; there is no interpretation without relationship. The therapeutic impact of interpretation lies in becoming attuned to the client's affective states.

In the context of contemporary psychodynamic practice with its widening scope, some interventions are of importance in building the therapeutic alliance and the sense of safety and trust that facilitates the expression of affects. For example, the use of *clarification*, distinct from interpretation, consists in reformulating or resuming the thread of the client's speech to confer a more consistent image of what has been communicated by the client. Clarification serves to help the client to articulate something that is difficult for him or her to verbalize, such as a difficult memory and the strong emotions it brings. In the following example, 17-year-old "Paul," in the midst of an affective storm fueled by the therapist's comment "that seems to make you feel annoyed," expresses his feelings:

> *Paul* (screaming):   I can't believe that you are confused by my face too! Ever since I was a small kid I have had to deal with nobody getting that I just make strange faces! I am so fed up of having to overexplain shit to people! How can you jump to conclusions like that? Now I am really angry! Really!
>
> [The therapist listens and pays attention to her physical reaction in response to Paul's screams. She monitors her facial expression and bodily posture. After a few minutes of silence, she decides to offer clarification.]
>
> *Therapist:*   Paul, I think my comment truly offended you and made you feel very alone. Your anger is helping me understand how strongly you felt about being misunderstood. Is that so?
>
> *Paul:*   Yes . . . it is really lonely feeling like a weird freak people don't get. . . . It really is.

By staying with Paul during his expression of strong affects and responding with a genuine curious and humble clarification, the therapist is conveying to Paul her desire to understand and her capacity to stay calm and offer containment with a clarification.

CONCLUSION

Psychoanalysis has been accused of being better at helping people to manage unhappiness than to become happier. Freud (1895/1950) stated that the aim of psychoanalysis was to change human misery into "ordinary unhappiness" (p. 308). It is my impression that one of the main reasons so many misconceptions and accusations surround psychoanalytic think-ing and practice is because they are a response to its own developmental history, which has been plagued with adversarial parents and inconsistent and confusing definitions and technical debate. Historically, psychoanalysis has not done a good job at developing an interdisciplinary language and integrating itself into the landscape of new treatments. Ironically, though, elements of psychoanalytic thinking and technique appear in most thera-peutic models (Shedler, 2010). When it comes to emotions, as I hope I have demonstrated, psychoanalysis and psychodynamic psychotherapy are at an important moment in the evolution of theory and practice as the result of increased interdisciplinary dialogue and collaboration.

An example of such development has been the increase in links between psychoanalytic thinking and research into psychosomatic states. Most now agree that affects initially are experienced in one's body as physiological states, which gradually can become what might be called *subjective states*—feelings or emotional experience—but the origin of such a sense of having feelings is intersubjective. Research has shown that symptoms sometimes are unprocessed emotional states lodged in the body (Luyten, van Houdenhove, Lemma, Target, & Fonagy, 2012). This new understanding, which combines the findings of neuroscience, psychoanalysis, and infant research, validates a long argued psychoanalytic premise and, most important, brings to the fore the importance of the body in psychotherapy. Emotional knowledge is vis-ceral and held within procedural memories that are deeply ingrained in our bodies and personalities. There is a decidedly greater emphasis in contem-porary psychodynamic theory and therapy on encouraging the experience and expression of emotion. Affects and not just drives are viewed as primary motivators of behavior and as carrying information that needs attention. If inner feelings are not attended to and made conscious, they automatically will maintain the client's behavior, often in maladaptive directions. Unlike drives, affective connections can be unlearned and relearned (McCullough et al., 2003).

Contemporary psychoanalytic theory and practice has shifted from its original one-person psychology focus to a two-person psychology. In this con-text, the core belief in the unconscious continues to be central and the thing that differentiates it from other psychotherapy approaches. Psychoanalysts differ in their views of the mutative effect assigned to the diverse aspects of the analytic process. Depending on the psychotherapist's theoretical persuasion, his or her personality, cultural background, or own personal experiences as a client in psychotherapy, different combinations of the new cognitions, internalizations, insights, and experiences in the context of the therapeutic dyad will lead to therapeutic change. Psychoanalysts all agree, though, that the ideal outcome of a psychotherapy process is a greater capacity for self-observation and agency over positive and negative feelings, as manifested in the form of a progressive resumption of development and the capacity to love and be loved.

REFERENCES

Allen, J. G. (2013). *Mentalizing in the development and treatment of attachment trauma.* London, England: Karnac Books.

Anderson, T., Ogles, B. M., Patterson, C. L., Lambert, M. J., & Vermeersch, D. A. (2009). Therapist effects: Facilitative interpersonal skills as a predictor of therapist success. *Journal of Clinical Psychology, 65,* 755–768. http://dx.doi.org/10.1002/jclp.20583

Baranger, M. (2012). The intra-psychic and the inter-subjective in contemporary psychoanalysis. *International Forum of Psychoanalysis, 21,* 130–135. http://dx.doi.org/10.1080/0803706X.2012.659285

Bateman, A., & Fonagy, P. (2016). *Mentalization-based treatment for personality disorders: A practical guide.* Cambridge, England: Oxford University Press. http://dx.doi.org/10.1093/med:psych/9780199680375.001.0001

Bateman, A. W., & Fonagy, P. (2004). Mentalization based treatment of BPD. *Journal of Personality Disorders, 18,* 36–51. http://dx.doi.org/10.1521/pedi.18.1.36.32772

Beebe, B. (2000). Co-constructing mother–infant distress: The micro-synchrony of maternal impingement and infant avoidance in the face-to-face encounter. *Psychoanalytic Inquiry, 20,* 421–440. http://dx.doi.org/10.1080/07351692009348898

Bion, W. R. (1962). *Learning from experience.* London, England: Maresfield.

Bion, W. R. (1970). *Attention and interpretation.* London, England: Maresfield.

Bion, W. R. (1979). The dawn of oblivion [Book 3]. In A *memoir of the future* (pp. 427–578). London, England: Karnac Books.

Blum, H. (1991). Affect theory and the theory of technique. *Journal of the American Psychoanalytic Association, 39,* 265–289.

Blum, H. (2000, April). *Language of affect.* Paper presented at the Third International Margaret S. Mahler Symposium in Child Development, Tokyo, Japan.

Bollas, C. (1979). The transformational object. *International Journal of Psychoanalysis, 60,* 97–107.

Breuer, J., & Freud, S. (1955). Studies on hysteria. In J. Strachey (Ed. & Trans.), *The standard edition of the complete psychological works of Sigmund Freud* (Vol. 2, pp. 1–335). London, England: Hogarth Press. (Original work published 1895)

Carlson, D. A. (2002). Free-swinging attention. *Psychoanalytic Quarterly, 71*, 725–750. http://dx.doi.org/10.1002/j.2167-4086.2002.tb00024.x

Chodorow, N. (1999). *The power of feelings: Personal meaning in psychoanalysis, gender, and culture.* New Haven, CT: Yale University Press.

de Bianchedi, E. T. (2001). The passionate psychoanalyst or learning from the emotional. *Fort Da, 7*, 19–28.

Fenichel, O. (1945). *The psychoanalytic theory of neurosis.* New York, NY: Norton.

Ferro, A. (2007). *Evitare le emozioni, vivere ler emozioni* [Avoiding emotions, living emotions]. Milan, Italy: Cortina.

Fonagy, P. (1991). Thinking about thinking: Some clinical and theoretical considerations in the treatment of a borderline patient. *International Journal of Psycho-Analysis, 72*, 639–656.

Fonagy, P. (2005). An overview of Joseph Sandler's key contributions to theoretical and clinical psychoanalysis. *Psychoanalytic Inquiry, 25*, 120–147. http://dx.doi.org/10.1080/07351692509349124

Fonagy, P., Gergely, G., Jurist, E. L., & Target, M. (2002). *Affect regulation, mentalization, and the development of the self.* New York, NY: Other Press.

Freud, S. (1950). Project for a scientific psychology. In J. Strachey (Ed. & Trans.), *The standard edition of the complete psychological works of Sigmund Freud* (Vol. 1, pp. 281–394). London, England: Hogarth Press. (Original work published 1895)

Freud, S. (1953). The interpretation of dreams. In J. Strachey (Ed. & Trans.), *The standard edition of the complete psychological works of Sigmund Freud* (Vols. 4–5, pp. 48–65 & pp. 460–488, respectively). London, England: Hogarth Press. (Original work published 1900)

Freud, S. (1957a). Instincts and their vicissitudes. In J. Strachey (Ed. & Trans.), *The standard edition of the complete psychological works of Sigmund Freud* (Vol. 14, pp. 109–139). London, England: Hogarth Press. (Original work published 1915)

Freud, S. (1957b). Papers on metapsychology. In J. Strachey (Ed. & Trans.), *The standard edition of the complete psychological works of Sigmund Freud* (Vol. 14, pp. 105–215). London, England: Hogarth Press. (Original work published 1915)

Freud, S. (1957c). Repression. In J. Strachey (Ed. & Trans.), *The standard edition of the complete psychological works of Sigmund Freud* (Vol. 14, pp. 141–157). London, England: Hogarth Press. (Original work published 1915)

Freud, S. (1959). Inhibitions, symptoms and anxiety. In J. Strachey (Ed. & Trans.), *The standard edition of the complete psychological works of Sigmund Freud* (Vol. 20, pp. 75–173). London, England: Hogarth Press. (Original work published 1926)

Freud, S. (1961a). Civilization and its discontents. In J. Strachey (Ed. & Trans.), *The standard edition of the complete psychological works of Sigmund Freud* (Vol. 21, pp. 57–146). London, England: Hogarth Press. (Original work published 1930)

Freud, S. (1961b). The ego and the id. In J. Strachey (Ed. & Trans.), *The standard edition of the complete psychological works of Sigmund Freud* (Vol. 19, pp. 1–65). London, England: Hogarth Press. (Original work published 1923)

Freud, S. (1963). Introductory lectures on psycho-analysis. In J. Strachey (Ed. & Trans.), *The standard edition of the complete psychological works of Sigmund Freud* (Vols. 16–17, pp. 13–463 & pp. 1–240). London, England: Hogarth Press. (Original work published 1916)

Gergely, G. (2013). Ostensive communication and cultural learning: The natural pedagogy hypothesis. In J. Metcalfe & H. S. Terrace (Eds.), *Agency and joint attention* (pp. 139–151). Oxford, England: Oxford University Press. http://dx.doi.org/10.1093/acprof:oso/9780199988341.003.0008

Heimann, P. (1950). On counter-transference. *International Journal of Psychoanalysis, 31*, 81–84.

Joseph, B. (1985). Transference: The total situation. *International Journal of Psychoanalysis, 66*, 447–454.

Kernberg, O. F. (1982). Self, ego, affects, and drives. *Journal of the American Psychoanalytic Association, 30*, 893–917. http://dx.doi.org/10.1177/000306518203000404

Kernberg, O. (1988). Psychic structure and structural change: An ego psychology-object relations theory viewpoint. *Journal of the American Psychoanalytic Association, 36S*(Suppl.), 315–337.

Kernberg, O. (2009). The concept of the death drive: A clinical perspective. *International Journal of Psychoanalysis, 90*, 1009–1023. http://dx.doi.org/10.1111/j.1745-8315.2009.00187.x

Klein, M. (1946). Notes on some schizoid mechanisms. *International Journal of Psychoanalysis, 27*, 99–110.

Lambert, M. J., & Ogles, B. M. (2004). The efficacy and effectiveness of psychotherapy. In M. J. Lambert (Ed.), *Bergin and Garfield's handbook of psychotherapy and behavior change* (5th ed., pp. 139–193). Hoboken, NJ: Wiley.

Laplanche, J., & Pontalis, J. B. (1973). *The language of psycho-analysis.* New York, NY: Norton.

Lingiardi, V., & McWilliams, N. (2017). *The psychodynamic diagnostic manual: PDM-2* (2nd ed.). New York, NY: Guilford Press.

Loewald, H. W. (1960). On the therapeutic action of psycho-analysis. *International Journal of Psychoanalysis, 41*, 16–33.

Loewald, H. W. (1986). Transference-countertransference. *Journal of the American Psychoanalytic Association, 34*, 275–287. http://dx.doi.org/10.1177/000306518603400202

Luyten, P., van Houdenhove, B., Lemma, A., Target, M., & Fonagy, P. (2012). A mentalization-based approach to the understanding and treatment of functional somatic disorders. *Psychoanalytic Psychotherapy, 26*, 121–140. http://dx.doi.org/10.1080/02668734.2012.678061

Mahler, M. S., Pine, F., & Bergman, A. (1975). *The psychological birth of the human infant: Symbiosis and individuation.* New York, NY: Basic Books.

McCullough, L., Kuhn, N., Andrews, S., Kaplan, A., Wolf, J., & Hurley, C. (2003). *Treating affect phobia: A manual for short term dynamic psychotherapy.* New York, NY: Guilford Press.

Music, G. (2001). *Affect and emotion: Ideas in psychoanalysis.* Cambridge, England: Icon Books.

Nacht, S. (1962). The curative factors in psycho-analysis: Contributions to discussion. *International Journal of Psychoanalysis, 43,* 206–211.

Ogden, T. H. (1992). *The primitive edge of experience.* New York, NY: Aronson.

Ogden, T. H. (1994). The analytic third: Working with intersubjective clinical facts. *International Journal of Psychoanalysis, 75,* 3–19.

Rapaport, D. (1950). *Emotions and memory* (2nd ed.). New York, NY: International Universities Press.

Rapaport, D. (1953). On the psychoanalytic theory of affects. *International Journal of Psychoanalysis, 34,* 177–178.

Safran, J. D., Muran, J. C., & Eubanks-Carter, C. (2011). Repairing alliance ruptures. In J. C. Norcross (Ed.), *Psychotherapy relationships that work: Evidence-based responsiveness* (2nd ed., pp. 224–238). New York, NY: Oxford University Press. http://dx.doi.org/10.1093/acprof:oso/9780199737208.003.0011

Sandler, J. (1960). The background of safety. *International Journal of Psychoanalysis, 41,* 352–356.

Sandler, J., Holder, A., Dare, C., & Dreher, A. (1997). *Freud's models of the mind: An introduction.* London, England: Karnac Books.

Sandler, J., & Sandler, A. M. (1978). On the development of object relationships and affects. *International Journal of Psychoanalysis, 59,* 285–296.

Shedler, J. (2010). The efficacy of psychodynamic psychotherapy. *American Psychologist, 65,* 98–109. http://dx.doi.org/10.1037/a0018378

Stern, D. N. (1985). *The interpersonal world of the infant.* New York, NY: Basic Books.

Stern, D. N. (2010). *Forms of vitality: Exploring dynamic experience in psychology, the arts, psychotherapy, and development.* Cambridge, England: Oxford University Press.

Winnicott, D. W. (1949). Hate in the counter-transference. *International Journal of Psychoanalysis, 30,* 69–74.

Winnicott, D. W. (1953). Transitional objects and transitional phenomena: A study of the first not-me possession. *International Journal of Psychoanalysis, 34,* 89–97.

Winnicott, D. W. (1958). The capacity to be alone. *International Journal of Psychoanalysis, 39,* 416–420.

Wolf, E. S. (1993). Disruptions of the therapeutic relationship in psychoanalysis: A view from self psychology. *International Journal of Psychoanalysis, 74,* 675–687.

3

COGNITIVE BEHAVIOR PSYCHOTHERAPY AND EMOTION

MICHAEL A. TOMPKINS

Over the years, I have taught many classes in cognitive behavior therapy (CBT). Whether from experienced clinicians or novice trainees, I typically hear the same assumptions regarding the role of emotion in this psychotherapeutic approach. For example, they may say that there is no place for emotion in CBT and that cognition is the only domain of interest to cognitive behavior therapists. Or they may say that CBT focuses only on teaching clients to manage their emotions without regard to the value of emotions themselves. They also may say that CBT focuses exclusively on teaching skills and, as such, is a string of techniques without a coherent theory or conceptualization to guide therapists in their therapeutic work. Given these assumptions about CBT, I'm not surprised that many clinicians view CBT and cognitive behavior therapists as robotic, mechanical, and with little concern for the emotional overlay inherent in psychotherapy. In this chapter, I hope to clarify and underscore the importance of emotion in CBT and to correct the

http://dx.doi.org/10.1037/0000130-003
Working With Emotion in Psychodynamic, Cognitive Behavior, and Emotion-Focused Psychotherapy,
by L. S. Greenberg, N. T. Malberg, and M. A. Tompkins

misguided assumption that emotion is secondary to cognition. CBT is effective because it recognizes the importance of emotion as a mediator of deep and lasting cognitive and behavioral change, and vice versa.

The chapter begins with a brief description of CBT and of the cognitive model on which this treatment approach rests. I then explain the role of emotion in the efficacy of this psychological treatment. The chapter next describes the role of emotion in five domains: learning, motivation, emotional responses, interpersonal relationships, and the therapeutic relationship itself. In each of these sections, I discuss strategies that cognitive behavior therapists typically use to evoke emotion to elicit relevant thoughts and beliefs, facilitate new and deep learning, or enhance the client's confidence that the skills he or she has learned will help in the face of strong negative emotions. Throughout, clinical vignettes are used to convey these practical considerations; all case materials have been disguised to protect client confidentiality.

COGNITIVE BEHAVIOR THERAPY AND THE COGNITIVE BEHAVIOR MODEL

A number of cognitive behavior approaches have been developed over the years by major theorists, such as Albert Ellis (1962) and his rational-emotive therapy, Donald Meichenbaum (1977) and his cognitive behavior modification, and Arnold Lazarus (1976) and his multimodal therapy. Other contributors have added to the richness of the theory and practice of CBT, and interested readers can find several reviews of the origin and growth of the different streams of CBT (Dobson, 2001).

Cognitive Behavior Psychotherapy

This chapter presents the cognitive therapy or CBT developed in the 1960s by Aaron T. Beck at the University of Pennsylvania as an alternative to psychoanalysis, the dominant psychological treatment at the time for depression (Beck, 1964). Cognitive behavior psychotherapy then and today is structured, problem focused, and short term. The client is an active participant in the approach, collaborating with the therapist to modify the maladaptive cognitions hypothesized to contribute to the maintenance of emotional distress and problem behaviors. The goal of CBT is to reduce symptoms of the condition in the service of improving the individual's day-to-day functioning. Since its inception, the treatment has been adapted to a wide range of psychiatric diagnoses, problems, and populations (Barlow, 2014), and has developed numerous disorder-specific treatments, including but not limited to depressive disorders (Di Giulio, 2010; Jorm, Morgan, & Hetrick, 2008; Tolin, 2010), anxiety disorders (Fedoroff & Taylor, 2001; Hofmann & Smits, 2008), insomnia (Irwin, Cole, & Nicassio, 2006; Okajima, Komada, & Inoue, 2011), addiction and substance use disorders (Dutra et al., 2008; García-Vera & Sanz, 2006; Leung & Cottler, 2009), and schizophrenia and other psychotic disorders (Gould, Mueser, Bolton, Mays, & Goff, 2001; Rector & Beck, 2001). Although these disorder-specific treatment protocols may vary regarding specific techniques, they all share the same core cognitive conceptualization and the general approach to treatment. Furthermore, hundreds of thoughtful empirical studies have repeatedly supported the efficacy of this treatment approach (Butler, Chapman, Forman, & Beck, 2006; Hofmann, Asnaani, Vonk, Sawyer, & Fang, 2012).

CBT translates then into three fundamental propositions that are central to understanding the rationale for the treatment approach and its components (Dozois & Dobson, 2001). First, cognitive activity affects behavior. To date, the evidence overwhelmingly supports the proposition that cognitive appraisals of events can influence or mediate the behavioral response to those events. A phobic client who believes that cats are dangerous will avoid them. A depressed client who predicts that pleasant activities that were once pleasant will not feel pleasant if tried again will avoid engaging in these activities.

The second fundamental proposition of CBT is that cognitive activity can be monitored and altered. This proposition is essential to several strategies used in CBT, such as self-recording and cognitive restructuring. Monitoring and recording cognitive activity are a prelude to the modifying cognitive activity. Clients who monitors their automatic thoughts will learn that they tend to appraise situations in an inflexible and predictable manner, and that their predictions are persistently inaccurate and unhelpful. Through monitoring and self-recording using a daily record of dysfunction thoughts (Beck, Rush, Shaw, & Emery, 1979), for example, depressed clients will learn that when they feel the most depressed, they tend to view events in particular ways; when they are less depressed, their view of the same event can differ. That is, clients who monitor and record their cognitive activity gain perspective on their cognitive processes, and this perspective is essential to the process of modifying thoughts and beliefs. Furthermore, clients who understand the role that their cognitive activity plays in their emotional response to events are more willing to learn and implement strategies to influence that cognitive activity.

The third fundamental proposition of CBT is based on the first proposition. That is, if cognitive activity mediates or influences behavioral change, then altering maladaptive cognitive activity can change maladaptive behavior. Therefore, according to cognitive behavior therapists' point of view, the role of cognitive change techniques, such as a dysfunctional thought record (a form clients use to identify and evaluate dysfunctional thoughts) or even psychoeducation, is to influence behavioral change. For example, a client who fears domestic house cats may be willing to approach rather than avoid house cats if, through a series of thought records, the client modifies his or predictions of danger and thereby develops an alternative and more accurate view of house cats—that they are not dangerous. Or, a client who often is angry and aggressive because the client assumes that people intend to thwart him or her or put that client down may feel less angry and thereby willing to try more adaptive behaviors or skills, such as assertiveness or conflict resolution, if the client learns that his or her assumption often is inaccurate and tends to fuel his or her angry responses.

The fundamental propositions that cognition affects behavior; that cognition can be monitored and altered, and that behavior change is mediated or influenced by cognitive change reflect the objective of the most notable interventions in CBT. Later, we take up the important and essential role that emotion plays in the success of these interventions.

Cognitive Behavior Model

Beckian CBT is based on a cognitive behavior model or conceptualization that assumes that cognitive appraisals (i.e., perceptions, expectations, and interpretation) of situations and events, rather than the situations and events themselves, influence our emotional responses. Most times, our appraisals of events are adaptive and therefore our emotional and behavioral responses are helpful and contribute to effective functioning. At other times, our appraisals are maladaptive and result in disproportionate emotional distress and repeated problem behaviors, such as avoidance in the case of anxiety disorders or withdrawal in the case of depressive disorders.

The following example illustrates the role of cognitive appraisals in emotional and behavioral responses to an event:

> "Jason" is home when his phone rings. He considers three possibilities about who the caller might be and why the person is calling him. "It might be my wife calling to tell me that she's working late again." "It might be my boss calling to tell me he didn't like the report I submitted today." "It might be my next-door neighbor calling to ask if he can borrow my lawn mower again." The assumption that Jason favors is likely shaped by his psychological set or belief about himself, others, and the future. If Jason's thinking is dominated by the concept that he is unlovable, he may conclude that his wife doesn't love him, and then feel sad or disappointed and withdraw to his room. If Jason's thinking is dominated by the concept

that the future is dangerous and unpredictable, he may conclude that his boss is calling to fire him, then feel anxious and avoid picking up the phone. If Jason's thinking is dominated by the concept that others care only about themselves, he may conclude that his neighbor is taking advantage of him, then feel angry and yell at his neighbor next time he sees him.

According to the cognitive model, then, the same initial event (i.e., the ringing of the phone) elicits different emotions, depending on how the individual interprets the event. The ring of the phone itself elicits little emotion, other than perhaps curiosity if the interpretation elicited by the ring is neutral. As suggested in the example, the tendency to interpret a neutral event in a particular way is influenced by the individual's psychological set, that is, what that individual believes about himself or herself, others, and the future. In the cognitive model, these broad psychological sets are termed *core beliefs*. However, other factors can influence the tendency to interpret events in a particular way. The current context in which the event occurs, as well as early experiences, can play a role. In Jason's case, he might not have concluded that his boss was calling to fire him if he had not submitted the report earlier that day, nor might he have concluded that his boss was about to fire him if he had not been fired from his previous job.

Human cognition consists of two separate systems, each of which is reflected in the cognitive behavior conceptualization of psychological problems. The first system includes appraisals or cognitions that are generated quickly and require little effort. These cognitions are intuitive and spontaneous, and are linked to the context in which they occur. The second system includes appraisals or cognitions that are generated slowly, require deliberate effort, and are logical (Kahneman, 2011). CBT targets both cognitive systems and uses the second system to shift the first. That is, CBT strives to assist clients to become rational and critical thinkers and to apply empiricism to identifying, testing, and modifying maladaptive appraisals.

Beck's (1964) cognitive behavior model assumes a hierarchy of relevant cognitions at three levels: core beliefs; intermediate beliefs; and automatic thoughts and images. Core beliefs, once triggered by a life event, drive intermediate beliefs, and both result in automatic thoughts. The goal of CBT is to teach clients to first recognize the role of their cognitive misappraisals in their emotional and behavioral responses, and then to learn strategies to replace maladaptive appraisals with more realistic and adaptive appraisals. CBT has substantial empirical support for its efficacy for a number of problems in a variety of populations. Furthermore, CBT recognizes that early experiences in interaction with temperament and culture influence the formation of mal-adaptive beliefs and maladaptive coping strategies that maintain ongoing problems. The focus of CBT is on the here-and-now; it strives to teach clients practical skills to manage chronic psychological disorders and thereby live fulfilling and productive lives.

UNDERSTANDING AND WORKING WITH EMOTION

In the 1960s, behavior therapy began a measured shift from its exclusive focus on specific behaviors and on classical and operant learning models to the role of cognitive and affective factors in human functioning. In light of the developments in basic cognitive science, cognitive therapy or CBT expanded conceptualizations to include cognitions as a maintaining factor in emotional disorders and thereby a focus of intervention. In the 1980s, CBT acknowledged the growing evidence of the critical role emotion plays in the process of change (Barlow, 1991, 2002; Bower, 1981; Greenberg & Safran, 1984, 1987; Leventhal, 1979; Zajonc, 1980).

A growing body of evidence has suggested that actively working to intensify a client's engagement with emotion in therapy can improve out-comes in a variety of psychotherapies (Borkovec & Sides, 1979; Jaycox, Foa, & Morral, 1998), including CBT (Jones & Pulos, 1993). Evidence also has indicated that emotional arousal during exposure may be critical in producing change and that without an adequate level of arousal, exposure procedures are less effective (Lang, 1979).

Deepening emotion within therapy is associated more often with psychodynamic or existential–humanistic therapies (Blagys & Hilsenroth, 2002; Goldfried, 2013). However, CBT uses emotion in the service of change too. For example, emotional processing theory posits that to modify excessive or disproportionate fear responses, it is necessary to activate the underlying fear circuitry to modify it (Foa & Kozak, 1986). Evoking elements of the original fear stimulus activates emotion (i.e., fear in the case of an anxiety disorder) through CBT or exposure therapy and enhances the modification of the underlying cognitive–affective mental structures. Neurobiological research has supported the fundamental assumptions of emotional processing theory in animal models, whereby the existing learned fear circuitry becomes both labile and modifiable when reactivated through evoking elements of the original fear stimulus (Tronson & Taylor, 2007). Activating emotion to enhance the modification of the underlying cognitive–affective mental struc-tures has been applied to emotional disorders, in general, and is the basis of a variety of interventions across emotional disorders or difficulties (Allen, McHugh, & Barlow, 2008).

However, it appears that evoking emotion in therapy is insufficient in itself for change. For example, in the case of exposure therapy, habituation or attenuation of the fear response may be less important than assisting the client to build tolerance and acceptance of negative affect (Arch, Wolitzky-Taylor, Eifert, & Craske, 2012; Bluett, Zoellner, & Feeny, 2014; Craske et al., 2008). Building distress tolerance skills is a consistent feature of CBT. Furthermore, the processing of emotions through attending, accepting, and differentiating cognitive–affective experience are related to positive outcomes in CBT, as well as to treatment approaches more often associated with emotion, such as emotion-focused therapy and client-centered therapy (Castonguay, Goldfried, Wiser, Raue, & Hayes, 1996; Pos, Greenberg, & Warwar, 2009; Watson & Bedard, 2006).

Although CBT emphasizes the role of cognitive factors in the maintenance of psychological conditions, the approach also recognizes the important role of the physiological, behavioral, and emotional components in the maintenance of psychological disorders. Cognitive behavior psychotherapy includes a variety of interventions to target these cognitive and behavioral factors, including emotion-focused techniques (Hofmann, 2011; Hofmann, Asmundson, & Beck, 2013). CBT borrows many of these techniques from other therapeutic approaches. Examples of these techniques are role plays, imagery role plays, two-chair dialogues, and the catching of an emotion in the therapeutic moment and then exploration of the emotion and cognitions associated with it to amplify the emotion itself. In addition, the techniques (presented later) used to evoke and work with emotions in CBT present other opportunities to the cognitive behavior therapist and client.

Emotion Marks Clinically Relevant Cognitions

In session, the cognitive behavior therapist searches for signs or shifts of emotion. When the therapist asks a client a question, the therapist pauses and looks down. As a client speaks about a past event, the client's voice begins to tremble or his or her eyes fill with tears. These subtle signs often signal the fleeting presence of a clinically relevant cognition, and the watchful cognitive behavior therapist then asks, "What went through your mind just then?" In CBT, emotion signals cognition, typically a relevant cognition to target for change. Often these cognitions are automatic thoughts, such as, "Nothing will ever change for me" or "What if this time I have a serious illness?"

From where do automatic thoughts spring, though? In the cognitive model, automatic thoughts emerge from more enduring cognitive structures: the core beliefs of the individual. Emotion marks core belief activation, and whether the cognitive behavior therapist decides to target in that moment the automatic thoughts, intermediate beliefs, or core beliefs themselves, emotion in a therapy session is a relevant and important target for intervention.

Surprisingly, although automatic thoughts are the most accessible of cognitions within the cognitive model, it is not uncommon for clients to have little awareness of them:

Jessica (drops her head and sighs):   I should have called you.

Therapist: What went through your mind just then, Jessica?

Jessica: Nothing. I'm fine.

Therapist: I still see the presence, I think, of a feeling. Please share with me what thought or image went through your mind just now.

Jessica (hesitates):   Okay. Well, I don't feel like you want to work with me anymore.

Therapist: So, you had the thought that I don't want to work with you anymore. How did that thought make you feel?

Jessica (begins to cry):   Lousy.

Therapist: Lousy? Lousy as in sad?

Jessica (begins to cry harder):   Yes. I feel really sad. You're going to give up on me like everyone else in my life. You don't care about me. No one cares about me.

Therapist: You feel very sad because you believe that no one cares about you.

Jessica (more tears):   Yes. Yes.

At this point, the cognitive behavior therapist might inquire about the automatic thought "You don't want to work with me anymore," and shift the client to examine the evidence for that assumption. Alternatively, the cognitive behavior therapist might explore the attitude "No one cares about me" and implement the downward arrow technique (Burns, 1980):

Therapist: If this were true, Jessica, that no one cares about you, what would that mean about you?

Jessica (pauses):   If no one cares about me, what does that mean about me?

Therapist: Yes, if it were true that no one cares about you, what would that mean about you, then?

Jessica (sobbing intensely now):   I guess it would mean that I'm worthless. Yes, worthless.

In both examples, the therapist first acknowledged the possible presence of an emotion and then linked the emotion to the cognition, thereby enhancing the client's emotional response in the moment. Once the emotion is acknowledged, the therapist can teach the client the role that her cognitions play in her emotional responses, "You feel very sad because you believe no one cares about you," always linking emotion to cognition and thereby illustrating the cognitive model, as well as inviting the client to accept the emotion and the cognitions related to that emotion.

Emotion Builds Self-Awareness and Emotion Tolerance

The best skills in the world are useless to clients if they do not know when to use them. In CBT, many strategies focus on increasing the client's awareness of his or her emotional arousal in session. Self-recording outside of session serves a similar function. Typically, self-recording involves the client's recording situations that trigger the targeted emotion (e.g., anxiety, depression, anger) or problematic behaviors and then recording the automatic thoughts triggered at the time. In this way, the client becomes more aware of his or her emotional responses and the features of his or her emotional responses (i.e., cognitions, emotions, behaviors). Self-recording also provides clients with an arm-distance perspective on their emotional responses that can contribute to an attenuation of the emotion. Furthermore, clients who monitor their emotional responses learn important lessons about emotions themselves, for example, that emotions rise and fall rather than increasing indefinitely. Emotions do not come out of nowhere but are linked to cognitions. In addition, emotions can be tolerated. These lessons also provide some distance on the emotion itself, particularly when the client fears his or her emotional response.

At the same time, many clients report an increase in the intensity of the emotion they are recording, and it is a good idea to predict this effect when training the client to self-record. Thus, self-recording not only increases the client's awareness of his or her emotional arousal but can indirectly enhance that client's tolerance to the emotion too. Self-recording invites the client to observe and interact with his or her emotional responses rather than avoid them. The act of self-recording, then, can enhance the client's tolerance of an emotion.

CBT now includes strategies and approaches, such as mindfulness, that build awareness and tolerance. *Mindfulness* is "moment-by-moment" awareness, whereby clients learn to pay attention on purpose, in the present moment, and without judging the unfolding experience moment by moment (Kabat-Zinn, 2003). Mindfulness is both a process and a practice, such as meditation. Three forms of mindfulness are typical of the Western practice of mindfulness meditation: focused attention, open monitoring, and loving-kindness and compassion (Salzberg, 2011). Focused attention and open monitoring are attention-regulation strategies. *Focused attention* calms the mind by repeatedly returning attention to a single object, such as the breath. *Open monitoring* turns attention to what arises, such as a body sensation, or an emotion that the client then labels. *Loving-kindness and compassion* meditation adds an element of care, comfort, and soothing to awareness. Regardless of the form of meditation, with practice, they all enable clients to accept and tolerate emotions.

Emotion Increases Confidence in the Effectiveness of Skills

Cognitive behavior therapists identify the skill deficits that result in the client's ongoing difficulties and then work with the client to build new adaptive skills to manage emotion and alter maladaptive behaviors. Cognitive reappraisal is a core skill that clients learn to help them manage their emotional and behavioral problems. A number of studies have supported the efficacy of reappraisal strategies (Hofmann et al., 2013), but CBT includes a variety of other skills, such as communication, problem-solving, and mindfulness, that may assist clients to regulate their emotions in the moment or before a situation in which problematic behaviors tend to arise (Hofmann, 2011).

New skills are new behaviors, and it is essential that clients believe that the skills work not only in session with the therapist but that they can deliver the new behavior (i.e., skill) in the presence of strong negative emotion. The belief that the client has the skills and knowledge to achieve the desired outcome is *self-efficacy* (Bandura, 1977, 1982). Confidence is the strength of that belief. Typically, Cognitive behavior therapists use strategies, such as role plays or imagery, to evoke emotion in session to enable the client to practice a newly learned skill during intense negative affect. For example, a client who is too anxious to decline additional work the supervisor insists he or she take can benefit from assertiveness skill training. However, once learned, the true test of the effectiveness of the newly acquired assertiveness skill is that the client is assertive when he or she is feeling anxious. Similarly, a client who struggles with intense anger can use a variety of coping skills to manage his or her anger, but the true test of the effectiveness of these skills is that they work when he or she is angry.

To summarize, emotion is an essential leg in the three-legged stool of CBT: cognition–emotion–behavior. Emotion is front and center in the cognitive conceptualizations of psychological disorders, and cognitive behavior therapists recognize emotion as a driver of deep psychological change. In CBT, emotion is not always viewed as a state that clients learn to manage, but often, when used effectively, emotion can enhance new learning, skill acquisition, and adaptive functioning.

EMOTION AND LEARNING

The cognitive behavior model is a learning model, and, as such, the goal of CBT is to facilitate new learning in the service of new and more adaptive behaviors. Emotion serves an important role in a client's learning process, particularly in questioning deeply held and often unquestioned beliefs, and learning new adaptive beliefs to override them.

Several information processing theories support the role of emotion in learning and behavioral change: the dual representation theory (Brewin, 1996, 2001); schematic, propositional, analogical, and associative representational systems model (Power & Dalgleish, 1997, 1999); cognitive-experiential self-theory (Epstein, 1994; Epstein & Pacini, 1999); interacting cognitive subsystems (ICS) model (Teasdale, 1997; Teasdale & Barnard, 1993); and metacognitive theory (Wells, 2000; Wells & Matthews, 1994).

The ICS model and the metacognitive model provide a broad and multilevel representation of the influence of emotion on qualitatively different information processing systems. The first system is a rational, verbal, logical, propositional information processing system without links to emotion. Cognitive behavior strategies, such as cognitive restructuring (described later), focus on activating this first system. The second system is a more holistic, non-linguistic, automatic, and rapid information processing system with deep and extensive links to emotion. Cognitive behavior strategies, such as behavioral experiments (BEs; described later), along with other strategies, such as imagery role plays or two-chair role plays, focus on activating this second system.

Although clients tend to believe with their "head" the alternative or new learning from thought records, they tend to believe with their "heart" the alternative beliefs derived through these emotion-linked interventions. The experience clients have between their "intellectual" beliefs versus their "emotional" beliefs may reflect different levels of information processing that reasoning strategies and experiential strategies access, and the different kinds of experience necessary to promote cognitive change in each case (Teasdale & Barnard, 1993). At the same time, although the ICS model implies that experiential exercises impact the implicational system and therefore render greater cognitive, emotional, and behavioral change, it is likely that emotion impacts both levels. That is, interventions that target the *propositional* (i.e., verbal/logical) level, such as thought records and guided discovery, may impact the *implicational* (i.e., deeper) level too when the client engages in this propositional process in the presence of emotion.

Experimental research on memory has supported the value of emotion in the process of learning. Heightened emotion usually facilitates remembering, although the accuracy can be compromised (Heuer & Reisberg, 1992). In addition, the enactment effect supports the usefulness of experiential learning. The *enactment effect*, or the self-performed tasks effect, suggests that individuals better remember a verbal phrase that describes an action when they enact or perform the action (Engelkamp, 1998) than when another person only describes the task or when the individual only observes another person doing the task. For example, individuals may better remember the phrase "brush the teeth" when they enact the task (i.e., act as if they are brushing their teeth). The robustness of the enactment effect may result from encoding memory among several modalities (e.g., visual, auditory, kinesthetic) such that the information is emotionally/experientially acquired. Information acquired this way may result in a more widespread effect on cognition, emotion, and behavior than purely verbal information.

The metacognitive theory may further support the value of emotional/experiential strategies to facilitate deep and lasting learning (Wells, 2000) through emotion. The experimental psychology literature distinguishes between declarative and procedural memory. *Declarative memory* holds knowledge and beliefs that are recalled as factual information (e.g., "The earth orbits around the sun" or "I cannot control my worry"). These beliefs might be called "thought beliefs." *Procedural memory* holds knowledge about plans or procedures that often are automatic and implicit (e.g., "Don't look into the sun" or "Take a medication to control my worry"). These might be called "felt beliefs."

Metacognitive theory implies that cognitive change depends not only on developing both a new declarative memory or thought belief (e.g., "I can control my worry") but also on developing a different procedural memory or felt belief through repeated enactments of a new plan or procedure (e.g., "Postpone worry until 5 p.m. each day"). Applying this implication to the cognitive behavior model, one might assume that particular events may elicit the declarative belief "I'm incompetent" for a socially anxious client; the client then avoids social situations or engages in overcautious behaviors when in social situations, such as peppering people with questions rather than sharing personal opinions when people ask. Metacognitive theory argues that effective psychotherapy changes both declarative thought beliefs and procedural felt beliefs.

It is insufficient to focus solely on changing declarative beliefs through verbal-strategies, such as cognitive restructuring. It is necessary to also change procedural beliefs. Clients who alter their behavior in the face of strong emotion, as is the case in experiential strategies, directly target procedural memory and likely alter declarative beliefs too.

What, then, is the argument for cognitive restructuring that identifies and tests declarative thoughts and beliefs, as is the case in cognitive restructuring, if deep and lasting cognitive change occurs through activating procedural beliefs and memories? Metacognitive theory argues that overt or covert declarative beliefs are just as much a part of cognition as the automatic and implicit knowledge that form procedural memory. These automatic and implicit procedural beliefs may be less susceptible to change through verbal-only strategies. However, identifying and testing declarative thoughts and beliefs can encourage clients to undertake experiential strategies that involve repeated enactment (i.e., new behaviors) of new plans and procedures. Experiential strategies then activate learning at the deeper implicational level and the declarative level. Targeting both these information processing levels encompasses and influences lasting change in cognition, emotion, and behavior. Through experiential learning, clients engage in a process that brings together what they know to be true "in their head" with what they know to be true "in their gut."

Behavioral Experiments to Facilitate Learning

Although cognitive restructuring strategies are useful, these thought experiments may only loosen an old belief and enhance a client's willingness to explore further and consider alternative views of events, and perhaps test new beliefs through the process of changing his or her behavior. Most cognitive behavior therapists believe that significant change in CBT may occur through behavioral reattribution (Wells, 1997) or BEs (Clark, 1989). The experiential approach of BEs may reflect a greater synchrony across the cognitive, affective, and behavioral systems (Rachman & Hodgson, 1974), thereby making BEs some of the most powerful strategies for bringing about change in CBT (Beck et al., 1979; Clark, 1989; Greenberger & Padesky, 1995; Wells, 1997) and a key intervention in CBT. The power of BEs rests, in part, on the use of emotion to activate and facilitate new learning.

BEs are planned experiential activities, based on experimentation or observation, that clients undertake in a CBT session or between CBT sessions (Bennett-Levy et al., 2004). The primary objective of BEs is to obtain new information that may help to test the validity of a client's existing beliefs about self, others, and the world and, to construct and/or test new, more adaptive beliefs.

BEs focus on changing behavior and following behavior therapy's formulation but with a focus on cognition and the recognition that doing things differently is a powerful means to change both cognition and affect. Changing behavior to change emotional and behavioral responses was a significant break from much of previous psychotherapy, which primarily or exclusively used in-session dialogue as the method of change.

Beck's (1964) formulation of cognitions as hypotheses to be tested—and testing them via BEs—oriented therapist and client to viewing cognitions as assumptions or predictions to be tested. The orientation of BEs, then, is an elaboration of the empirical foundation of CBT itself, whereby the cognitive behavior therapist applies the empirical scientific approach to the client's experience (i.e., beliefs, emotions, and behaviors). In science, experiments play an important role in testing scientific theories. In CBT, the theory that is to be tested is the client's belief rather than a scientific law or theory, but the philosophical approach is similar.

In science, there are two broad approaches to experimentation. The first—what some consider the only true form of experimentation—involves the scientist's deliberately manipulating some aspect of the world. For example, Isaac Newton designed an experiment to test the dominant theory of the day that white light was pure and fundamental by directing sunlight through a prism, which spread the light into an oblong spectrum. In this simple and elegant experiment, Newton proved that light was not pure but was a combination of different rays or wavelengths of light.

Design and Implementation of Behavioral Experiments

Cognitive behavior therapists can design BEs in this same way. The therapist and client can manipulate the environment to test the validity of a client's hypothesis or belief, thoughts, or perceptions. For example, a healthy client with panic disorder who believes that a racing heart means that he or she will have a heart attack and thereby avoids exercising can test that prediction by running up a flight of stairs to increase his or her heart rate and then observe whether he or she has a heart attack or not.

A second experimental approach is the observational experiment. It is impossible in many sciences, such as astronomy, evolution, archeology, and anthropology, to manipulate the environment to test a theory or hypothesis. The scientist cannot change the sun's gravitational field to observe what happens to planetary orbits under new conditions. Instead, scientists can gather data and observe the world in an effort to build a coherent theory about how people, social systems, and cultures work. For example, an archaeologist may gather and analyze potsherds unearthed in the ruins of an ancient village to develop a theory about the day-to-day life of the people who lived there.

Cognitive behavior therapists can use BEs in this discovery-oriented approach too. Rather than manipulating the environment, the therapist assists the client to develop a plan to observe and gather evidence relevant to the client's specific belief or theory. For example, to test the client's belief that people will think that he or she is weird if they see the client sweating in social situations, the client might survey a group of friends and family members about what they would think if they observed a person sweating at a party. Similarly, a man who believes that women are attracted only to men who are ruggedly good-looking might create a survey questionnaire and anonymously solicit women to complete this "attractiveness" survey.

There is a long-standing recognition of the value of personal experience in learning (Kemmis & McTaggart, 2000; Kolb, 1984; Lewin, 1946; Schon, 1983). Behavioral experiments use experiential learning in the service of cognitive change. The process of designing and implementing BEs follows an experiential learning model (Kolb, 1984; Lewin, 1946) and proceeds through four stages: plan, experience, observe, and reflect.

Based on the conceptualization of the problem (reflect), the client and therapist clarify a declarative belief to test and plan an appropriate experiment to test it (plan). The client then carries out the experiment (experience), perhaps altering a feature of the client's typical experience or behavior (e.g., a client who fears that people will think he or she is weird if the client blushes, so avoids wearing red clothing; for the BE, the client agrees to wear a red scarf) and observes the results of the experiment (observe). The client and therapist then explore the implications for the belief (reflect) and perhaps plan another experiment (plan). This cycle continues throughout a session or throughout a treatment until a new belief forms and solidifies. The client and therapist can begin the BE process at any stage in the experiential learning circle.

To illustrate how cognitive behavior therapists plan and implement BEs, consider "John," who worried excessively about sweating. When he met with the therapist, he was able to state that he was worried that if people saw him sweating without a good reason (i.e., exercising), they would think he was weird or sketchy. John avoided going to restaurants and movies, and interacting with people he did not know well. When he left his home, John wore a jacket to hide the sweat under his arms if he began to sweat in social situations.

Therapist: John, it sounds like you're very worried that people will think you're weird if they see that you're sweating.

John: Yeah. I'm afraid they'll think I'm weird if I'm all sweaty for no good reason.

Therapist: What's a good reason for sweating?

John: If I've been exercising or it's very hot. Those would be good reasons.

Therapist: So, you're afraid that people will think you're weird if they see that you're sweating and you don't have a good reason to sweat. Do I have that right?

John:	Yeah. I guess it's kind of dumb when you say it like that but, yeah, that's what I believe.
Therapist:	How strongly do you believe that prediction on a scale of 0 to 100%, where 100 is that you believe it completely?
John:	I don't know, maybe 80%.
Therapist:	Okay, so 80%. And, how anxious do you feel on that scale when you think about that prediction being true?
John:	Maybe an 80% too.
Therapist:	So, how could we test out this prediction of yours? You know, how could we test your prediction that if people see that you're sweating without a good reason then they'll think you're weird?
John:	Gee, I don't know. Can we test out something like this?
Therapist:	Sure. I have an idea, and I'll do it first so that you can watch. How about if I make it so that I look like I'm sweating, and we go into the bookstore down the street and speak with one of the clerks there? We might be able to test out your prediction that way. What do you say?
John:	Sure, I guess so. You're going to do the experiment, right?
Therapist:	You bet!

John and his therapist then designed the experiment (plan). First, the therapist and client clarified how they would know whether the person thought the therapist was weird or not. They agreed that the clerk would have a particular look on his or her face (i.e., distaste or shock), and the therapist practiced these faces with John so that he would recognize the look if it occurred. John and the therapist agreed that if the clerk thought the therapist was weird, he or she would cut the conversation short and make an excuse to walk away quickly. It is crucial when designing BEs that the therapist work with the client to identify objective evidence that the prediction is true or false. The impact of the BE on the client's learning often depends on how well the therapist controls contaminating or confounding variables so that results of the experiment are unambiguous.

Once the therapist planned the experiment, it was time to conduct it. John watched as the therapist sprayed water under his arms with a spray bottle to make large and noticeable wet spots. John then accompanied the therapist to the bookstore. The therapist instructed John to observe the results of the experiment, in particular, to watch for evidence that the clerk thought the therapist was weird. The therapist, with John watching, walked into the bookstore and asked the clerk to recommend a good book for a trip he was about to take (experience). The clerk smiled and took him to a section of the bookstore. She spoke to him at length about the author and the book. She nodded her head. She laughed. She continued to speak to the therapist (observe) until the therapist excused himself: "This sounds like a great book. Will you set it aside for me, and I'll come back later and buy it?"

John and the therapist returned to the office and discussed what John had observed (reflect). Did John observe the look that suggested that the clerk thought the therapist was weird? Did the clerk cut the conversation short and walk away? John admitted that he did not observe any evidence that his prediction was true.

> *Therapist:* How strongly do you believe your prediction now on that 0 to 100% scale?
>
> *John:* Well, that was pretty impressive, doc. Maybe I'm at 50% now.
>
> *Therapist:* Why not 25%, John?
>
> *John:* Well, maybe she didn't see the wet circles under your arms. Maybe they were too small.
>
> *Therapist:* So, how could we test that out?
>
> *John (with a smile):* More water?

The therapist nodded and then sprayed more water under his arms until the wet spots were larger, perhaps 8 to 10 inches in diameter (plan). He and John repeated the experiment (experience), watching for the same evidence and observing the same results (observe). To satisfy John's concern that the clerk may not have noticed the wet spots, the therapist raised his arms to point to areas of the bookstore and stood and chatted with the clerk with his hands clasped behind his head. John was satisfied that the clerk likely had seen the wet spots under the therapist's arms.

> *Therapist:* So, John, how strongly do you believe your prediction now?
>
> *John:* Wow. It's definitely getting lower. I'd say it's a 20% now.
>
> *Therapist:* And your anxiety on that scale? What would you rate that?
>
> *John:* Oh, maybe 25%. The prediction still makes me pretty anxious.
>
> *Therapist:* John, what did you learn from this experiment that is helpful to you now?

John:	Well, I guess I learned that my prediction may be wrong. It's strange because when I was watching you do the experiment, I felt like she was going to think you were weird for sure.
Therapist:	John, did you see any evidence of the alternative belief that the clerk saw that I was sweating but didn't seem to care?
John:	Oh, yeah. She smiled at you and seemed like she enjoyed talking with you. She didn't seem to be bothered at all by the wet spots under your arms.
Therapist:	Yes. The alternative prediction seems more likely, doesn't it? If people see you sweating, they likely don't care that much and aren't likely to think you're weird.
John:	Yeah. This is cool, but, I don't know, maybe she didn't think you were weird because you're an adult and I'm just a teenager. Maybe she would think a teenager is weird if he was sweating for no good reason.
Therapist:	Hmm. John, how could we test that out?
John (smiling):	I knew you were going to ask me that.

John then repeated the same experiment. He was quite anxious but completed the experiment as he and his therapist had planned. This successful BE set the stage for John to complete additional BEs, whereby he dropped other safety behaviors.

To summarize, emotion plays a critical role in learning at both the thought belief and felt belief levels. Cognitive restructuring activates reason to alter cognitions and typically begins with capturing a cognition to restructure: "What went through your mind just then?" This purely verbal/logical enterprise results in new learning and, when the client is experiencing negative affect, can result in lasting cognitive change. Altering cognition at the logical level often is a precursor to orienting the client to primarily experiential strategies, such as BEs, and begins with an invitation to test the cognition: "How can we test that out?" The power of experiential strategies rests, in part, on the activation of deep, automatic, and intuitive emotional learning that results in deep and lasting cognitive, emotional, and behavioral change. Cognitive behavior therapists use both logical and experiential strategies because, although reason can teach us a great deal, experience can teach us more.

EMOTION AND MOTIVATION

Motivation or motivational tendencies are part of every emotion. When we feel anxious, we tend to avoid or leave the anxiety-evoking situation. When we feel sad, we tend to slow down and withdraw from pleasurable activities. When we feel irritated or angry, we tend to strike out. The link between motivation and emotion is more obvious for certain emotions than others and more pronounced when the emotional responses are extreme, as in the case of psychological disorders, such as mood disorders and particularly depression, addictions, or eating disorders.

The objective of motivational tendencies is either to attain reward and pleasure or to avoid punishment and misery (Carver & Scheier, 1998; Gray & McNaughton, 2000; Mowrer, 1960). Early behaviorists viewed motivation as initiated and maintained through drive reduction (Hull, 1943; Spence, 1956). For example, we are motivated to drink water because it reduces the thirst drive, or we are motivated to eat because it reduces the hunger drive. However, motivation theorists have broadened our understanding of motivation to include incentive expectancies (Bindra, 1974; Bolles, 1972; Pfaffmann, 1960; Toates, 1986). Motivated behavior, then, is a function of not only satisfying biological drives but doing so by the learned association between stimulus and rewarding or positive experiences. For example, we are motivated to eat tasty foods, seek attractive sexual partners, or use illicit drugs because they satisfy both biological drives, and we associate (through learning) these stimuli with rewarding experiences. Therefore, the sights, smells, and sensations associated with rewarding experiences predict the likelihood of the rewarding experience and thereby contribute to the likelihood that we will seek the rewarding experiences.

Many motivations, therefore, are driven by biological needs. Other motivations are primarily driven by incentives or rewards. Still other motivations are driven by a combination of both. For example, when we experience hunger, we have a strong need-driven motivation to eat and thereby reduce the hunger drive. In contrast, after a full meal, the motivation to eat the baked apple pie is more incentive driven than need driven. The more complex the behaviors, such as social behaviors, the more likely these behaviors are motivated by a number of need-driven and incentive-driven experiences. For example, going on a date is likely linked to sexual need and also the need for intimacy and social affiliation.

Emotion and motivation are closely linked. For emotional disorders, motivational tendencies typically contribute to the maintenance of the disorder through avoidance motivation. Pleasant positive affect is associated with approaching a desirable state or object. Reducing or escaping unpleasant negative affect is associated with an undesirable object or situation. Depression and anger, for example, arise when the desire to avoid unpleasant situations or experience pleasant situations or experiences is difficult or impossible to achieve. Unlike other organisms, the emotional responses of humans are particularly associated with this mechanism because of our capacity to anticipate and predict future events. The decision to engage in a particular behavior therefore is closely linked to the expectation of the pleasantness or the relief associated with the motivated behavior (Cox & Klinger, 1988).

Many of the strategies in CBT function to increase the willingness or motivation of clients to act in ways that often are contrary to the way they feel. For example, a client who is depressed may show little willingness or motivation to do the things he or she once did that were pleasant or from which the client derived a sense of mastery. Instead, the client waits to feel less depressed before taking a bike ride with friends or accompanying a coworker to lunch. An overly anxious client may exhibit little willingness or motivation to approach the situations that make him or her anxious and, instead, may favor avoiding or quickly leaving these situations.

The tendency to avoid unpleasant experiences, such as those that make us anxious, is an intuitive behavioral response to that emotional state. These behavioral responses are intuitive and often automatic because of the survival value for humans over millions of years. However, clients with emotional disorders are trapped in a cycle of managing their emotional responses in this intuitive manner. That is, when anxious or fearful, the client with an anxiety disorder will avoid. When feeling down or overwhelmed, the client with a depressive disorder will withdraw or give up. The goal of CBT is to assist clients to act counter to the behavioral tendency of their emotional responses. Acting counterintuitively enables clients to learn something important that their intuitive responses prevent. For example, a client who is afraid of dogs because he or she believes dogs are dangerous will not learn anything new about dogs (i.e., that most dogs are not dangerous) if the client continues to avoid them. Or, avoiding negative affect interferes with the client's learning that he or she can tolerate and manage negative affect. Willingness to confront, accept, and tolerate negative affect may be the most effective skill a client with an emotional disorder can learn, particularly in the case of anxiety disorders (Wirtz, Hofmann, Riper, & Berking, 2014).

Similarly, the cognitive behavior therapist might teach the client mindfulness to increase the client's willingness to remain in an anxiety-evoking situation and observe rather than flee his or her emotional responses. Even an exposure hierarchy is a willingness strategy. An *exposure hierarchy* is a list of exposure tasks, ranked from least to most anxiety-evoking, that target the client's key internal and external fear cues. The exposure therapy then is graded or graduated, that is, the client moves through the exposure process one exposure task at a time, beginning with exposure tasks that evoke relatively low fear responses. Graduated exposure is no more effective than a single-step exposure (i.e., evoking the highest level of fear in a single step) as long as the client remains in the fear-evoking situation for a sufficient period. However, few clients are willing to undertake a single-step exposure task. Therefore, the cognitive behavior therapist and client collaboratively develop an exposure hierarchy. The hierarchy provides the client with a path forward and some perceived "control" over the exposure process. The perceived control, in addition to a curious stance toward the client's emotional response, increases the client's willingness to approach rather than avoid the feared situations.

To summarize, motivation is closely linked to emotion. All emotions include motivated behaviors or action tendencies and therefore are adaptive and helpful. Generally, we act in accordance or intuitively with these action tendencies. When we are anxious, we are cautious. When we are sad, we slow down and do less. However, it is essential that clients with emotional disorders learn the importance of responding counterintuitively to their motivational tendencies. Responding intuitively is a feature of the problem, not a solution to it. CBT includes a variety of strategies to enhance the willingness or motivation of clients to act counter their emotional responses. Once clients learn these strategies, they can restore their emotional systems and the motivations that are a feature of them to adaptive responses to the situations and problems in their lives.

EMOTION AND EMOTIONAL CHANGE

Most clients who seek CBT wish to change how they feel. Whether they wish to feel less depressed, less angry, less anxious, or less guilty, CBT targets these emotional responses when they are a problem. At the same time, CBT uses emotion to change a client's emotional responses to events. Through evoking the client's emotion responses, the cognitive behavior therapist introduces clients to new and novel information that challenges and destabilizes the maladaptive associative network of cognitions, behaviors, affect, and somatic experiences that maintain their problematic emotional and behavioral responses (Foa & Kozak, 1986; Lang, 1977). The dissonance between the old learning (i.e., what the client believes) and new information creates the opportunity for emotional processing, which translates into new emotional responses to stimuli, life events, and shifts in perspectives and meaning (Foa, Huppert, & Cahill, 2006). In the case of exposure therapy for anxiety disorders, through exposure, clients learn to distance (or decenter) from conditioned fear responses, which thereby increases their tolerance for distress (Arch et al., 2012).

Researchers have asserted that affective engagement is a critical condition of therapeutic change (Foa & Kozak, 1986; Foa et al., 2006). *Affective engagement* reactivates old learning and makes it more labile and plastic, and, if novel and unexpected information is presented during affective engagement, the old memory is updated to include this new information (Nadel, Hupbach, Gomez, & Newman-Smith, 2012). As new learning strengthens over time and within different contexts, new learning then competes or inhibits previous learning held within the anxiety network (Bouton, 2002). Developing a healthier or adaptive associative fear network enables the client to inhibit or challenge old learning. Emotion plays a vital role in this process.

Researchers have applied the idea of affective engagement to depressive disorders and have identified several common processes hypothesized to maintain these disorders. For example, experiential avoidance (i.e., avoiding the thoughts, emotions, and other internal stimuli associated with their emotional response) occurs for clients with emotional disorders (Hayes, Wilson, Gifford, Follette, & Strosahl, 1996), as well as maladaptive beliefs, and rumination (i.e., unproductive repetitive processing) of future or past events. Clients with depressive disorders and anxiety disorders share similar maladaptive emotion regulation styles (i.e., experiential avoidance, thought suppression, disengagement, emotional blunting, and hopelessness; Hayes et al., 1996; Trew, 2011). A central goal of CBT, whether it is the treatment of anxiety disorders or major depression, is to use an approach and a series of strategies to facilitate healthy emotional processing. Many strategies in CBT evoke emotion in the service of processing the old meanings and cognitions that contribute to the client's problematic emotional responses, and facilitating new learning that will contribute to a more effective life. I present two strategies to use emotion in the service of new learning: imagery rescripting and imagery dialogues.

Imagery Rescripting to Change Emotion

Imagery rescripting is a set of clinical strategies that focus on changing unpleasant memories (Stopa, 2009). Researchers and clinicians have applied imagery rescripting strategies to a variety of clinical problems: borderline personality disorder (Giesen-Bloo et al., 2006), bulimia (Cooper, Todd, & Turner, 2007), posttraumatic stress disorder arising from childhood sexual abuse (Smucker & Niederee, 1995), and posttraumatic nightmares (Long et al., 2011). Typically, the imagery rescripting procedure includes a cognitive restructuring component followed by three imagery-related stages (Smucker, Dancu, Foa, & Niederee, 1995; Smucker & Niederee, 1994): imaginal reliving, mastery imagery, and self-calming imagery.

Recently, cognitive behavior therapists have applied imagery rescripting in the treatment of clients with social phobia (Wild & Clark, 2011; Wild, Hackmann, & Clark, 2008). Many clients with social anxiety disorder report negative images linked to identifiable past social or interpersonal events (Hackmann, Clark, & McManus, 2000), and for some of these clients, the negative imagery is unrelated to an identifiable past event. For these clients, standard present-focused imagery modification techniques, such as BEs and video feedback, are likely sufficient. However, clients who have not responded adequately to the present-focused techniques and who report recurrent negative images and memories related to past socially traumatic events from which the client's negative self-image stems, may benefit from including imagery rescripting in standard CBT for the disorder.

The first step is to identify the client's recurrent image, the memory to which it is linked, and the encapsulated belief that captures the meaning of both. To illustrate, in the following clinical vignette, the therapist asked "Walt," a 32-year-old software engineer, "What kinds of things go through your mind when you're feeling anxious in social situations? Do you have any spontaneous pictures or images when you're anxious in social situations?"

Walt: I don't know. Maybe that people are pointing at me and laughing.

Therapist: Yes. Please close your eyes now, Walt, and describe everything about the image to me. Try to describe in the present tense, if you can.

Walt: I was maybe 12 years old.

Therapist: Try, I'm 12 years old.

Walt: Okay. I'm 12 years old, and I'm standing in the schoolyard. I'm drinking from the water fountain, and water splashes all over my pants. I turn around, and there are a bunch of kids pointing at me and laughing. They're saying that I peed in my pants. I feel humiliated. I close my eyes and run to the office. I call my mom, and she picks me up. I feel horrible.

Therapist: What is the worst thing about the memory, Walt? What does it mean about you?

Walt: I'm useless. I can't even drink water from a water fountain. I'm a total reject.

Therapist: Walt, would you please describe this in shorthand, perhaps one or two sentences, of the image of people pointing and laughing at you, and the memory of this event when you were in middle school?

Walt: Okay. How about: I'm a loser and always will be. Everyone will reject me and laugh at me because I can't do anything right.

Once the therapist has identified the belief that encapsulates the image and memory, the therapist guides Walt through a cognitive restructuring strategy, whereby Walt and the therapist examine the evidence that confirms and disconfirms this belief. Earlier cognitive restructuring and BEs may provide some of the evidence that disconfirms the belief. The cognitive restructuring phase of imagery rescripting invites Walt to consider the evidence that encapsulates the belief when he was a child (i.e., then) and alternatives with new information to what he perceives to be evidence supporting his encapsulated belief (i.e., now; see Exhibit 3.1).

EXHIBIT 3.1
Walt's Evidence for Then and Now

Encapsulated belief: I'm useless	
Then	Now
Evidence for the encapsulated belief	Alternatives with new information
I was a clumsy kid.	I was clumsy because I was really tall for my age. I couldn't do anything about my size. A lot of the tall kids were a little clumsy like me. I eventually grew into my body, and being tall became a good thing. I became a pretty good basketball player. Kids liked me for that. I certainly wasn't useless, even if I was in a clumsy phase.
Some of the kids didn't like me.	A lot of kids are mean, especially in middle school. I was kind of mean sometimes. Some of the kids didn't like me because I did pretty good in school. Some of the kids didn't like me because I was tall and played basketball pretty good. If I was honest with myself, I didn't like some of the kids either. Just because some kids didn't like me doesn't mean I'm useless. I was useful in a lot of ways. I helped the coach and the teachers, and sometimes kids didn't like me for that.
I soaked my pants.	The kids laughed at me for only a couple of minutes, and then they forgot about it. One or two kids laughed at me the next day, but after that, no one said anything. Yes, it was mean of the kids to laugh and point at me, but kids can be mean. Even though I was upset, this didn't stop me from studying hard and helping my teachers and friends. I was useful even after the water fountain event.

Following the cognitive restructuring phase, Walt and the therapist move into the imagery rescripting procedure. The therapist begins with a rationale to explain the process and how it can help Walt feel less anxious in social situations:

> Walt, the water fountain event led you to develop certain beliefs about yourself and to feel anxious because you assume people will treat you today the way they treated you in the past. In a sense, you've been viewing the events of today through the restricted lens of the past. It isn't a helpful or even accurate lens because it does not include all the new information you have as an adult. We've examined your tendency to overestimate the likelihood that people will reject you, and you now see that is seldom true and that the world doesn't expect you to be perfect— to never have another water fountain accident.
>
> Still, every time this memory is triggered in social situations today, you feel the pain that you felt as a kid. In order to feel less anxious in your relationships with people, it's important to update that memory with the new information we've discovered over the past few weeks.
>
> The best way to process this memory is to revisit it again. In a minute, I want you to close your eyes and tell the memory again in the first-person present tense as though you are the 12-year-old Walt again. And then I want you to bring in the new information as the 32-year-old Walt. This may mean that the 32-year-old Walt talks the 12-year-old Walt through that painful few minutes. You will tell the 12-year-old Walt what you know now or perhaps speak to the other kids who laughed and pointed at you.
>
> The goal of this process is to update the memory so that it no longer is an event that colors your present so that you can accurately process the present as it is really happening. Are you ready to begin?

The therapist then asks Walt to close his eyes and talk the therapist through the memory of the water fountain event at the age it occurred. This phase is similar to imaginal reliving of traumatic memories in CBT for post-traumatic stress disorder (Ehlers & Clark, 2000; Foa & Rothbaum, 1998):

Therapist: You're 12 years old, Walt, and you've just splashed water on your pants. Tell me what's happening now. Take me through it as if it's happening right now.

Walt: Okay, so I'm bending down to get a drink, and I twist the knob of the water fountain, and water goes everywhere. I'm soaking wet. There is a huge wet spot on my lap. I'm wearing chinos, so it looks like I peed on myself. I freeze and stand up, and then I hear kids behind me laughing. They're calling me a loser. I turn around, and they're all pointing at my crotch and laughing. Some of the kids are choking, they're laughing so hard. They're shouting to other kids, "Walt peed in his pants!" They're screaming it now, and other kids are turning to look at me. (Begins to cry) This is so hard. I hate this! I feel so humiliated.

Therapist: You're doing great, Walt. I know this is hard, but you're doing great. Stay with what's happening and tell me what happens next.

Walt (clears voice and wipes his eyes): I look at all the kids and tell them that it was an accident. They keep laughing. I can feel my face turning red. I'm crying, and I don't want them to see me crying. A kid yells at me that I'm a baby. He says I'm crying because I'm a useless baby that can't do anything. I start running to the office. I still hear the kids yelling, "Baby! Baby! Baby!" I want to disappear. I want to be someone else. Anybody else. (Sobs)

The next phase of the imagery rescripting procedure is to invite the client to relive the socially traumatic event again, but this time, the older self describes the event he or she observes happening to his or her younger self:

Therapist: You're doing a great job, Walt. Please keep your eyes closed, and let's move to the next step. I now would like you to talk me through the water fountain event again, but this time, I want you to tell it to me as though you're observing what is happening, as though you're standing there in the school-yard watching what is happening to 12-year-old Walt. This time, I want you to describe the event in the third person: "I see Walt standing at the water fountain. He freezes as water splashes on his shirt and pants." Now, please continue.

Walt: Um, okay. Walt is covered with water, and I watch him slowly stand up. He doesn't turn around because kids are shouting at him. They're calling him a loser and saying that he peed in his pants. Finally, he turns around, and the kids are pointing and calling him a baby. They're saying he's a baby and can't even drink from a water fountain. I see Walt looking around, and then he starts to run toward the office. The kids keep calling him names. They're so mean to him.

Therapist: Yes, the kids are very mean to Walt. What happens next? What do you see happening next?

Walt: A kid runs after him and waves to other kids. He's pointing at Walt's crotch and yelling that he peed in his pants. The kids keep shouting and pointing until Walt enters the school. This is so wrong. These kids are little idiots! (Clenches his fists and pounds them on his thighs)

The final phase of the imagery rescripting process invites the client to relive the socially traumatic event again at the age it occurred, but this time, the wiser and older self is with the client and offers compassion, new information, and support:

Therapist: Great work, Walt. We're almost done. The final step is to give your older self a chance to help your younger self. Please close your eyes again and go through the event one more time. I want you to talk me through it again as if you were your 12-year-old self, and it's happening right now. But this time, your wise 32-year-old self is in the schoolyard and standing next to you. The older Walt has all the information you've learned in our prior sessions, and the older Walt can help, if you want him to. He can talk to the other kids or talk to you or do anything else that feels helpful and right in this situation. Are you ready? . . . Okay, take me back to the schoolyard and the water fountain.

Walt: I'm standing at the water fountain with Walt. We're thirsty, and Walt drinks first. He turns the knob, and water splashes everywhere. It soaks Walt, and I get wet too—not as much but still pretty wet. The kids are laughing and calling me and Walt babies. They're saying we peed in our pants. They're pointing at our crotches and shaking their heads. I tell them to shut up. (Begins crying a little)

Therapist: Yes. That's right. What else do you want to do?

Walt: I want to tell them to get a life. To grow up.

Therapist: Please have older Walt say this to younger Walt.

Walt: So, older Walt steps in front of the younger Walt. He says to the kids, "Hey, you're the losers. You know that he didn't pee in his pants. The water fountain did it, but you want to pump yourselves up by putting Walt down. You're the losers here, not Walt!"

Therapist: What are the kids doing now?

Walt: They're still laughing, but they're walking away, at least some of them.

Therapist: What happens next?

Walt: I lift my head and tell Walt to do the same. We lift our heads and point and laugh back at them. (Stops crying)

Therapist: So, you and young Walt are lifting your heads and looking at the other kids. What happens next?

Walt:	The kids are walking away. They're looking down, and we're looking up.
Therapist:	And what does young Walt see?
Walt:	He sees a bunch of kids who are just kids. He knows that every kid is teased and laughed at and that today is Walt's turn.
Therapist:	Is there anything that young Walt wants to say?
Walt:	Yes. He wants to say that although today is his turn to be teased, he's showing them that they can't hurt him—that he's not a loser, that he's not useless.
Therapist:	How is young Walt feeling now?
Walt (hits his thigh as he says each sentence):	He is strong. He is confident. He's not a loser. He's not useless.
Therapist:	Is there anything else that young Walt needs to know?
Walt:	Yes. He needs to know that everything is going to work out for the best. That kids are mean sometimes, but most adults aren't mean, and even if he runs into a mean adult, he's not 12 years old anymore. He can take care of himself.
Therapist:	Would you say that to young Walt now.
Walt:	Yes. "You're strong, Walt. You're not useless, and a lot of people can learn from you. You're a great teacher."
Therapist:	Okay. When you're ready, bring yourself back to this room and open your eyes.

Imagery Dialogue to Change Emotion

Imagery dialogue is a powerful experiential technique that cognitive behavior therapists use to work with maladaptive core beliefs that drive strong emotional responses to situations and events (Young, Klosko, & Weishaar, 2003). Typically, imagery dialogues focus on the clients in conversations with people who contributed to the development of their maladaptive core beliefs or with people who reinforce their maladaptive core beliefs in their current lives. The goal, then, is to assist clients to develop and strengthen adaptive core beliefs, and this deep change must occur in the presence of strong negative affect, at least as strong as the negative affect the client experienced when developing the original maladaptive beliefs.

Most often, imagery dialogue work begins with dialogues the client imagines with his or her parents, or other significant childhood figures, such as a grandfather or brother. The cognitive behavior therapist begins by asking the client to close his or her eyes and to picture himself or herself with a parent (or other significant other) in an upsetting situation from the past or a recent event. The therapist then assists the client to express strong affect, often anger, toward the parent for failing to meet the client's fundamental needs. This often is new territory for the client. The client may never have even imagined expressing his or her anger toward a parent, and this in itself can be of value. However, imagery dialogues provide so much more to clients. Through imagery dialogues, they can imagine a different outcome, such as standing up for their rights with an offending parent: "All I wanted was you to love me, and you didn't give it to me"; "I have the right to take care of myself, and I'm finished taking care of you"; "No, I won't let you abuse me anymore"; "No, I won't let you criticize me." Imagery dialogues also can empower clients to push against or distance themselves from their maladaptive core beliefs. Typically, clients feel powerless against these deeply held beliefs about themselves and others. Imagery dialogues can create a sense of purpose and self-efficacy, and foster an alternative and more adaptive core belief. Through imagery dialogues, the client who believes that he or she is defective can learn that all children are entitled to love and respect, and that this can "feel" true for this client too. The client who believes that he or she is invisible can learn that all children are entitled to express themselves and that, through imagery dialogue, can begin to "feel" this is true for this client too.

Expressing anger often is difficult for clients and, at times, they will try to talk the cognitive behavior therapist out of doing experiential work of this sort. They may insist that they are past this and that they have already dealt with the anger they harbor. They may question whether feeling angry is necessary and argue that they sought CBT because they wanted to change the way that they think about past events, not how they feel about them. At times, clients may seek CBT expressly to avoid experiencing the emotions that trouble them and are baffled that the therapist would suggest that they interact with these experiences. Other clients will explain that they have forgiven their parent, which is unlikely if they have not moved beyond the anger of being wronged. There is a place for forgiveness and in accepting the limitations of a parent, but at this stage, most clients follows the stage of expressing and feeling what they may have suppressed or tried to explain away for years.

At times, clients believe that it is wrong to feel such intense anger toward a parent, and they feel guilty. They might believe that their parents did they best they could, which may be true, but this does not mean that the mistakes the parents made did not hurt the client. Furthermore, so long as the client feels too guilty to feel and express anger toward a parent, the client is unable to grieve adequately for what might have been. Grieving for what they lost in their childhood makes it possible for clients to put aside further attempts to change a parent and, at last, get today as an adult what they had wanted then as a child.

"Pam" is a 58-year-old married woman with two young children. She sought CBT for help with her depression that begin when she was an adolescent. When Pam was a child, her brother sexually molested her for several years. A preschool teacher reported the abuse to child protective services, which investigated the incident and removed her brother from the home. Pam's mother blamed Pam for the abuse, for the brother's removal from the home, and for her feeling humiliated. Pam has a strained relationship with her mother, who is cold and distant. Pam's mother continues to criticize and blame Pam for the smallest mistake, often shaming her in front of other family members or even strangers. Pam has not been able to assert herself with her mother and has never acknowledged the anger she feels toward her mother then and now.

Therapist: Pam, please close your eyes and bring back that moment in your mind when you're standing alone in your house. Can you bring that moment to life now? Now, what is little Pam feeling right now? Would you tell your adult part to ask little Pam how she's feeling? How is little Pam feeling?

Pam: She feels alone.

Therapist: I see. Would you ask her why she feels so alone?

Pam: There's no one around. There's no one to play with. The kids are either older or much younger than me. There's no one that matches my age.

Therapist: Yes, I understand. Now, please bring your mother into the image with little Pam. Imagine that your mother is angry with you. Imagine that she's blaming you for something. Would you bring your mother into the image like that? Tell me what you see. What's the expression on her face?

Pam: She looks mad. She seems tall standing there looking down at me. There're scuff marks on my shoes, so maybe she doesn't like that.

Therapist: Okay. Now, you are your mother now, and say to little Pam what your mother might have said to little Pam about the scuff marks on her shoes. Have her get mad at you over the scuff marks and be her so I can hear how she might have sounded.

Pam: "Couldn't you be more careful?" It just sounds like noise. I can't put words to it. She's unhappy, and I've made her that way.

Therapist: So, it's your fault. It's your fault again. And how's little Pam feeling right now?

Pam (holds back tears):   She wants to cry.

Therapist: Please try to bring me into the scene, even if it's a little out of focus. Obviously, I don't really quite fit there, but please try.

Pam: Yeah, I can see you now, a little bit, I think.

Therapist: Good. I'm going to talk to your mother now in the image. Would you feel safer with some kind of wall in the image, perhaps a barrier between you and me on one side and your mother on the other side?

Pam: I don't need a wall. I'll just stand behind you. Is that okay?

Therapist: Yes. Please stand behind me. Okay, now you play your mother and speak to me. I'm going to talk to your mother. Now, I'm not talking to you, meaning little Pam. I'm talking to your mother. Please imagine that now.

Therapist (to "Pat," the name of Pam's mother): "Pat, Pam is a child, and children scuff their shoes. Pam is just being a child."

Pam (as Pat):   "She's a horrible child. She's selfish and doesn't take care of her things. She's a bad child."

Therapist (to Pat):   "Pam is not a bad child, Pat. You expect her to act like an adult, but she's a child. You expect too much from her. She's not a bad child. She's not a horrible child. You're the adult. It's your job to love Pam and take care of Pam and to accept that she is a child and has not yet learned the things you expect her to know now."

(Pam is crying very hard now. She is trying to stifle her sobs, but her shoulders are shaking, and she is looking at the floor.)

Therapist (to Pam):   I'm going to coach you now. I'm going to give you things to say because it may be hard for you to come up with what to say. I'm going to be little Pam saying that I'm bad, that I'm a horrible child. And I want you to be you as a caring mother. I want you to speak as the mother the way you would speak to your own children. I want you to speak to little Pam and say to me what you would say to your own children, not the way your mother spoke to little Pam.

Pam: Okay.

Therapist (as little Pam):   "I'm a horrible girl. I scuffed my shoes. Mother told me I shouldn't. I'm horrible. It's my fault."

Pam (as a caring mother): "No, you're not a horrible girl. You're just a little girl. It was an accident. It's shoes. It's not a big deal."

Therapist (as little Pam): "I should have known better. I've ruined my shoes. I should have been more careful. I'm a bad girl, a horrible little girl."

Pam (as a caring mother): "It's not a big deal. They're only shoes. It's not a big deal. You didn't hurt yourself. It doesn't matter. They're only shoes."

Pam (as caring mother): "You're not bad. You're not bad."

Therapist (as little Pam): "But I have to believe her because she is always right."

Therapist (to caring mother): "Tell Pat that she wasn't always right."

Pam (as caring mother): "You weren't always right. You made mistakes. You were wrong sometimes."

Therapist: I would like to include one more thing in this scene, Pam. It's a little touchy. I hope it's okay that I bring this up. I'm going to be Pat again, and she's going to speak to you about your brother. Is that okay?

Pam: It's okay. Go ahead.

Therapist (as Pat to little Pam): "I wish you hadn't told me about your brother. You know that I'm busy. You should have handled this yourself. You should have told him to stop. Why did you have to get me involved in this business?"

Pam (as little Pam to Pat): "Because you're the mother. You're supposed to protect me."

Therapist: That was wonderful. That was great. Please say that again to Pat.

Pam (to Pat): "You're the mother. You were supposed to protect me."

Therapist (as Pat to little Pam): "No, I told you to cut the waterworks. I told you to shut up and to stop complaining. You're always complaining about things. What's the big deal? So what that he's sexually abusing you. Why are you so upset over that?"

Pam (as little Pam to Pat): "Because it hurt. It's wrong. I don't like it."

Therapist (to little Pam): Tell Pat that a good mother would stop it. A good mother wouldn't tell her child to stop it herself. She would stop it.

Pam (as little Pam to Pat):   "A good mom would protect me. A good mom would keep me safe. A good mom would tell him to stop."

Therapist (to Pam):   Now speak to Pat as a caring mother. Tell her that you would never let this happen to your children. Tell her that you would protect them for something like this.

Pam (as the caring mother speaking to Pat):   "I would never let that happen to my child. If it happened, I would stop it. It wouldn't continue. It wouldn't happen. I wouldn't let someone hurt my child that way."

Therapist: Good. Tell Pat that you're done protecting her.

Pam (to Pat):   "And I'm done protecting you. You should have done it. It was your job."

Therapist: Tell her that it's not your fault.

Pam (to Pat):   "It's not my fault. I didn't do anything wrong. I didn't do anything wrong."

Therapist: Good. Pam, please open your eyes now and tell me how you're feeling right now?

Pam: Angry. Very angry.

Therapist: Angry at her (Pat)?

Pam: Yes.

Therapist: Yes. How does it feel to be angry at her? Does it feel better than being angry at yourself, or are they about the same?

Pam: It feels better to be angry at her because it's outside of me. It's not inside of me.

Therapist: Yes. It seemed that you truly believed it wasn't your fault. It wasn't coming from the intellectual side. You felt angry about something that was wrong and were able to speak the anger you were feeling. The anger came out. Was it difficult to say those things to your mother, or did it happen automatically?

Pam: I didn't know it was going to come out. It just came out. It just came out.

Therapist: It was the caring mother side of you that came out. The caring mother who would protect her children against anything. You wouldn't fail your children the way your mother failed to protect you.

Pam: Yes. She didn't protect me, and it's her fault, not mine. I see that at last. I kind of knew that in my head, but it was still really difficult for me to be angry with her. It's still hard for me to be angry with her, but that all feels different now. I feel different.

To summarize, CBT includes many strategies to evoke emotion to enable clients to master their problematic emotional responses. Through these emotion-evoking strategies, clients learn to tolerate negative affect, which then enables clients to accept emotions that they have suppressed for many years or perhaps never acknowledged having.

Imagery is a powerful intervention for evoking emotion to change emotion. Imagery rescripting and imagery dialogues are just two strategies, and CBT includes many others (Hackmann, Bennett-Levy, & Holmes, 2011) that are applied to the treatment of a variety of problems.

EMOTION AND INTERPERSONAL RELATIONSHIPS

Many clients seek CBT because they have problems in their relationships with others. Often the relationship distress is due to clients' poor emotion regulation skills. Clients who do not have effective skills to manage their emotional responses may strike out at others when they are angry or depend too much on others when they are anxious. CBT teaches clients skills to manage their emotional responses to improve their interpersonal relationships.

At the same time, interpersonal problems arise from the avoidance of emotions themselves. Anxious clients often are unaware of the interpersonal consequences of their worry behaviors (Erickson & Newman, 2007); for example, a client who fears the loss of intimate relationships may seek repeated reassurances from his wife, who then, after many years of an inability to reassure her partner, distances herself from her husband to cope with the distress he feels. Clients with chronic anxiety disorders, such as generalized anxiety disorder, have reported having greater interpersonal problems (Przeworski et al., 2011), few close friends (Whisman, Sheldon, & Goering, 2000), and an increased likelihood of divorce or separation, or low marital satisfaction (Whisman, 2007; Whisman et al., 2000). Those interpersonal difficulties may reflect a tendency of anxious clients to avoid experiencing, accepting, and expressing their emotional responses in relationships with others (Newman, Castonguay, Borkovec, & Molnar, 2004).

CBT strives to teach clients skills both to regulate maladaptive emotional responses and to fully experience those emotional responses when avoiding them is creates problems for them. Regardless of the focus of the intervention, regulation, or acceptance, emotion is vital to that process of interpersonal change.

Imagery to Break Maladaptive Interpersonal Patterns

Clients with interpersonal difficulties often cope through avoidance or overcompensation in their relationships with others. For example, a client with the core belief "I'm incompetent" may avoid asking his or her supervisor for help and then fail to meet the supervisor's expectations, thereby reinforcing the client's belief that he or she is incompetent. A client with the core belief "I'm defective" may overcompensate by adopting a superior stance with coworkers or friends, who then call the client "uppity" thereby reinforcing the client's belief that he or she is defective.

The cognitive behavior therapist can use imagery techniques to evoke emotion, whereby clients can push through their typical coping styles and discover new ways of relating to others. The goal of imagery is to assist the client to imagine acting in adaptive ways in the face of the emotions that arise rather than retreating into his or her typical maladaptive coping strategies. For example, a client who believes that he or she is a failure and ordinarily avoids self-advocating would imagine asking the boss for a raise. In the following clinical vignette, the cognitive behavior therapist, through the use of imagery, assists "Lisa" to break a lifelong pattern of avoidance in her intimate relationships. Lisa was the daughter of an alcoholic father who repeatedly belittled her. He called her stupid and a loser, and repeatedly ridiculed her any time she wished to improve herself. When an excellent college accepted Lisa, her father did not permit her to attend. He told her that she was not smart enough to attend college and that it would be a waste of money. Lisa did manage to attend a local community college, but her father refused to contribute anything toward her tuition, and she was unable to complete her education. Lisa now believes that she is a loser, and although she wants to establish an intimate relationship, she typically avoids dating. The relationships she has had in the past were with men who used her for sex and then left her.

The cognitive behavior therapist begins by asking Lisa to close her eyes and imagine that she is at dinner with a very nice man who is employed at a well-paying job, perhaps as a mechanic or a schoolteacher. The therapist then instructs Lisa to speak to her "I'm a loser" core belief, which pressures her to end the date and go home, with her healthy adult voice, which encourages her to stay rather than avoid so that she can master the emotions that situations like this evoke in her.

> Therapist: Lisa, now that your eyes are closed, I would like you to imagine that you are at dinner with a nice man with a good job. Can you picture yourself in a situation like that?

> Lisa: Yes. I'm at the table with him. He's very nice, and he's talking about his job and what he does. I'm feeling very uncomfortable. I want to make some excuse like I usually do, and leave, but I'm forcing myself to stay and speak to him.

> Therapist: Lisa, step outside yourself right now and tell me why that part of you wants to leave. Why do you want to leave right now?

> Lisa: I'm really scared. I've afraid that he's going to ask me what I do, and I'll have to tell him that I don't do anything. Then he won't like me. That will be it. He's a nice guy, and he'll dump me.

> Therapist: Why won't he like you?

> Lisa: The minute he finds out that I never finished college, he'll think I'm stupid. I'm not very smart. He probably wants a smart girlfriend, someone who is interesting and can carry on a conversation. That's not me.

Lisa is feeling the urge to avoid. She is feeling very anxious and uncomfortable, and if she were on a real date with a nice guy, she might not speak much, and that might lead the man to conclude that she is not very smart, or she would make an excuse and leave the restaurant. The therapist encourages Lisa to imagine breaking or pushing against her tendency to avoid and, instead, speak with the man.

> Therapist: Lisa, try to imagine speaking with him now. Tell him a bit about your interests. What you like to read and what you do for fun. Perhaps you can imagine telling him about your art class. Try to imagine speaking to him now, and tell me what you see happening.

> Lisa: I start to tell him about my art class. He's asking me questions. We're talking about it, and he seems interested. We're talking about music and art.

> Therapist: How's the conversation going?

> Lisa: So far, he seems interested in me. I still feel nervous, terrified really, but I'm forcing myself to tell him about the things I like to do. It's difficult though. I'm having a good time, but I'm really nervous.

Therapist:	Tell him that. Tell him that you're enjoying yourself, but you're feeling very nervous.
Lisa (to man):	"I feel really nervous. I'm enjoying myself, and I'm a little worried that you might not be enjoying yourself too."
Therapist:	What does he say?
Lisa:	He tells me that he's nervous too. He says that he's enjoying himself, but he's feeling nervous.
Therapist:	How do you feel hearing that from him?
Lisa:	I feel more relaxed.
Therapist:	Tell him about the things you're worried that he's going to find out about you that you can't show him. Tell him about the thing that you're ashamed of or afraid that he's going to find out.
Lisa (to man):	"I'm terrified to tell you this, but I'm worried that you don't think I'm very smart. I don't know if I'm smart. I'm worried that you're going to think I'm stupid and not call me back."
Therapist:	What does he say?
Lisa (crying now):	He tells me that he's afraid that I won't like him either. He tells me that he sometimes worries that he's not smart enough too. He doesn't think it's such a big deal. He tells me that we all have stuff that we're insecure about.
Therapist:	How do you feel now?
Lisa:	A little more comfortable because he's being honest with me. He's not judging me. He's sharing his own insecurities with me. That makes me feel less scared.

The cognitive behavior therapist is asking Lisa to imagine acting counter to her emotional pattern. It is less about what Lisa will say to the imagined man and more about her countering her avoidant coping pattern. Rather than shutting down and withdrawing into herself as she typically would do, Lisa imagines sharing with a man her insecurities in a genuine and accepting manner. Once Lisa is more comfortable sharing with a man her interests, the more likely it is that a man will find her interesting and smart. Through imagery, the cognitive behavior therapist works to strengthen the adaptive belief that Lisa is smart enough to hold her own in a conversation and smart enough to find a caring and thoughtful man.

Interpersonal Role Plays to Practice Interpersonal Skills

Interpersonal role plays are a powerful strategy that enables clients to practice newly acquired interpersonal skills in session with the cognitive behavior therapist. Interpersonal role plays are particularly effective when enhancing the client's confidence that he or she can engage the skill in the presence of negative affect.

Self-efficacy is the belief in one's ability to successfully accomplish a task (Bandura, 1982, 1994). Self-efficacy theory suggests that people generally will only attempt tasks that they believe that they can accomplish. The strength of this belief is self-confidence, and people with strong self-efficacy beliefs believe that they can accomplish even difficult tasks. Often, a feature of difficult tasks is that they evoke negative affect, and the individual must perform the task in the face of uncomfortable negative emotion. Stress, anxiety, worry, and fear all negatively affect self-efficacy and can lead to an inability to initiate and perform anxiety-evoking tasks (Bandura & Adams, 1977). For that reason, it is essential that clients who learn new interpersonal skills believe that they can perform these skills in high-emotion states.

"Nathan" is a 37-year-old copy editor who sought CBT because he was feeling overwhelmed and anxious in his personal and professional lives. Nathan struggles to assert himself with others, particularly his boss, who arrives at Nathan's desk daily with a new addition to Nathan's growing to-do list. Nathan grew up in a high-conflict home. Both his mother and father would scream at their children for the slightest mistake, and Nathan dreaded any hint of conflict in his relationships with friends and colleagues. The cognitive behavior therapist had worked with Nathan to identify his anxiety-evoking thoughts, and, through cognitive restructuring, Nathan reported that he was much less anxious when he thought about being assertive with other people, but he did not yet believe that he was "strong enough" to say no to his supervisor when she asked him to do another task. The cognitive behavior therapist had taught Nathan the four steps of assertive communication, and he could easily recall the steps and had practiced them with the therapist. However, Nathan reported that this practice was easy because he did not feel particularly anxious. The cognitive behavior therapist suggested that they try a series of interpersonal role plays to enhance Nathan's confidence that he can be assertive even when he is feeling anxious.

> *Therapist:* Nathan, I want to begin by reminding you of the four steps of an assertive request. First, describe the situation in objective and neutral language. Second, share how the situation is making you feel. Third, ask for the change. Fourth, secure the agreement: "Will you do that for me, please?" Do you remember these steps?

Nathan: Yes. We've gone over the steps a lot, so I think I've got them.

Therapist: Great. Now, how about if we practice with a situation that comes up a lot for you. I'm thinking that a good situation would be when your supervisor comes to your desk and asks you to add something to your to-do list at the end of the day, and then expects you to work late to complete it. I know you're feeling overwhelmed at work, and we've agreed that the best way to manage your stress at work is to control the number of tasks on your to-do list at any time. We agreed that assertiveness was a strategy that could help you with that.

Nathan: Yeah. It's like what Mark, my friend, told me. You remember what I told you, right? Mark said that the curse of being a smart and capable writer is that people will give you as much work as you'll take. That's the way the world works.

Therapist: That's so true, Nathan. You're great at your job, and people think that you can do anything. At the same time, you pay a big price for always saying yes to their requests. So, let's role play a situation with your supervisor, Joan. I'll come to your desk and ask you to add another task to your to-do list. You'll then practice saying no. You'll go through the four steps, and then I'll gradually turn up the heat in the role plays. This will give you a chance to practice when you're feeling anxious and stressed. How does that sound? Also, as the supervisor keeps at it, remember to practice the broken record strategy. That will help too. Before we begin, how confident are you, on that 0 to 100% scale, that you can be assertive when your supervisor is demanding you add another task to your to-do list?

Nathan: I'd say 20%.

Therapist: Okay, Nathan. Here we go.

Therapist (as supervisor, Joan): "Hi, Nathan. Say, I know you're busy, but marketing just asked us to review copy for the new ad that's going out this week. It won't take much time, and it's important. How about if I give this to you, and you take care of it?"

Nathan (to Joan): "This is the third small task you've given me today. I'm already working as fast as I can. The more tasks you add to my to-do list, the more overwhelmed I feel. Also, I'm concerned that I won't be able to complete everything before I leave for the day. If you want me to do this task, please take a look at the other tasks you've given me today and take one of them off the list. Will you do that for me?"

Therapist (as Joan): "Yeah, Nathan, I know you're busy, but this won't take long. You might have to work a little late today, but that's no big deal, right?"

Nathan (to Joan): "I'm not working late today, Joan. This is the third task you've given me today. I'm working as fast as I can, and I'm concerned that I won't complete everything today. If you want me to do this task, take something off my to-do list, and I'll do this one. What do you say?"

Therapist (as Joan): "Nathan, I thought you were a team player. You're letting us all down. The other team members aren't going to like that you are taking the easy way. Stop whining and add this task to your list. It won't take time. Geez."

Nathan: I'm feeling really stressed. That's just the kind of thing she'd say to me.

Therapist: Nathan, you're doing great. Hang in there. Use your coping responses. Go through all the reasons why Joan is not going to fire you, and remind yourself that if you don't get better at saying it now and continue to fall behind the way you are, then you may just disappoint your team and perhaps give Joan a reason to fire you.

Nathan: Yeah. That helps. Okay.

Nathan (to Joan): "I told you that I'm not working late today, and I'm a good team player. I rarely say no to the things you give me, even when other people here do. If you want me to do this task, please take something off my to-do list, and then I'll do this one. Will you do that?"

Therapist (as Joan): "Look, Nathan, I'm not kidding here. I'm telling you to do this, and I expect you to do this. We pay you to work, and this is the work I'm giving you."

Nathan: Wow. I don't think she would go that far. She's not mean or anything.

Therapist: I know, Nathan, but it's important that you practice even if someone says something outrageous. That way, you'll know that you can handle pretty much anything.

Nathan (to Joan): "Yeah. That's right, Joan. I'm not telling you that I won't work, I'm just trying to work smart. I'm happy to do this task when you take another off my to-do list. You decide. Take something off the list, and I'll do this. What do you say?"

Therapist: Nathan, that was awesome. Well done! How did that feel?

Nathan:	Well, I have to say, I was stressing. I could see that you were getting irritated and that made my anxiety spike, and I didn't think I could keep going, but I did.
Therapist:	Now, how confident are you that you can be assertive with Joan the next time she asks you to do one more thing before you leave for the day?
Nathan:	I'm at 80% now. I really think I can do this. Also, I liked when you reminded me to use my coping statements. That helped too.

To summarize, emotions enhance our relationships with others, and open emotional expression is the foundation of intimacy. Clients with interpersonal difficulties typically cope with their emotional responses in maladaptive ways, often through avoidance and overcompensation. CBT includes many strategies to evoke emotion in the service of correcting maladaptive interpersonal patterns. Imagery dialogues and role plays are two similar strategies. The goal of any of these strategies is to evoke emotion in the service of developing new learning that can then inhibit old learning. This new learning must then occur in the presence of the emotional responses in which the old learning occurred, and imagery dialogues and role plays enable cognitive behavior therapists to facilitate this process.

EMOTION AND THE THERAPEUTIC RELATIONSHIP

There is a tendency among clinicians to view the relationship in CBT as a factor that is independent from the active and critical mechanism of change (Castonguay, Constantino, McAleavey, & Goldfried, 2010). A number of researchers have challenged this view and have asserted that the therapeutic relationship is both a mediating variable for change and an important mechanism of change (Safran & Muran, 2000; Safran & Segal, 1996).

Psychotherapy, including cognitive behavior psychotherapy, requires a great deal from clients. Clients must be willing to disclose what is deeply personal and thereby become vulnerable with the therapist. Clients must be willing to experience feared emotions and to be open to feedback from the therapist. Clients also must be willing to tolerate discussing the therapeutic relationship itself. At the same time, clients often seek therapy because of the difficulties they have in relating to others. They may avoid processing or even accepting their emotional experiences through a host of cognitive and interpersonal strategies. These strategies are the focus of CBT, whether they occur outside or inside the therapy office.

Cognitive behavior therapists view the therapeutic relationship as one of many events that can trigger the thoughts and beliefs clients have that contribute to the problems in their lives. Therefore, the therapeutic relationship presents ample opportunities to work on these cognitions and behaviors directly. A client who believes he or she is incompetent may avoid trying a CBT skill because the client fears that he or she will implement the skill incorrectly. A client who believes others are quick to judge and criticize him or her may not share with the therapist what is truly troubling him or her. Therefore, a cognitive behavior therapist cannot separate the interventions—whether it is setting an agenda for the therapy session, using a thought record to identify and modify problematic cognitions, or completing out-of-session tasks (e.g., homework)—from the interpersonal and therapeutic relationship in which the intervention occurs.

CBT strives to find balance between relationship building and skill building. Clients benefit from skills to manage their emotional responses and the problems that arise in their lives. However, the willingness of clients to learn and implement these skills rests on the abilities of cognitive behavior therapists to remain affectively attuned to the subtle emotional and behavioral shifts that occur in a session and over the course of a therapy. Such attunement requires cognitive behavior therapists who are aware of these interpersonal and intrapersonal processes, and are skilled in broaching these delicate discussions with clients who may be unaware or aware but fear such discussions (Safran & Muran, 2000; Safran & Segal, 1996).

Even when clients are compliant with standard cognitive behavior interventions, it is important that cognitive behavior therapists attend to the subtle interpersonal patterns that arise or to the subtle moments in which the therapeutic alliance is bruised rather than ruptured. In cases in which the client is failing to engage in the treatment and comply with the tasks of CBT, the therapist may wish to set aside standard CBT interventions, explore their own contributions to the patterns, and explore with the client his or her emerging feelings in the context of the therapeutic relationship.

Many features of CBT contribute to a solid therapeutic working alliance, such as collaboration between client and therapist; solicitation of feedback from the client regarding an intervention, the session, or the therapist; and the judicious use of self-disclosure both to model adaptive interpersonal responses and to encourage the client's trust and openness. At the same time, the cognitive behavior therapist does not abandon CBT when encountering a clinically relevant behavior in the relationship. The therapist still may ask, "What just went through your mind?"

The cognitive behavior therapist also does not abandon the cognitive behavior conceptualization on which the therapist has based the treatment.

The cognitive behavior conceptualization is essential to identifying what may constitute a clinically relevant emotion or behavior in the therapeutic relationship. These emotional and behavioral markers reflect core belief activation, as described earlier, and identifying and effectively working with these emotional markers can enhance treatment adherence and response (Safran, Muran, & Eubanks-Carter, 2011).

It is important that the cognitive behavior therapist know how to speak to the client about these observations with skillful tentativeness and a recognition that the therapist's experience and observations may be accurate or inaccurate. For example, if a client who believes that he or she is incompetent appears to be anxious when the therapist discusses with that client a possible out-of-session therapeutic assignment (e.g., homework), the therapist might first note the observation and then tentatively suggest an explanation (based on the cognitive behavior case conceptualization for the client):

> As we were just discussing this homework assignment, I noticed that you cleared your throat and began to rub your hands together. I sensed, and I may be off the mark here, that you were feeling anxious about the assignment. Perhaps there was something about the assignment that made you a little nervous. Perhaps you are a bit worried that you might not do the assignment correctly? Again, I could be way off about this, and if I am, I hope you will tell me, but I wonder if what I observed relates to what you are feeling right now.

In the following clinical vignette, the CBT psychotherapist is working with "Scott," a 20-year-old college student who sought treatment for his excessive social anxiety, particularly regarding his fears that women will reject him. Scott grew up with a critical mother and a father who was a workaholic. Scott's mother was highly critical of him and highly dependent on him for emotional support that she did not receive from her husband. Scott has had several relationships with women over the years, even with women he liked, but none has lasted beyond 3 or 4 months. Scott has reported that the relationships gradually "burned out," but he could not recall what transpired.

The cognitive behavior therapist, a woman, was confused when Scott said that he was thinking about taking a break from therapy. She had just praised Scott for his progress in therapy and had shared that she thought he is "a great guy with great potential." She encouraged him to continue their work together:

> *Therapist:* Scott, I am certainly open to your taking a break from your therapy. You've made great progress over the past couple of months. At the same time, I find myself wondering a

little bit about the timing of this. Perhaps I've said or done something that upset you. I hope that you feel comfortable enough to tell me that if I have.

Scott (looks anxious):   Oh, no. You haven't done anything. You're great. It's not about you. I like you. That's not it. But I still think it's time to wrap up our meetings. Is that okay?

Therapist: Of course, it's okay, Scott. At the same time, as I said, I'm curious about the timing, particularly after I complimented your progress in therapy and said that I thought that you're a nice and decent man. I hope you can understand that I'm a bit puzzled that you want to finish up our work today. Are you feeling a little more nervous today than usual? And, if you are, can you recall when you began to feel a little nervous in our meeting today?

Scott: Yes. I guess I'm feeling more nervous. I guess it was when you complimented me. I wasn't expecting that.

Therapist: So that made you feel uncomfortable? So, what went through your mind between the compliment and feeling nervous? If you're comfortable sharing this with me, I think it could be really important for you and our work together. What went through your mind, Scott?

Scott (in a shaky voice):   Well, I guess—I mean—I guess that I thought that you were getting ready to fire me. I guess I assumed that you didn't want to meet with me anymore.

Therapist: So, it sounds like you're afraid I will end the therapy? If I did, I find myself wondering if you would take that as a rejection?

Scott: Yeah. Yes, I probably would.

The therapist's willingness to ask about the interaction and its impact on her (i.e., her confusion about whether she had said or had done anything that had caused Scott to dislike her) and to speculate (based on the cognitive behavior conceptualization for Scott) regarding the possible reasons for it (i.e., Scott's fear that she will reject him) led to an extended exploration of Scott's emotional response about receiving compliments and praise:

Scott: It's really hard for me, I guess, to hang in there when I realize that someone likes me. That's what Julia, one of the women I dated for a while, said to me. She said that as soon I realized that she liked me and was into me that I started to pull away. I'm becoming more aware of how that core belief we've talked about, that I'm unlikeable, hits me at this deep level. I don't even realize that I'm pulling away. It feels like it happens automatically.

Therapist: Yes.

Scott: I guess. . . . I guess I'm just so scared that women are going to reject me that I pull away before they can pull away. It's like the best defense is a good offense.

In later sessions, Scott and the therapist further explored Scott's fears of rejection and the ways he coped with that fear, such as building barriers to intimacy with women and leaving relationships if he thought that rejection was imminent.

Scott: I guess I'm terrified of rejection. I pull back when I realize that I like someone a lot.

Therapist: Yes. I see that so much more clearly now, Scott. And as you pull back, the woman senses that and then thinks you don't like her. She leaves, or you leave. So, you want an intimate relationship with a woman, but you are not fully in the relationship because you're so afraid that she'll reject you. I wonder where that leaves you, Scott? And where does that leave our relationship?

Scott: I'm not sure. You've helped me a lot, and I know that if I leave now, I might not get the thing I want a lot, which is an intimate and long-term relationship with a woman. But it's so scary to continue to meet with you if I can't be certain you won't fire me some day.

Therapist: Yes, Scott, it is scary. It sounds as though you don't have much faith that relationships will work out and that people will stay around for you.

Scott (drops his head and is tearful): It's so hard for me to trust women in that way. At the same time, I know that I've got to trust women enough if I want to have the kind of relationship I want.

Therapist: Yes, Scott. As I think about our relationship and this therapy, I'm wondering if you can trust me enough here so that we can work together to find the kind of relationship you want with a woman out there. I understand now, thanks to your willingness to share this with me, just how scary this is for you. This is particularly true since, at some point, this therapy and this relationship will end.

Scott: Yes, I know. I'm feeling very scared right now. I'm sweating I'm so scared. The idea that this could end really scares me and that this could continue scares me too.

Therapist: Yes, Scott, this is unchartered territory for you, but I think that if you can learn to tolerate that uncertainty, tolerate the risk that a relationship might end even when you're not ready for it to end, then I believe that you can have the kind of relationship you want with a woman someday. I feel very hopeful for you right now, Scott.

To summarize, a strong therapeutic alliance is the foundation on which any psychotherapeutic work rests. Many features of CBT contribute to a solid therapeutic working alliance, such as collaborative empiricism and soliciting feedback from the client regarding an intervention, the session, or the therapist. At the same time, the therapeutic relationship is a relationship, and most clients respond to the cognitive behavior therapist much in the same way they respond to other people in their lives. Clients may have little awareness of these automatic and established emotional and behavioral patterns of relating to others. Effective CBT psychotherapists attend to the subtle interpersonal patterns that arise that signal a disruption or rupture of the therapeutic alliance. When a client fails to engage in the treatment and comply with the tasks of CBT, the cognitive behavior therapist sets aside standard CBT interventions and explores with the client his or her emerging emotions and thoughts in the context of the therapeutic relationship.

CONCLUSION

This chapter has described cognitive behavior psychotherapy and the theoretical model on which it is based. CBT emphasizes the role of cognitions in emotional responses and assumes that clients who learn to identify and modify the cognitions that influence their emotional responses can then alter the maladaptive emotional and behavioral patterns for which they likely have sought treatment. Evoking emotion provides clients with the opportunity to practice the skills they learn when they feel what they are feeling, whether those skills are asserting themselves with a supervisor while feeling anxious or resolving conflicts with a family member while feeling angry.

However, the goal of CBT is not just to teach clients skills to regulate their emotional and behavioral responses. Cognitive behavior therapists use techniques to evoke and enhance emotion to facilitate learning and change. They have borrowed many of these experiential techniques from other therapeutic approaches, including psychodrama, Gestalt therapy, and psychodynamic therapy. From its beginnings in the 1970s, cognitive behavior therapists have used imagery, interpersonal role plays, BEs, and two-chair dialogues to bring the client's emotions into the therapy session.

Cognitive behavior psychotherapy continues to evolve. Each year, clinical researchers apply the model and approach to new problems that often use new strategies. However, regardless of the changes to the approach, emotion will always be an essential partner in the process of deep and lasting psychological change.

REFERENCES

Allen, L. B., McHugh, R. K., & Barlow, D. H. (2008). Emotional disorders: A unified protocol. In D. H. Barlow (Ed.), *Clinical handbook of psychological disorders: A step-by-step treatment manual* (pp. 216–249). New York, NY: Guilford Press.

Arch, J. J., Wolitzky-Taylor, K. B., Eifert, G. H., & Craske, M. G. (2012). Longitudinal treatment mediation of traditional cognitive behavioral therapy and acceptance and commitment therapy for anxiety disorders. *Behaviour Research and Therapy, 50,* 469–478. http://dx.doi.org/10.1016/j.brat.2012.04.007

Bandura, A. (1977). Self-efficacy: Toward a unifying theory of behavioral change. *Psychological Review, 84,* 191–215. http://dx.doi.org/10.1037/0033-295X.84.2.191

Bandura, A. (1982). Self-efficacy mechanism in human agency. *American Psychologist, 37,* 122–147. http://dx.doi.org/10.1037/0003-066X.37.2.122

Bandura, A. (1994). Self-efficacy. In V. S. Ramachandran (Ed.), *Encyclopedia of human behavior* (pp. 71–81). New York, NY: Academic Press.

Bandura, A., & Adams, N. (1977). Analysis of self-efficacy theory of behavior change. *Cognitive Therapy and Research, 1,* 287–310. http://dx.doi.org/10.1007/BF01663995

Barlow, D. H. (1991). Disorders of emotion. *Psychological Inquiry, 2,* 58–71. http://dx.doi.org/10.1207/s15327965pli0201_15

Barlow, D. H. (2002). *Anxiety and its disorders: The nature and treatment of anxiety and panic* (2nd ed.). New York, NY: Guilford Press.

Barlow, D. H. (2014). *Clinical handbook of psychological disorders* (5th ed.). New York, NY: Guilford Press.

Beck, A. T. (1964). Thinking and depression: II. Theory and therapy. *Archives of General Psychiatry, 10,* 561–571. http://dx.doi.org/10.1001/archpsyc.1964.01720240015003

Beck, A. T., Rush, J. A., Shaw, B. F., & Emery, G. (1979). *Cognitive therapy for depression.* New York, NY: Guilford Press.

Bennett-Levy, J., Butler, G., Fennell, M., Hackmann, A., Meuller, M., Westbrook, D., & Rouf, K. (Eds.). (2004). *Oxford guide to behavioural experiments in cognitive therapy*. New York, NY: Oxford University Press. http://dx.doi.org/10.1093/med:psych/9780198529163.001.0001

Bindra, D. (1974). A motivational view of learning, performance, and behavior modification. *Psychological Review, 81,* 199–213. http://dx.doi.org/10.1037/h0036330

Blagys, M. D., & Hilsenroth, M. J. (2002). Distinctive activities of cognitive-behavioral therapy: A review of the comparative psychotherapy process literature. *Clinical Psychology Review, 22,* 671–706. http://dx.doi.org/10.1016/S0272-7358(01)00117-9

Bluett, E. J., Zoellner, L. A., & Feeny, N. C. (2014). Does change in distress matter? Mechanisms of change in prolonged exposure for PTSD. *Journal of Behavior Therapy and Experimental Psychiatry, 45,* 97–104. http://dx.doi.org/10.1016/j.jbtep.2013.09.003

Bolles, R. C. (1972). Reinforcement, expectancy, and learning. *Psychological Review, 79,* 394–409. http://dx.doi.org/10.1037/h0033120

Borkovec, T. D., & Sides, J. K. (1979). The contribution of relaxation and expectancy to fear reduction via graded, imaginal exposure to feared stimuli. *Behaviour Research and Therapy, 17,* 529–540. http://dx.doi.org/10.1016/0005-7967(79)90096-2

Bouton, M. E. (2002). Context, ambiguity, and unlearning: Sources of relapse after behavioral extinction. *Biological Psychiatry, 52,* 976–986. http://dx.doi.org/10.1016/S0006-3223(02)01546-9

Bower, G. H. (1981). Mood and memory. *American Psychologist, 36,* 129–148. http://dx.doi.org/10.1037/0003-066X.36.2.129

Brewin, C. R. (1996). Theoretical foundations of cognitive-behavior therapy for anxiety and depression. *Annual Review of Psychology, 47,* 33–57. http://dx.doi.org/10.1146/annurev.psych.47.1.33

Brewin, C. R. (2001). A cognitive neuroscience account of posttraumatic stress disorder and its treatment. *Behaviour Research and Therapy, 39,* 373–393. http://dx.doi.org/10.1016/S0005-7967(00)00087-5

Burns, D. D. (1980). *Feeling good: The new mood therapy*. New York, NY: Morrow.

Butler, A. C., Chapman, J. E., Forman, E. M., & Beck, A. T. (2006). The empirical status of cognitive-behavioral therapy: A review of meta-analyses. *Clinical Psychology Review, 26,* 17–31. http://dx.doi.org/10.1016/j.cpr.2005.07.003

Carver, C. S., & Scheier, M. F. (1998). *On the self-regulation of behavior*. New York, NY: Cambridge University Press. http://dx.doi.org/10.1017/CBO9781139174794

Castonguay, L. G., Constantino, M. J., McAleavey, A. A., & Goldfried, M. R. (2010). The therapeutic alliance in cognitive-behavioral therapy. In J. C. Muran & J. P. Barber (Eds.), *The therapeutic alliance in cognitive-behavioral therapy: An evidence-based guide to practice* (pp. 150–171). New York, NY: Guilford Press.

Castonguay, L. G., Goldfried, M. R., Wiser, S., Raue, P. J., & Hayes, A. M. (1996). Predicting the effect of cognitive therapy for depression: A study of unique and common factors. *Journal of Consulting and Clinical Psychology, 64*, 497–504. http://dx.doi.org/10.1037/0022-006X.64.3.497

Clark, D. M. (1989). A cognitive approach to panic. In K. Hawton, P. M. Salkovskis, J. Kirk, & D. M. Clark (Eds.), *Cognitive behaviour therapy for psychiatric problems* (pp. 52–96). Oxford, England: Oxford Medical.

Cooper, M. J., Todd, G., & Turner, H. (2007). The effects of using imagery to modify core emotional beliefs in bulimia nervosa: An experimental pilot study. *Journal of Cognitive Psychotherapy, 21*, 117–122. http://dx.doi.org/10.1891/088983907780851577

Cox, W. M., & Klinger, E. (1988). A motivational model of alcohol use. *Journal of Abnormal Psychology, 97*, 168–180. http://dx.doi.org/10.1037/0021-843X.97.2.168

Craske, M. G., Kircanski, K., Zelikowsky, M., Mystkowski, J., Chowdhury, N., & Baker, A. (2008). Optimizing inhibitory learning during exposure therapy. *Behaviour Research and Therapy, 46*, 5–27. http://dx.doi.org/10.1016/j.brat.2007.10.003

Di Giulio, G. (2010). *Therapist, client factors, and efficacy in cognitive behavioural therapy: A meta-analytic exploration of factors that contribute to positive outcome.* Ottawa, Canada: University of Ottawa.

Dobson, K. S. (Ed.). (2001). *Handbook of cognitive-behavioral therapies* (2nd ed.). New York, NY: Guilford Press.

Dozois, D. J. A., & Dobson, K. S. (2001). Historical and philosophical bases of the cognitive-behavioral therapies. In K. S. Dobson (Ed.), *Handbook of cognitive-behavioral therapies* (2nd ed., pp. 3–39). New York, NY: Guilford Press.

Dutra, L., Stathopoulou, G., Basden, S. L., Leyro, T. M., Powers, M. B., & Otto, M. W. (2008). A meta-analytic review of psychosocial interventions for substance use disorders. *American Journal of Psychiatry, 165*, 179–187. http://dx.doi.org/10.1176/appi.ajp.2007.06111851

Ehlers, A., & Clark, D. M. (2000). A cognitive model of posttraumatic stress disorder. *Behaviour Research and Therapy, 38*, 319–345. http://dx.doi.org/10.1016/S0005-7967(99)00123-0

Ellis, A. (1962). *Reason and emotion in psychotherapy.* Oxford, England: Lyle Stuart.

Engelkamp, J. (1998). *Memory for actions.* Hove, England: Psychology Press.

Epstein, S. (1994). Integration of the cognitive and the psychodynamic unconscious. *American Psychologist, 49*, 709–724. http://dx.doi.org/10.1037/0003-066X.49.8.709

Epstein, S., & Pacini, R. (1999). Some basic issues regarding dual-process theories from the perspective of cognitive–experiential self-theory. In S. Chaiken & Y. Trope (Eds.), *Dual-process theories in social psychology* (pp. 462–482). New York, NY: Guilford Press.

Erickson, T. M., & Newman, M. G. (2007). Interpersonal and emotional processes in generalized anxiety disorder analogues during social interaction tasks. *Behavior Therapy, 38*, 364–377. http://dx.doi.org/10.1016/j.beth.2006.10.005

Fedoroff, I. C., & Taylor, S. (2001). Psychological and pharmacological treatments of social phobia: A meta-analysis. *Journal of Clinical Psychopharmacology, 21,* 311–324. http://dx.doi.org/10.1097/00004714-200106000-00011

Foa, E. B., Huppert, J. D., & Cahill, S. P. (2006). Emotional processing theory: An update. In B. O. Rothbaum (Ed.), *Pathological anxiety: Emotional processing in etiology and treatment* (pp. 3–24). New York, NY: Guilford Press.

Foa, E. B., & Kozak, M. J. (1986). Emotional processing of fear: Exposure to corrective information. *Psychological Bulletin, 99,* 20–35. http://dx.doi.org/10.1037/0033-2909.99.1.20

Foa, E. B., & Rothbaum, B. O. (1998). *Treating the trauma of rape: Cognitive-behavioral therapy of PTSD.* New York, NY: Guilford Press.

García-Vera, M. P., & Sanz, J. (2006). Analysis of the situation of treatments for smoking cessation based on cognitive-behavioral therapy and nicotine patches. *Psicooncología, 3,* 269–289.

Giesen-Bloo, J., van Dyck, R., Spinhoven, P., van Tilburg, W., Dirksen, C., van Asselt, T., . . . Arntz, A. (2006). Outpatient psychotherapy for borderline personality disorder: Randomized trial of schema-focused therapy vs transference-focused psychotherapy. *Archives of General Psychiatry, 63,* 649–658. http://dx.doi.org/10.1001/archpsyc.63.6.649

Goldfried, M. R. (2013). Evidence-based treatment and cognitive-affective-relational-behavior-therapy. *Psychotherapy, 50,* 376–380. http://dx.doi.org/10.1037/a0032158

Gould, R. A., Mueser, K. T., Bolton, E., Mays, V., & Goff, D. (2001). Cognitive therapy for psychosis in schizophrenia: An effect size analysis. *Schizophrenia Research, 48,* 335–342. http://dx.doi.org/10.1016/S0920-9964(00)00145-6

Gray, J. A., & McNaughton, N. (2000). *The neuropsychology of anxiety* (2nd ed.). Oxford, England: Oxford University Press.

Greenberg, L. S., & Safran, J. D. (1984). Integrating affect and cognition: A perspective on the process of therapeutic change. *Cognitive Therapy and Research, 8,* 559–578. http://dx.doi.org/10.1007/BF01173254

Greenberg, L. S., & Safran, J. D. (1987). *Emotion in psychotherapy: Affect, cognition, and the process of change.* New York, NY: Guilford Press.

Greenberger, D., & Padesky, C. A. (1995). *Mind over mood: A cognitive therapy treatment manual for clients.* New York, NY: Guilford Press.

Hackmann, A., Bennett-Levy, J., & Holmes, E. A. (Eds.). (2011). *Oxford guide to imagery in cognitive therapy.* New York, NY: Oxford University Press. http://dx.doi.org/10.1093/med:psych/9780199234028.001.0001

Hackmann, A., Clark, D. M., & McManus, F. (2000). Recurrent images and early memories in social phobia. *Behaviour Research and Therapy, 38,* 601–610. http://dx.doi.org/10.1016/S0005-7967(99)00161-8

Hayes, S. C., Wilson, K. G., Gifford, E. V., Follette, V. M., & Strosahl, K. (1996). Experimental avoidance and behavioral disorders: A functional dimensional approach to diagnosis and treatment. *Journal of Consulting and Clinical Psychology, 64,* 1152–1168. http://dx.doi.org/10.1037/0022-006X.64.6.1152

Heuer, F., & Reisberg, D. (1992). Emotion, arousal, and memory for detail. In S. A. Christianson (Ed.), *The handbook of emotion and memory: Research and theory* (pp. 151–180). Hillsdale, NJ: Erlbaum.

Hofmann, S. G. (2011). *An introduction to modern CBT: Psychological solutions to mental health problems.* Oxford, England: Wiley-Blackwell.

Hofmann, S. G., Asmundson, G. J. G., & Beck, A. T. (2013). The science of cognitive therapy. *Behavior Therapy, 44,* 199–212. http://dx.doi.org/10.1016/j.beth.2009.01.007

Hofmann, S. G., Asnaani, A., Vonk, I. J. J., Sawyer, A. T., & Fang, A. (2012). The efficacy of cognitive behavioral therapy: A review of meta-analyses. *Cognitive Therapy and Research, 36,* 427–440. http://dx.doi.org/10.1007/s10608-012-9476-1 (Erratum published 2014, *Cognitive Therapy and Research, 38,* 18, p. 368. http://dx.doi.org/10.1007/s10608-013-9595-3)

Hofmann, S. G., & Smits, J. A. J. (2008). Cognitive-behavioral therapy for adult anxiety disorders: A meta-analysis of randomized placebo-controlled trials. *Journal of Clinical Psychiatry, 69,* 621–632. http://dx.doi.org/10.4088/JCP.v69n0415

Hull, C. L. (1943). *Principles of behavior: An introduction to behavior theory.* New York, NY: Appleton-Century.

Irwin, M. R., Cole, J. C., & Nicassio, P. M. (2006). Comparative meta-analysis of behavioral interventions for insomnia and their efficacy in middle-aged adults and in older adults 55+ years of age. *Health Psychology, 25,* 3–14. http://dx.doi.org/10.1037/0278-6133.25.1.3

Jaycox, L. H., Foa, E. B., & Morral, A. R. (1998). Influence of emotional engagement and habituation on exposure therapy for PTSD. *Journal of Consulting and Clinical Psychology, 66,* 185–192. http://dx.doi.org/10.1037/0022-006X.66.1.185

Jones, E. E., & Pulos, S. M. (1993). Comparing the process in psychodynamic and cognitive-behavioral therapies. *Journal of Consulting and Clinical Psychology, 61,* 306–316. http://dx.doi.org/10.1037/0022-006X.61.2.306

Jorm, A. F., Morgan, A. J., & Hetrick, S. E. (2008). Relaxation for depression. *Cochrane Database of Systematic Reviews, 4,* CD007142.

Kabat-Zinn, J. (2003). Mindfulness-based interventions in context: Past, present, and future. *Clinical Psychology: Science and Practice, 10,* 144–156. http://dx.doi.org/10.1093/clipsy.bpg016

Kahneman, D. (2011). *Thinking fast and slow.* New York, NY: Farrar, Straus & Giroux.

Kemmis, S., & McTaggart, R. (2000). Participatory action research. In N. K. Denzin & Y. S. Lincoln (Eds.), *Handbook of quantitative research* (2nd ed., pp. 567–605). Thousand Oaks, CA: Sage.

Kolb, D. (1984). *Experiential learning: Experience as the source of learning and development.* Englewood Cliffs, NJ: Prentice Hall.

Lang, P. J. (1977). Imagery in therapy: An information processing analysis of fear. *Behavior Therapy, 8,* 862–886. http://dx.doi.org/10.1016/S0005-7894(77)80157-3

Lang, P. J. (1979). A bio-informational theory of emotional imagery [Presidential address, 1978]. *Psychophysiology, 16,* 495–512. http://dx.doi.org/10.1111/j.1469-8986.1979.tb01511.x

Lazarus, A. (1976). *Multimodal behavior therapy.* New York, NY: Springer.

Leung, K. S., & Cottler, L. B. (2009). Treatment of pathological gambling. *Current Opinion in Psychiatry, 22,* 69–74. http://dx.doi.org/10.1097/YCO.0b013e32831575d9

Leventhal, H. (1979). A perceptual-motor processing model of emotion. In P. Pilner, K. R. Blankstein, & I. M. Spiegel (Eds.), *Perception of emotion in self and others* (pp. 1–46). New York, NY: Plenum Press. http://dx.doi.org/10.1007/978-1-4684-3548-1_1

Lewin, K. (1946). Action research and minority problems. *Journal of Social Issues, 2,* 34–46. http://dx.doi.org/10.1111/j.1540-4560.1946.tb02295.x

Long, M. E., Davis, J. L., Springer, J. R., Elhai, J. D., Rhudy, J. L., Teng, E. J., & Frueh, B. C. (2011). The role of cognitions in imagery rescripting for posttraumatic nightmares. *Journal of Clinical Psychology, 67,* 1008–1016. http://dx.doi.org/10.1002/jclp.20804

Meichenbaum, D. (1977). *Cognitive-behavior modification.* New York, NY: Plenum Press. http://dx.doi.org/10.1007/978-1-4757-9739-8

Mowrer, O. (1960). *Learning theory and behavior.* New York, NY: Wiley. http://dx.doi.org/10.1037/10802-000

Nadel, L., Hupbach, A., Gomez, R., & Newman-Smith, K. (2012). Memory formation, consolidation and transformation. *Neuroscience and Biobehavioral Reviews, 36,* 1640–1645. http://dx.doi.org/10.1016/j.neubiorev.2012.03.001

Newman, M. G., Castonguay, L. G., Borkovec, T. D., & Molnar, C. (2004). Integrative psychotherapy. In R. G. Heimberg, C. L. Turk, & D. S. Mennin (Eds.), *Generalized anxiety disorder: Advances in research and practice* (pp. 320–350). New York, NY: Guilford Press.

Okajima, I., Komada, Y., & Inoue, Y. (2011). A meta-analysis on the treatment effectiveness of cognitive behavioral therapy for primary insomnia. *Sleep and Biological Rhythms, 9,* 24–34. http://dx.doi.org/10.1111/j.1479-8425.2010.00481.x

Pfaffmann, C. (1960). The pleasures of sensation. *Psychological Review, 67,* 253–268. http://dx.doi.org/10.1037/h0045838

Pos, A. E., Greenberg, L. S., & Warwar, S. H. (2009). Testing a model of change in the experiential treatment of depression. *Journal of Consulting and Clinical Psychology, 77,* 1055–1066. http://dx.doi.org/10.1037/a0017059

Power, M. J., & Dalgleish, T. (1997). *Cognition and emotion: From order to disorder.* Hove, England: Psychology Press.

Power, M. J., & Dalgleish, T. (1999). Two routes to emotion: Some implications of multi-level theories of emotion for therapeutic practice. *Behavioural and Cognitive Psychotherapy, 27,* 129–141.

Przeworski, A., Newman, M. G., Pincus, A. L., Kasoff, M. B., Yamasaki, A. S., Castonguay, L. G., & Berlin, K. S. (2011). Interpersonal pathoplasticity in individuals with generalized anxiety disorder. *Journal of Abnormal Psychology, 120,* 286–298. http://dx.doi.org/10.1037/a0023334

Rachman, S., & Hodgson, R. (1974). I. Synchrony and desynchrony in fear and avoidance. *Behaviour Research and Therapy, 12,* 311–318. http://dx.doi.org/10.1016/0005-7967(74)90005-9

Rector, N. A., & Beck, A. T. (2001). Cognitive behavioral therapy for schizophrenia: An empirical review. *Journal of Nervous and Mental Disease, 189,* 278–287. http://dx.doi.org/10.1097/00005053-200105000-00002

Safran, J. D., & Muran, J. C. (2000). *Negotiating the therapeutic alliance: A relational treatment guide.* New York, NY: Guilford Press.

Safran, J. D., Muran, J. C., & Eubanks-Carter, C. (2011). Repairing alliance ruptures. *Psychotherapy, 48,* 80–87. http://dx.doi.org/10.1037/a0022140

Safran, J. D., & Segal, Z. V. (1996). *Interpersonal process in cognitive therapy.* New York, NY: Basic Books.

Salzberg, S. (2011). *Real happiness: The power of meditation.* New York, NY: Workman.

Schon, D. A. (1983). *The reflective practitioner.* New York, NY: Basic Books.

Smucker, M. R., Dancu, C. V., Foa, E. B., & Niederee, J. (1995). Imagery rescripting: A new treatment for survivors of childhood sexual abuse suffering from posttraumatic stress. *Journal of Cognitive Psychotherapy, 9,* 3–17.

Smucker, M. R., & Niederee, J. (1994). Imagery rescripting: A multifaceted treatment for childhood sexual abuse survivors experiencing posttraumatic stress. In L. VandeCreek, S. Knapp, & T. L. Jackson (Eds.), *Innovations in clinical practice: A source book* (Vol. 13, pp. 96–98). Sarasota, FL: Professional Resource Press.

Smucker, M. R., & Niederee, J. (1995). Treating incest-related PTSD and pathogenic schemas through imaginal exposure and rescripting. *Cognitive and Behavioral Practice, 2,* 63–92. http://dx.doi.org/10.1016/S1077-7229(05)80005-7

Spence, K. W. (1956). *Behavior theory and conditioning.* New Haven, CT: Yale University Press. http://dx.doi.org/10.1037/10029-000

Stopa, L. (2009). How to use imagery in cognitive-behavioural therapy. In L. Stopa (Ed.), *Imagery and the threatened self* (pp. 65–93). New York, NY: Routledge. http://dx.doi.org/10.4324/9780203878644

Teasdale, J. D. (1997). The relationship between cognition and emotion: The mind-in-place in mood disorders. In D. M. Clark & C. G. Fairburn (Eds.), *The science and practice of cognitive behavioural therapy* (pp. 67–93). Oxford, England: Oxford University Press.

Teasdale, J. D., & Barnard, P. J. (1993). *Affect, cognition and change: Re-modeling depressive thought.* Hove, England: Erlbaum.

Toates, F. (1986). *Motivational systems.* New York, NY: Cambridge University Press.

Tolin, D. F. (2010). Is cognitive-behavioral therapy more effective than other therapies? A meta-analytic review. *Clinical Psychology Review, 30,* 710–720. http://dx.doi.org/10.1016/j.cpr.2010.05.003

Trew, J. L. (2011). Exploring the roles of approach and avoidance in depression: An integrative model. *Clinical Psychology Review, 31,* 1156–1168. http://dx.doi.org/10.1016/j.cpr.2011.07.007

Tronson, N. C., & Taylor, J. R. (2007). Molecular mechanisms of memory reconsolidation. *Nature Reviews Neuroscience, 8,* 262–275. http://dx.doi.org/10.1038/nrn2090

Watson, J. C., & Bedard, D. L. (2006). Clients' emotional processing in psychotherapy: A comparison between cognitive-behavioral and process-experiential therapies. *Journal of Consulting and Clinical Psychology, 74,* 152–159. http://dx.doi.org/10.1037/0022-006X.74.1.152

Wells, A. (1997). *Cognitive therapy of anxiety disorders: A practice manual and conceptual guide.* Chichester, England: Wiley.

Wells, A. (2000). *Emotional disorders and metacognition.* Chichester, England: Wiley.

Wells, A., & Matthews, G. (1994). *Attention and emotion: A clinical perspective.* Hillsdale, NJ: Erlbaum.

Whisman, M. A. (2007). Marital distress and DSM–IV psychiatric disorders in a population-based national survey. *Journal of Abnormal Psychology, 116,* 638–643. http://dx.doi.org/10.1037/0021-843X.116.3.638

Whisman, M. A., Sheldon, C. T., & Goering, P. (2000). Psychiatric disorders and dissatisfaction with social relationships: Does type of relationship matter? *Journal of Abnormal Psychology, 109,* 803–808. http://dx.doi.org/10.1037/0021-843X.109.4.803

Wild, J., & Clark, D. M. (2011). Imagery rescripting of early traumatic memories in social phobia. *Cognitive and Behavioral Practice, 18,* 433–443. http://dx.doi.org/10.1016/j.cbpra.2011.03.002

Wild, J., Hackmann, A., & Clark, D. M. (2008). Rescripting early memories linked to negative images in social phobia: A pilot study. *Behavior Therapy, 39,* 47–56. http://dx.doi.org/10.1016/j.beth.2007.04.003

Wirtz, C. M., Hofmann, S. G., Riper, H., & Berking, M. (2014). Emotion regulation predicts anxiety over a five-year interval: A cross-lagged panel analysis. *Depression and Anxiety, 31,* 87–95. http://dx.doi.org/10.1002/da.22198

Young, J. E., Klosko, J. S., & Weishaar, M. E. (2003). *Schema therapy: A practitioner's guide.* New York, NY: Guilford Press.

Zajonc, R. B. (1980). Feeling and thinking: Preferences need no inferences. *American Psychologist, 35,* 151–175. http://dx.doi.org/10.1037/0003-066X.35.2.151

4

EMOTION-FOCUSED PSYCHOTHERAPY

LESLIE S. GREENBERG

Emotion-focused therapy (EFT) starts with the proposition that emotions influence cognition and behavior, and that one can work directly with emotion to change it, which subsequently will change thoughts and actions. EFT (Greenberg, 2017) encourages a focus on and an exploration of lived emotional experience in therapy, and, in particular, an acceptance of dreaded, disowned emotions. EFT helps clients to make sense of emotions by attending to them, symbolizing them in awareness, expressing them congruently, accepting them, feeling an agent of them, and regulating and differentiating them (Auszra, Greenberg, & Herrmann, 2013). The therapy is designed to help clients process emotion by first moving past unhelpful secondary, symptomatic emotions to arrive at more informative, primary vulnerable emotions and to develop new emotion-based narratives (Angus & Greenberg, 2011; Greenberg, 2015, 2017; Herrmann, Greenberg, & Auszra, 2016). Spinoza (1677/1967) claimed that a passive emotion ceases to be passive as soon as

http://dx.doi.org/10.1037/0000130-004
Working With Emotion in Psychodynamic, Cognitive Behavior, and Emotion-Focused Psychotherapy,
by L. S. Greenberg, N. T. Malberg, and M. A. Tompkins

one forms a clear and distinct idea of it. It is for this reason that EFT brings cognition to emotion to help people develop a sense of agency in relation to their emotions.

EFT is a neohumanistic therapy. Initially, the approach to individual therapy was called *process experiential therapy* (Greenberg, Rice, & Elliott, 1993; Rice & Greenberg, 1984) to emphasize both its experiential nature and its focus on moment-by-moment process. The original couple therapy was called *emotionally focused couple therapy* (Greenberg & Johnson, 1988) because it emphasized the importance of emotion in interaction and communication. Later, because of a growing understanding of the importance of emotion in change and to bring the name in line with general North American language use, *emotionally focused*, which had been used more generally in the psychology coping literature, was changed to *emotion-focused therapy*. The approach emanated from an integration of the author's background training in client-centered experiential and gestalt therapies with his training in systemic therapies. The integration was all framed within emotion theory and affective neuroscience concepts, and informed by psychotherapy process research.

This chapter begins with an explanation of emotion and functioning as viewed within the EFT framework. The next two sections are theoretical; they offer an emotion-based explanation of human functioning as an alternative to a learning theory–based and a motivational view of functioning. Readers who are more interested in practice might choose to skip these two sections, returning to them later, if interested. Subsequent sections are more practical in nature; they focus on the role of emotion in change, in interpersonal relationships, and in the therapeutic relationship. A case study of an EFT session is presented to ground the ideas on practice.

WHAT IS EMOTION?

Although there no clear agreement yet among emotion scientists on what emotion is (Ekman, 1993; Ekman & Davidson, 1994; Frijda, 1986, 2016; Scherer, 2015), EFT posits that *emotions* are an adaptive form of information processing and action readiness that orients people to their environment and promotes their survival and well-being. Emotions are embodied connections to our most essential needs (Frijda, 1986). Rapidly alerting us to situations important to our well-being, emotions provide information about what is good and bad for us—and must be distinguished from *cognition*, which evaluates if something is true or false. Essentially, emotions organize us to react adaptively and tell us if things are going our way.

Emotions arise as appraisals of an object or event in relation to a person's concerns (Frijda, 1986). They therefore are strongly influenced and shaped by the appraising individual's current needs, goals, sensitivities, interests, and values. It is not just an appraisal that activates an emotion but an appraisal in relation to a concern. Once activated, emotions provide basic action tendencies developed evolutionarily to promote survival (Izard, 1991; LeDoux, 2012). Emotional action tendencies involve a rapid, automatic evaluation by the brain, without language, of the immediate repercussions and consequences of a situation for the individual's concerns.

THEORY OF FUNCTIONING

A major premise of EFT is that emotion is the fundamental datum of human experience, is foundational in the construction of the self, and is a key determinant of self-organization. Rather than "I think, therefore I am," EFT is based on the idea that "I feel, therefore I am" and that in any significant personal experience, we think only inasmuch as we feel. In everyday life, emotion increases peoples' ability to respond adaptively to situations as they arise and to use the information provided by emotion to live vitally and adaptively. Our lived emotional experience is the product of a complex synthesis of many processes, including cognitive, memory, motivational, and behavioral ones.

EFT views emotion as fundamentally adaptive. Emotion provides us with our basic mode of information processing such that we react rapidly and automatically with fear processing, or shame processing, or sadness processing, or joy processing. With the aid of this type of emotion processing, people react automatically to their apprehension of patterns of sounds, sights, and smells, and to other signs of people's intentions in a way that has served humans well as a species for centuries and as individuals for years. Fear-induced flight produces safety, disgust expels a noxious intrusion, and, in sadness, one calls out for the lost object. People respond emotionally in an automatic fashion to patterns of cues in their environment that signal novelty, comfort, loss, or humiliation. Emotions also direct attention to information that seems immediately relevant to maintaining well-being or attaining goals.

Automatic thoughts and conscious reflective evaluations, however, also can produce emotion. For example, we can think our way into being afraid and thus activate a defensive motive state. But the emotions produced by these more conscious linguistic, orbital frontal cortex processes are not nearly as important as the more primary emotions produced by our limbic systems and other automatic processes. Automatic processes make appraisals—not in language or thought—of the relevance of a situation to organismic needs or concerns. It is these nonlinguistic appraisals of relevance, goal congruence, novelty, danger, and control that are more impenetrable to reason and harder to change.

As Frijda (2016) argued that rather than considering emotions as "basic," what probably is basic are the modes of action readiness that aim to establish, modify, maintain, or terminate a given self-object relationship. What then may well be universal are not emotions as feelings but, rather, emotions as dispositions for various forms of action readiness that act as emotionally based motive states. Facial and other expressions, for example, are implementations of the individual's action tendencies and occur automatically in relation to an underlying concern. Action tendencies have an aim, the most basic of which is to survive. If the current situation lends itself to it, the state of readiness will activate an action or action sequence from the individual's repertoire that appears capable of achieving the aim of modifying or maintaining relationships. Actual actions appear when the subthreshold activations turn into full-blown action. From this viewpoint, feelings are reflections in consciousness that accompany action inclinations.

In EFT, two fundamental levels of emotion generation are important. One, the *experiential level of processing*, involves the automatic processes that produce primary emotional responses following automatic perceptual appraisals. The other, the *conceptual level of processing*, is a conscious narrative level of processing that makes sense of automatic experience (Gazzaniga, 1988).

As individuals have more lived experience and develop more cognitive-linguistic capacities, their early automatic emotional responses develop into more complex processing and form emotion schemes in which sensory, memorial, and ideational information is combined to form an internal network-based structure. It is the activation of these schemes that generate bodily felt emotional experience. Conscious meaning, on the other hand, is created by an integration of language and bodily experience of reason and emotion via an ongoing circular process of making sense of experience. Individuals symbolize bodily felt sensations in awareness and articulate them in language, thereby constructing new experience and ultimately new narratives (Greenberg & Angus, 2004; Greenberg & Pascual-Leone, 1995; Greenberg et al., 1993). In this *dialectical constructivist view* (Greenberg, 2017; Greenberg & Pascual-Leone, 2001; Greenberg & Watson, 2006), a set of sensations from the world (i.e., cues) are synthesized with a set of internal bodily reactions (i.e., interoception) that consist mainly of action tendencies and sensations, which are labeled as, say, anger, sadness, or fear to provide a situated conceptualization of what one is experiencing (i.e., symbolization). In EFT, the dialectic is between evolutionarily based affect motor programs, which generate bodily felt experience, and cultural and social learning processes, which influence how we label the feeling. Emotion therefore is a complex construction process synthesizing biology, culture, emotion, and language. Behavior is seen as being generated often by our brains for reasons that we are not consciously privy to; we then interpret our behaviors in such a way as to create a coherent narrative about our current experience that makes sense in terms of our past and future. Our narrative explains ourselves to ourselves and provides self-understanding (Gazzaniga, 1988) but is more or less representative of both internal and external lived experience. EFT works with these two fundamental systems—the automatic generation of emotion by the experiential system and the reflexive narrative meaning-making of experience by the conceptual system—and the interaction between them.

Although EFT focuses on awareness and acceptance of emotion, a distinguishing characteristic of being human is the ability to evaluate one's own desires, feelings, and needs (Taylor, 1985). In determining the self that one will become, a person has the ability either to desire or not desire his or her first-order feelings and desires. In this second, higher order, evaluation, the person evaluates the worth of the desire against an ideal or standard to which that person aspires. Being a self involves being self-evaluatively reflective and developing and acting according to higher order desires—essentially, developing feelings and desires about feelings and desires. For the emotion system, the evaluation is simply, "Is it good or bad for me?" whereas in the stronger, self-reflective evaluation, there also is a judgment of the value of the emotion and its accompanying desire. People evaluate whether their emotions and desires are good or bad, courageous or cowardly, or useful or destructive, thus forming subjective judgments of the worth of their own desired states and courses of action (Taylor, 1985). Thoughtful reflection—where conscious thought plays its essential role—on emotional prompting is a crucial part of EFT. Thought is used to judge whether emotional prompting coheres with what people value as worthwhile for themselves and others. So, being aware of feelings does not mean simply doing what feels good!

Emotion Schemes

Emotion schemes are organized, internal structures or networks that are at the base of the adult emotional response system. They synthesize affective experience with motivational, cognitive, and behavioral elements into internal organizations that are activated rapidly out of awareness. We come into the world with basic psychoaffective motor programs for emotions with action tendencies for emotions, such as anger, sadness, fear, and shame. We do not learn how to be angry, sad, afraid, or ashamed; however, experience soon influences what we become angry at, sad about, and afraid or ashamed of. Emotion schemes are internal representations of our lived experience.

Emotion schemes consist largely of procedural, preverbal, and affective elements (e.g., bodily sensations, action tendencies, visual images, smells), rather than beliefs in language. When activated, they produce experience and action; when synthesized with other schemes, they form into higher order organizations of experience, such as feeling worthless or unlovable, or feeling confident or desirable (Greenberg, 2015, 2017).

How do schemes operate? Schemes are activated by cues that match the input features of the scheme or nodes of the neural network. When activated, emotion schemes produce experience and responses. The notion of schemes as experience and action producing, as opposed to schemas as beliefs, was developed by Piaget (1954) and elaborated on by neo-Piagetians (J. Pascual-Leone, 1987, 1991; J. Pascual-Leone & Johnson, 1991, 2011). This view offers an alternative to a simple conditioning view of learning.

Important life experiences that are significant by virtue of having previously activated emotional responses become coded into emotion schematic memory. Once emotional responses have been experienced, they are organized into a schematic system that synthesizes a variety of levels and types of information, including sensorimotor stimuli, perception, motivation, action, and conceptual-level information. These newly acquired and more complex emotional responses become automatic—as automatic as the in-wired biologically adaptive responses that they integrate. When activated, they are synthesized with higher level processes, such as attention and executive processes (J. Pascual-Leone & Johnson, 1991, 2011), and set into action the basic mode of processing that guides our life. In contrast to a cognitive schema, the emotion scheme is a network that produces action tendencies and experience as opposed to conceptual knowledge.

Development of Emotion Schemes

Core emotion schemes develop in early interactions and continue developing throughout life. For example, an emotion scheme based on the in-wired joy and calm at human contact will develop in infancy into the overarching goal of seeking contact or comfort and familiarity because it feels good. Initially, this scheme will have components of the smell of the mother and her milk, sound of her voice, particular rhythm of sucking, and feeling of joy at satisfaction and comfort at contact. This scheme soon becomes more differentiated: The face of the mother, her approaching steps, and the way in which she turns to the child become components of the scheme along with the lived experience of the interactions with her. Neural activation patterns emerge that represent these components together. Cells with increasingly more specific response properties are created, at higher processing levels, through progressive convergence of the wiring until schemes serving as specific detectors for complex situations and patterns rise to the top of the hierarchy.

With each episode of satisfying proximity to the mother, the neural connections associated with this emotion scheme are strengthened such that, over time, the corresponding neural circuits are activated more easily. Ultimately, these neural connections form a scheme with the highest excitability of all such that the scheme can become active spontaneously, even by the image of or the voice of the mother. The child then experiences a wish, a longing for the mother. The need for the mother also will be easily activated with the advent of internal states, such as hunger or cold, that the mother previously has alleviated. Now, when the child feels hungry or lonely, the feeling of need for comfort is activated, the utterances that previously have been effective for this purpose are emitted, and attention is deployed to notice whether mother can be heard or seen anywhere. When the mother appears, the sight of her triggers positive emotions, and the child calms down; or, alternately, if there is no soothing response, the child begins to develop emotion schemes of painful feelings, such as fear and shame, that can become the source of later emotional difficulties.

Over time, lived experiences of situations are associated with representations of the bodily states individuals experienced in the situations; the situations thereby are given affective meaning. In this way, a somatic state, a visceral experience, or a feeling becomes a marker for a specific experience and is stored in memory (Damasio, 1999). When cues evoke an emotion schematic organization formed from a past bad experience, the person will experience an unpleasant gut feeling (Damasio, 1994), and the feeling will have an implicit meaning that what is currently occurring is bad. Emotion schemes also determine peoples' future experience of that emotion: To protect themselves from feeling bad, they will tend to make decisions to avoid this kind of unpleasant event. The body is used as a guidance system: Emotions guide decisions, helping people to anticipate future outcomes based on previous experience stored in emotion schemes that activate gut feelings.

Although adaptive, emotions can become maladaptive through a variety of negative life experiences, thus generating maladaptive responses to current situations. They are the source of much dysfunction and the targets of change in EFT. Because in-wired emotion response programs are open to input and learning, emotions are a flexible adaptive processing system; however, that system could become maladaptive via the formation of emotion schematic memories of negative experiences. In life, if emotions become dysregulated and are not soothed or understood, and if not enough safety or validation is given to feelings, emotions develop into painful emotion schematic memories. These memories of emotionally significant experiences are stored at emotion addresses; for example, memories of sadness-producing experiences are stored at a sadness address; anger-related memories, at an anger address; and fear-related experiences, at a fear address. Emotion schematic memories are activated by cues relevant to the emotion around which they were formed; so, for example, a current loss or a feeling of sadness will activate emotion schematic memories of sadness. A threat cue, such as the look of anger on another's face that often is perceived subliminally, will produce fear and activate schemes related to previous fear experience. Once activated, these schemes synthesize to generate a fear response with its associated motivation to escape, an action tendency to flee, and rudimentary forms of cognitive processing, such as focusing of attention and scanning for threat. On activation of this basic mode of processing, the person begins to process more consciously for sources of danger; he or she ultimately symbolizes in words the appraised danger and generates ways of coping with it. It is this basic mode of processing generated by the activation of emotion schemes that need to be changed in therapy. In EFT, the maladaptive schemes are activated to open them to new emotional experience.

Emotion schemes themselves, though, are not conscious; the emotions they generate, however, can become conscious. The important issue is that the emotionally motivated, basic mode of processing set into motion by scheme activation occurs out of awareness and influences conscious processing. The activation of a fear scheme sets into motion a basic mode of processing for the threat, and this conscious processing works in the service of the affective goal activated by the scheme: safety in the case of fear and contact in the case of sadness.

EFT posits that experience is generated by a tacit synthesis of a number of schemes that are coactivated and coapply to a situation, and by processing at numerous further levels (Greenberg & Pascual-Leone, 2001; A. Pascual-Leone & Greenberg, 2007; J. Pascual-Leone, 1991). A number of activated emotion schemes synthesize at a higher level into an operating self-organization that provides the person's emotional experience and reaction in a situation: the person's experiential state or current state of mind. This synthesis of multiple schemes forms the "self I find myself to be" in a situation, such as feeling organized as confident or feeling organized as shaky, or worthless, or secure. It is this self-organization in a situation that provides the bodily felt referent of experience and the feeling of what happens (Damasio, 1999; Gendlin, 1996; Greenberg, 2011) to which "I" need to attend to experience "myself." These experiences are not a product of will or deliberation but, rather, of an automatic dynamic self-organizing process that occurs outside of awareness. EFT sees that the first response activated automatically is an emotional one, whether it is fear, sadness, or anger processing. Beliefs and relational patterns come later.

Subjective Experience

Experienced emotion is a complex idiosyncratic felt meaning rather than a primitive or general response. For example, a person's conscious experience of danger is fear that itself is a synthesis of a variety of emotion schemes built from the person's basic neurochemistry and physiology, and from their unique experience. Our unique experience is synthesized from our activated schemes much like the flavor of a recipe emerges from its ingredients. When all ingredients from the various schematic components are synthesized in consciousness with information about the external stimulus and long-term memories about what that stimulus means, and the particular characteristics of the schemes aroused in the brain, the resulting feeling that emerges is some personal variant of fear.

To understand emotions, one needs to understand individuals' idiosyncratic construction of their felt experience—the feelings that orient them to the world and are the basis for the personally relevant meaning they construct. Feelings are not necessarily fully formed and awaiting expression. Moreover, people do not feel one thing at a time in response to situations; they may have multiple or sequential feelings. The key word in working with emotion work is *complexity*; therapists must adopt a "not knowing" position in relation to a client's feeling and recognize that although they have a perspective on what clients are feeling, their clients are experts on their own experience. Therapists must encourage clients to pay attention to, explore, and make sense of what they feel; given that emotion schemes ultimately are the source of experience and the source of distress, they need to be activated in therapy to be changed.

Dysfunction

In EFT, dysfunction is seen as lacking the ability to creatively adjust to situations and to be able to produce novel responses, new experiences, and new narratives (Greenberg, 2017). In general terms, emotion is seen as dysfunctional when it gives poor information. This dysfunction occurs when responses are not adaptive or are inappropriate to the situation and when the emotional reactions cannot be monitored and regulated nor effectively communicated. In studying EFT work in therapy, my research group and I have observed that it is core painful emotions generated by maladaptive emotion schemes that synthesize into maladaptive self-organizations that are at the center of dysfunction and are the targets of therapeutic change.

EFT posits that emotional processes underlie most, if not all, psychological dysfunction. A good example of this view is a look at ruminative thinking or repetitive thought, which has been shown to be related to dysfunction and has been suggested as an underlying mechanism of disorder (Nolen-Hoeksema & Watkins, 2011; Watkins, 2008). EFT views *rumination* as a symptom of protection against or avoidance of and attempts to cope with underlying painful emotions. Treatment involves helping clients to concretely describe their underlying feelings and to differentiate complaints (often expressed in asking pleadingly why bad things have happened) into their constituent unresolved anger and sadness. Once accepted and experienced, these core feelings need to be processed according to EFT principles of emotional change (described later).

The four major sources of dysfunctional emotional processing are

1. *Lack of emotion awareness:* An example is the inability to symbolize a bodily felt experience of sadness or fear in awareness, which often results from the avoidance or disclaiming of primary experience.

2. *Maladaptive emotional responses:* These responses are generated by emotion schemes formed from unprocessed emotion (e.g., fear of abandonment, shame of humiliation). They often result from traumatic learning in interpersonal situations, frequently with primary caregivers.

3. *Emotion dysregulation:* This source involves the under- or overregulation of emotion often resulting from failures in the early dyadic regulation of affect. One example is the traumatic fear that overwhelms. Another example is the addictive behaviors that come from an inability to soothe or regulate the automatic emotion system; those behaviors take control using substances to soothe despite the deliberate conceptual system's desire to stop.

4. *Problems in narrative construction and meaning creation:* These problems stem from people's inability to make sense of their experience and to develop adaptive narrative accounts of self, other, and world (e.g., incoherent narratives, maladaptive narratives of self, blaming others).

EMOTIONAL DEVELOPMENT AND LEARNING

Emotional development from infancy to adulthood occurs through an interaction of a person's emotional temperament, his or her experience in the world, and the emotional attunement from others to that person's experience. Attachment relationships and achievements in social and school settings are seen as directly promoting emotional development and self-organization. People who experience severe lack of affective attunement in their formative relationships with significant others (particularly, but not limited to, caregivers) are vulnerable to more emotional disorder in their lives than people who have received empathic attunement to affect (Schore, 1994, 2003; van der Kolk, 2014). Affect regulation is seen as a core aspect of development.

The goal of EFT is self-development. To appreciate what this means, we need to understand what the self is and what development means. The self is a process of self-organization that is constantly being created to take particular forms. Development can be contrasted with learning: Development is seen as a change in the self-organizing process, such as becoming more regulated, whereas learning is seen as involving a change within the self-organization, such as having an increase or decrease in the intensity of a particular response (e.g., becoming less angry).

The Self

In EFT, the self is a temporal process unfolding in the present and in interaction with the environment. It is arising in the moment in contact with the environment (Perls, Hefferline, & Goodman, 1951). The self is formed in relation to the environment; it is decentralized and unfolds in time. As the organism engages in ongoing transactions with the environment, the self is organized moment by moment into different forms, such as happy, self-critical, worthless, cautious, or bold. It is more like a constantly flowing river than a structure, much more constituted by the passing of time than by spatial location and a fixed form. Thus, the self is a dynamic self-organizing process that creates the self the person is about to become. It is the forming of forms. The person is constantly putting the self together in the situation. Just as touch only exists in touching, so the self only exists in experiencing something in a situation. EFT is concerned with the self-organizing processes and with the flexibility of this process rather than with finding a "true self."

How then does EFT explain stability? Although people organize in different ways at different times, they do develop more characteristic ways of organizing emotionally to give a certain stability to the way in which personality and character structure are repeatedly constructed. People have certain patterned sequences and ways of being that are more likely to occur than others. These more frequently organized states are called *attractor states* in dynamic systems theory. EFT suggests that development involves change in the rules that guide these characteristic patterns; the result is change in the ways of being or in character structure across the life span but also in therapy. People, for instance, change from being self-critical to self-accepting, from being a person who easily gets angry at others—responding to shame with anger or to requests with irritation—to being a more calm, considerate person. These are changes in ways of functioning that indicate self-development.

Development Through Synthesis

It is helpful to contrast the kind of developmental change in the self that EFT strives to promote with the type of change produced by learning new skills. *Development* is the process of changes that happen over time in which the original structure is transformed, and the person moves to higher level and more complex forms of organization. According to Piaget (1954, 1973), development involves a progressive reorganization of mental processes through the experience of discrepancies between what people already know (i.e., experience) and what they discover (i.e., new experience), and then adjust their ideas accordingly

To contrast an emotion schematic view of development with a learning theory view of learning, we need to understand how functioning based on emotion schemes and "development by synthesis" differs from a stimulus response type of view of learning. In EFT, emotional change does not occur by reduction of arousal by exposure or by changing one's thoughts and beliefs via means of new information or reasoning; rather, development occurs through a synthesis of existing schemes. Instead of learning by association or by logical or empirical analysis, the EFT developmental perspective offers a view of functioning in which development occurs by synthesis (Neisser, 1976). In this view, rather than stimulus–response connections, schemes are internal network structures that are cued by multiple stimuli and have multiple outputs (J. Pascual-Leone & Johnson, 1991, 2011). They are coactivated and coapply, and many schemes are synthesized with each other and with other higher level attention and other cognitive operating processes to determine output. Schemes also are not simply reactive; they actively process information constantly, evaluating situations to aid survival. In addition, a scheme is "thoughtfully" anticipatory (J. Pascual-Leone & Johnson, 1991, 2011; Piaget, 1954, 1973), possessing outcome expectancies. Schemes, unlike associations, are not blind or dumb associations; rather, they are complexly multidetermined and evaluative, and can anticipate the result of their application. For this reason, they offer an alternate conceptualization to stimulus–response conceptualizations (Greenberg & Pascual-Leone, 1995, 2001; Greenberg & Safran, 1987; J. Pascual-Leone, 1991).

It also is useful to contrast an emotion schematic view in which the emotion scheme is the fundamental processing unit with an attachment theory view of internal working models (Bowlby, 1988), or with the object relations view of internal representations of self–other relationships (Kernberg, 1976/1984; Schore, 1994, 2003). These psychodynamic conceptualizations posit much more complex internal structures as the fundamental unit of processing—structures based on a relationship between self and other and the affects that glue them together (Guntrip, 1969; Kernberg, 1976/1984). In my view, these represent much more complex, higher forms that are built up from the basic emotional response. The brain's first response to a stimulus is the action tendency of fear or shame or joy, not a complex perception that the other is abandoning and that the self is abandoned, resulting in fear.

Emotional development can be contrasted with the learning that involves the acquisition of knowledge or skills through skill training or psychoeducation. Learning of the skill training or psychoeducation type focuses on the strengthening of correct responses and the weakening of incorrect responses, as well as the addition of new information to memory. Learning, in this view, involves conditioning, which occurs as a function of positive and negative reinforcement. Reinforcement is seen as establishing a change in behavioral responses to environmental stimuli. In a more cognitive approach to learning, people are viewed as not merely responding deterministically to environmental stimuli; rather, they are seen as cognitive beings who actively participate in learning and whose actions are a consequence of information processing that involves internal mental processes, including thinking, reasoning, and memory. From these viewpoints, it is believed that fear of saying "spiders" or "heights" can be negatively or positively reinforced by mere exposure or by reasoning with people to illuminate their errors in thinking, or by changing their beliefs mainly by success experience. In my view, these processes lead to the learning of coping skills but not to transformation or development. This difference has been referred to as first-order versus second-order change (von Foerster, 1995).

First- and Second-Order Changes

Change in psychotherapy can be thought of as occurring in two ways. *First-order change* occurs when the parameters of the system change in a continuous manner, but the structure of the system does not alter. In *second-order change*, the system changes qualitatively and in a discontinuous manner. This second type of change in systems requires changes in the body of rules governing the structure or internal order of a system (Bateson, 1999; Watzlawick, Weakland, & Fisch, 1974). First-order change deals with change in the existing structure: doing more or less of something. This type of change often refers to the gaining of new knowledge, skills, and behaviors within a particular stage of development. First-order change does not change a problem but helps a person become better equipped to deal with the problem. If you have too much anger, you learn anger management skills; if you are not assertive, you get assertiveness training. In my view, the acquisition of coping skills along the lines of learning theory involves first-order change. In EFT, modification of symptoms of emotion dysregulation by learning and psychoeducation, although possibly helpful, involves improved coping; this is first-order change.

The development sought after in EFT involves second-order change in which something new emerges and results in a completely new way of being in the world. It involves experiencing and seeing things differently. Second-order change involves transformation: The problem goes away. So, someone with too much anger comes to address his or her underlying shame or fear, which leads the person to be angry; and when he or she has changed the primary underlying feeling, that person is are no longer angry. Rather than expanding capability within the same stage of development, the learner moves to a new, more integrated—and what could be considered a higher stage of development—moving from anger to feeling worthy. In addition, the development is not only limited to a particular instance or task but aims to improve the person's personality and attitude, thus changing their mindset. It makes them more resilient. It provides all-around growth, which helps people face future challenges.

Many psychoeducational methods for dealing with dysregulated emotion work to get first-order symptom change. For example, training people to breathe when distressed, count backward from 100, or take a warm bath may help for immediate coping with the problem but does not deal with underlying emotions. Improved emotion regulation skills, distress tolerance, and distraction are all first-order changes that help people cope. Desensitizing by exposure or habituation reduces fear responses to activating cues, but the hypothesis is that the underlying emotional determinants of all these problems—the core attachment insecurities or core feelings of shame generating the symptomatic self-organization—do not change. Over time, coping may even generalize to other situations through the reinforcement of success experience, leading to second-order change in the core problem; however, this second-order change is not assured because the core problem was not the target of change.

Framing now in terms of a dialectical constructivist approach (Greenberg, 2017; Greenberg & Pascual-Leone, 1995, 2001), transformational change comes from the development of truly novel responses by means of synthesizing existing emotion schemes into new more functional schemes (Piaget, 1973) that create new ways of being. This is second-order change of existing schemes. For example, a 1-year-old child's schemes of standing and falling can be dynamically synthesized into a higher level scheme of walking by a process of dialectical synthesis (Greenberg & Pascual-Leone, 1995; J. Pascual-Leone, 1991) rather than by being taught how to walk. Similarly, schemes of different emotional states can be synthesized to form new integrations. In development, when opposing schemes with opposing action tendencies are coactivated, compatible elements from the coactivated schemes synthesize to form new higher level schemes. Thus, a schematic emotional memory of shame and a withdrawn worthless self-organization from prior abuse can be synthesized with current empowering anger against violation—which motivates approach rather than withdrawal—to form a new confident or assertive self-organization. This process develops into a new way of feeling more deserving and more confident. Similarly, a self-organization of insecurity based on fear from attachment ruptures in the past can be changed by processing the sadness of loss: feeling deserving of having had the unmet need met and grieving the loss of what was missing. EFT treatment does not involve direct modification of the symptom, such as psychoeducational retraining of attention but, rather, helps clients reexperience the feelings that underlie the symptom and transform these feelings with new experience.

EMOTION AND MOTIVATION

EFT sees the following as major human processes that serve the basic macromotive of survival common across species: *affect regulation*, the effort to have the feelings we want and not have the feelings we do not want, and *meaning creation*, the making of narrative sense of ourselves and our world. The attempt to identify specific content motives, such as attachment, autonomy, achievement, or control, however, is so strong in Western thinking that it is hard for people to not see these content motivations as fundamental givens. Maslow (1954) even attempted to specify five hierarchical levels of human need: physiological, safety, belonging, self-esteem, and actualization. In contrast, emotion theory suggests that these content-specific motivations are derivatives of emotion and that human psychological needs are emergent phenomena constructed in a complex process of development.

Origins of Psychological Needs

In general, *need* or *motivation* refers to what a person wants, wants to do, desires, or intends; *motivation* is derived from the Latin *motivus* (to move). Although EFT does not deny the importance of hypothesized motives, such as attachment, achievement, mastery, power, esteem, and many others, it does hypothesize that emotions are the in-wired givens and that motives, needs, wishes, and desires develop from emotion and the processes of affect. Psychological needs are not simply inborn; they emerge out of affect, and they represent basic likes and dislikes, things that the organism desires to preserve a state of well-being. They are created and coconstructed in interaction with the environment by the operation of affect regulation and meaning construction. Basically, we come to desire what has helped achieve the survival aim of the emotion and therefore felt good. The aim in anger, for example, is one of protecting boundaries or overcoming hurdles. In fear, the aim is to flee from danger; in sadness, the aim is to reach or cry out for contact or comfort, or withdrawing when there is no response; and in disgust, the aim is to dispel what is noxious and tastes bad. All of these evolved as action-oriented systems to aid survival, and all are desirable in situations in which they promote survival. As unusual as it may seem, I came to like feeling anger when violated because it protected me; I came to like sadness at loss because it brought me comfort; and I liked feeling fear because it led me to attach, which promoted survival, and I would not become an attachment-seeking being at separation if it did not feel good to connect.

Rather than postulate a set of basic motivations, such as attachment, mastery, or control, EFT sees psychological needs as arising from a process of construction from an interaction between basic in-born biases, preferences, and affective values of what is good and bad for us, and lived experience. Thus, for example, the infant is prewired through the affect system to favor warmth, familiar smell, softness, smiling faces, high-pitched voices, and shared gaze. These all produce neurochemical reaction, action tendencies, and positive affects that support life, and once experienced, begin to be sought after. Similarly, infants have negative reactions to restraint, loud noises, interoceptive discomfort, loud noise, and overstimulation, and move away from them. Experience leads to the development of emotion schematic memories with expectancies of what feels good and bad, and, as cognition develops, likes and dislikes become further consolidated in consciousness as needs and desires. Need or desire is created from the seeking or avoidance of those things that helped one survive and made one feel good or bad. Feelings are the rewards or punishments that lead to desiring more or less of something.

People come into the world with basic motives to survive and thrive, and these motives are serviced by affect regulation and meaning creation. Out of an interaction of these processes with inborn emotional biases and, later, lived experience are sculpted our other needs, such as for connection, validation, and achievement. Without emotions, we would not have attachment or mastery, control, or nurturing motives.

There is, however, a puzzling circularity in the relationship between emotion and need that is seen especially in the theory of emotion generation in which emotion arises from automatic appraisals in relation to need (Frijda, 1986), which seems to imply that need may be primary and may preexist emotion. There clearly is a close relationship between emotion and need, so much so that some emotion theorists like Buck (2014) have suggested the use of the term *emotivation* to describe the interdependence of emotion and motivation. The question arises: Which comes first, emotion or need? In my view, once needs are developed from basic emotions, they become barometers of what the organism has found good in the past and guide the organism's current strivings.

The emotion brain is constantly reading the environment in terms of its potential to meet or thwart need satisfaction (i.e., survival). Need attainment or frustration generates emotion, which provides a readout of the organism's progress toward or failure to meet need satisfaction. There clearly is a circular causal relationship between emotions and needs in the process of living, but it is in the process of need development that emotion comes first. Although needs are intimately connected to emotion generation, this does not mean they developmentally precede emotion nor that they were wired in. A need for contact or comfort, as Harlow's (1958) monkeys showed by clinging to the cloth-covered wire mother monkeys over their need for milk from a bottle, developed because the cloth felt good; this feeling was more important than the need for food. A child looks at the mother's face, seeking to again experience the joy that was produced by the smile on the mother's face. What was wired in was the preference for or positive feelings of softness and smiles.

Need Satisfaction Versus Need Frustration

An important feature of working with motivation is whether need satisfaction or need frustration leads to change in therapy. Need satisfaction is seen as leading to the abatement of the need. For example, satisfaction of the need for closeness leads to a person's need being satisfied, resulting in moving on to explore and meet other needs. When the need to achieve is satisfied, the person relaxes and moves on to meet other needs. This view of need gratification is important for a therapy in which accessing previously unresolved feelings and unmet needs is seen as necessary to satisfy or change needs. Rather than leading to a reinforcement of the activated feelings and needs, activation makes them amenable to new input. Need frustration is seen as leading not to extinction of the need but to repetition of efforts to get it met and possibly intensify it.

Perls, Hefferline, and Goodman (1951) viewed need satisfaction as leading potentially to completion of the need and moving on to other concerns. Maslow (1954) argued that people actively look to satisfy their needs and once a need is satisfied, they pursue higher needs based on his hierarchy. It seems fairly self-evident, for example that—controlling for other factors— if you are suffering from danger or cold and hunger, then safety, food, and warmth are a priority. You do not have the time or energy to pursue self-esteem needs until other needs are met.

In therapy, accessing the need for attachment in childhood of a distant parent or of protection from an abusive father does not lead to reinforcement of the needs or the emotions of sadness or fear but to their reduction. When the needs, sadness, and fear are empathized with and soothed by the therapist's attunement, and the unmet needs for security or protection are met in therapy, they are transformed by this corrective emotional experience. In addition, the experience of resolution and need validation in the present leads to positive expectations of future need satisfaction and less overall future anxiety or concern about need satisfaction. Activating, encouraging, and responding to the painful need and emotion could be viewed, in simple learning theory terms, as positive reinforcement that would lead to an increase in frequency of these behaviors. From a need satisfaction view, though, activating, encouraging, and responding to the painful need and emotion leads to a reduction in feelings and need, and leads to the experience of a sense of greater security or confidence. That experience produces a reduction in preoccupation with getting the need met based on positive expectations of its satisfaction.

In summary, affect regulation and meaning creation are primary processes serving the motivation to survive. Rather than positing specific content motives, EFT theory suggests that specific motivations are derivatives of emotion and hundreds of human psychological needs are developed from life experience and the emotions we have experienced and liked. EFT does not analyze the content of clients' lives and interactions to look for patterns or explanations of why a client does or does not do certain things. Rather, EFT accesses emotions and makes sense of the motivations and action tendencies within them.

EMOTIONAL CHANGE

A number of studies have shown that making sense of moderately aroused emotions predicts good therapy outcome (Carryer & Greenberg, 2010; Greenberg, 2017; Missirlian, Toukmanian, Warwar, & Greenberg, 2005). Rather than a cathartic getting rid of emotion, emotion-focused therapists help people experience their emotions in the present, relate to them from a working distance, and make sense of them. Making sense of emotion and bringing cognition to emotion are the best predictors of change. However, it is not the understanding or awareness that are crucial to change, but, rather the experience and expression of new emotions to change old emotions that bring with them the bodily change crucial to rewiring at an experiential level. It is the newly accessed and transformed experience that then needs to be made sense of in new narratives that consolidate the change.

This section describes elements that must be considered in any successful treatment. Discussed first are the four main compasses that guide EFT treatments: emotion assessment, principles of emotional change, case formulation, and marker-guided intervention. The section then discusses general EFT methods and skills, and concludes with a description of emotional change processes.

Emotion Assessment

Emotion assessment involves distinguishing between primary and secondary emotion and adaptive and maladaptive emotion. Once primary emotions have been reached, practice is guided by six major principles of emotional change in therapy (discussed later). *Primary emotions* are a person's first, immediate gut response to a situation, such as sadness about loss or fear at threat. *Secondary emotions*, in contrast, are responses to preceding emotional reactions; they often obscure or interrupt these more primary emotional reactions (e.g., depressed hopelessness covering shame at not being good enough, rage covering shame at loss of self-esteem). For example, an individual who feels fear at the possibility of danger subsequently may experience the secondary emotion of anger or shame in response to the fear. Secondary emotions also can be secondary to more cognitive processes (e.g., anxiety in response to catastrophic thinking). Most secondary emotions are symptomatic feelings, such as phobic fear, feelings of depletion, and hopelessness in depression. For example, a client with tears running down his or her face, says, in a complaining tone, "I just can't take this anymore. I want it [my depression] to change." There is a hopeless quality as well as a tone of protest in the client's voice and expression; this is secondary hopelessness or resignation. The therapist needs first to acknowledge the secondary emotion and then guide the client to the underlying primary vulnerable emotion: in this case, feelings of shame and worthlessness. Emotions are generated by top-down and bottom-up processes. People have automatic emotions generated bottom up by emotions schemes and cognitively derived emotions generated by top down by deliberative processes that are based on such things as beliefs, idealized view of self, and socially derived expectations and moral standards and values. Those emotions that are influenced more by cognition and social factors generally are, in my view, secondary emotions, such as when catastrophic thoughts lead to anxiety.

An additional nonprimary emotional response category is *instrumental emotion*, an emotion experienced or expressed primarily to achieve an aim. It has been thought of as the manipulative use of emotion to get what one wants or for secondary gain; typical examples are the expression of anger to control or to dominate, or crocodile tears to evoke sympathy Instrumental emotion can be generated with different degrees of conscious or unconscious intent. Here, therapists need to help people become aware of the aim of their emotional expression and explore more direct ways to communicate their emotions.

Although secondary emotions generally are not adaptive responses to the environment, primary emotions can be either adaptive or maladaptive. Primary *adaptive emotions* are those automatic emotions in which the implicit evaluation, verbal or nonverbal emotional expression, action tendency, and degree of emotion regulation fit the stimulus situation and are appropriate to it (e.g., sadness at loss that reaches out for comfort, fear at threat that prepares the individual to escape). Primary *maladaptive emotion* responses are a person's first, automatic reaction to a situation; however, they are overlearned responses based on previous and often traumatic experiences. These emotional responses may have been adaptive in the original situation but are no longer helpful in the present one. So, these emotional responses are more a reflection of past unresolved issues than reactions to the present situation, and they do not prepare the individual for adaptive action in the present. Maladaptive emotions are those old familiar feelings that people know well. They are like good old friends who are bad for someone.

Principles of Emotional Change

The six principles gleaned from the literature on how emotions are worked with are (a) emotion *awareness:* symbolizing core emotional experience in words; (b) *expression:* saying or showing what one feels using words or action; (c) *regulation:* soothing or reducing emotional arousal; (d) *reflection:* making narrative sense of one's experience; and (e) two principles of *transformation:* (i) undoing one emotion with another emotion and (ii) corrective emotional experience, which involves new lived experiences with another person (Greenberg, 2017). These processes are viewed as best facilitated in the context of an empathic therapeutic relationship. The first three—awareness, expression, and regulation—can be thought of as serving emotion use; regulation and the two principles of transformation serve emotional development. These principles have been described in detail elsewhere (Greenberg, 2015; Greenberg & Watson, 2006).

Emotional Awareness

Increasing awareness of emotion is the most fundamental overall goal of treatment. Once people know what they feel, they reconnect to their needs and are motivated to meet them. Increased emotional awareness is therapeutic in a variety of ways. Becoming aware of and symbolizing core emotional experience in words provide access to the adaptive information and the action tendency in the emotion. Emotional awareness, however, is not thinking about feeling; it involves feeling the feeling in awareness. Only once emotion is felt does its articulation in language become an important component of its awareness.

Clients' ability to articulate what they are experiencing in their inner world is a central focus of this treatment. It has been shown that naming a feeling in words helps decrease amygdala arousal (Kircanski,

Lieberman, & Craske, 2012; Lieberman et al., 2007). Emotion-focused therapists work with clients to help approach, tolerate, accept, and symbolize their emotions. The first step in awareness work is acceptance of emotional experience as opposed to its avoidance. Once the client has accepted the emotion rather than avoided it, the therapist can help the client to improve coping.

Emotional Expression

Emotional expression has been shown to be a unique aspect of emotional processing that predicts adjustment to such things as breast cancer (Stanton et al., 2000), interpersonal emotional injuries, and trauma (Foa & Jaycox, 1999; Greenberg & Malcolm, 2002; Paivio, Hall, Holowaty, Jellis, & Tran, 2001; Paivio & Nieuwenhuis, 2001). Expressing emotion in therapy does not involve the venting of secondary emotion, but, rather, overcoming avoidance to strongly experience and express previously constricted primary emotions (Greenberg & Safran, 1987). Expressive coping also may help one attend to and clarify central concerns, and it serves to promote pursuit of goals.

Emotion Regulation

The first step in helping emotion regulation is to provide a safe, calming, validating, empathic environment. This type of environment helps soothe automatically generated, underregulated distress (Bohart & Greenberg, 1997) and helps strengthen the self. After this step is the teaching of emotion regulation and distress tolerance (Linehan, 1993) skills; this teaching involves, among other things, identifying triggers, avoiding triggers, identifying and labeling emotions, allowing and tolerating emotions, establishing a working distance, increasing positive emotions, and reducing vulnerability to negative emotions, as well as self-soothing, diaphragmatic breathing, relaxation, and distraction. Forms of meditative practice and self-acceptance often are most helpful in achieving a working distance from overwhelming core emotions. The ability to regulate breathing, observe one's emotions, and let those emotions come and go are important processes to help regulate emotional distress.

Another important aspect of regulation is developing clients' abilities to self-soothe. Emotion can be down-regulated by soothing at a variety of different levels of processing. Physiological soothing involves activation of the parasympathetic nervous system to regulate heart rate, breathing, and other sympathetic functions that speed up under stress. At the more deliberate behavioral and cognitive levels, promoting clients' abilities to receive and be compassionate to their emerging painful emotional experience is the first step toward tolerating emotion and self-soothing.

Reflection

In addition to recognizing emotions and symbolizing them in words, promoting reflection on emotional experience helps people make narrative sense of their experience and furthers its assimilation into their ongoing self-narratives. What we make of our emotional experience makes us who we are. Reflection helps to create new meaning and develop new narratives to explain experience (Goldman, Greenberg, & Pos, 2005; Greenberg & Angus, 2004; Greenberg & Pascual-Leone, 1995; Pennebaker, 1995). Pennebaker (1995) showed the positive effects that writing about emotional experience has on autonomic nervous system activity, immune functioning, and physical and emotional health. He concluded that through language, individuals are able to organize, structure, and assimilate their emotional experiences and the events that may have provoked the emotions.

Transformation

Probably the most important way of dealing with maladaptive emotion in therapy involves not its regulation but its transformation by other emotions. Activation of new emotions in therapy helps change obsolete emotional responses and transforms previously disowned dreaded feelings from the past.

Changing Emotion With Emotion. The process of changing *emotion with emotion* applies most specifically to transforming primary maladaptive emotions such as fear and shame with other adaptive emotions (Greenberg, 2015). Maladaptive emotional states are best transformed by undoing them by activating other more adaptive emotional states. Spinoza (1677/1967) was the first to note that emotion is needed to change emotion, proposing that "an emotion cannot be restrained nor removed unless by an opposed and stronger emotion" (p. 195).

Newly activated experience, such as anger to change fear, compassion to change shame, and even love to change hate, helps transform peoples' persistent, memory-based, problematic emotional states and their interactions with the environment. In this view, enduring change of maladaptive emotional responses occurs by generating a new emotional response—not through a process of insight or understanding of unconscious conflicts but by through generation of new responses to old situations and incorporation of those new responses into memory.

The process of changing emotion with emotion goes beyond ideas of catharsis, completion and letting go, exposure, extinction, or habituation in that the maladaptive feeling is not purged, nor does it simply attenuate by the person feeling it. Rather, another feeling is used to transform or undo it. Although dysregulated secondary emotions, such as the fear and anxiety in phobias, obsessive compulsiveness, and panic and fear-laden intrusive images, may be overcome by mere exposure, in many situations, primary maladaptive emotions (e.g., the shame of feeling worthless, anxiety of basic insecurity, sadness of abandonment) are best transformed by contact with other emotions with opposing action tendencies. For example, change in primary maladaptive emotions, such as core shame or fear of abandonment that lead to withdrawal, is brought about by the coactivation of an incompatible, more adaptive approach experience, such as empowering anger and pride or compassion for the self to the same situations. The new emotion undoes the old response rather than attenuate it (Fredrickson, 2001). This change involves more than simply feeling or facing the feeling, which leads to its diminishment. Rather, the withdrawal tendencies of primary maladaptive fear or shame (for example) are transformed into staying in contact by activating the approach tendencies in anger or comfort-seeking sadness.

EFT works to transform maladaptive emotion schematic memories of past childhood losses and traumas by activating them in the therapy session. The aim is to transform those memories through a recently proposed process called *memory reconsolidation* (Lane, Ryan, Nadel, & Greenberg, 2015), which involves the assimilation of new material in the present into memories of the past (Nadel & Bohbot, 2001). Introducing new present experience into currently activated memories of past events has been shown to lead to memory transformation through this process (Nadel & Bohbot, 2001). This a key way of changing emotion with emotion. The traditional view on memory suggested that once memories had been consolidated and become part of long-term memory, they were more or less permanent. It was found, however, that every time a memory is retrieved, the underlying memory trace seems to be labile and fragile once again, thus requiring another consolidation period (Moscovitch & Nadel, 1997). This *reconsolidation* period allows for another opportunity to disrupt the memory. Because memory reconsolidation only occurs once a memory is activated, it follows that to be able to change emotional memories, they have to be activated in therapy. Emotional memories can be changed by activating the experience of the memory in a session; if, after about 10 minutes of working on the painful experience related to this memory, a new emotion is experienced, it will in some way be incorporated into the memory and can change the experience of the original memory. By being activated in the present, the old memories are updated by the new current experience. The new experience comes from being in the context of a safe relationship and through activation of more adaptive emotional responses and new adult resources in an enactment, in the session, of reacting to the old situation in a new way. The memories are reconsolidated to incorporate these new elements. It is important in therapy to activate emotionally painful memory and then, after about 10 minutes—a time frame after which the memory is labile (Nader, Schafe, & LeDoux, 2000)—help introduce a new experience.

In therapy, maladaptive fear of abandonment or annihilation from past childhood maltreatment—once aroused in the present—can be transformed into security by activating more empowering, boundary-establishing emotions of adaptive anger or disgust at the maltreatment that were felt in the past but not expressed, or by evoking the previously inaccessible softer soothing feelings of sadness at loss and need for comfort or compassion toward the self. Similarly, maladaptive fear can be undone by adaptive sadness. Maladaptive shame internalized from the contempt of others can be transformed by accessing anger at the violation resulting from the abuse one suffered, self-compassion, and pride and self-worth; anger at being unfairly treated or thwarted is an antidote to hopelessness and helplessness. The tendency to shrink into the ground in shame or to collapse in helplessness can be transformed by the thrusting forward tendency in anger at violation or by the reaching out in sadness. Approach emotions change withdrawal emotions: After the alternate emotion has been accessed, it transforms or undoes the original state, and a new state is forged. As discussed earlier, introducing new present experience into currently activated memories of past events can lead to transformation through the assimilation, during memory reconsolidation, of new material into past memories. Often a period of calming the maladaptive emotion and making sense of it is needed before activating an opposing transforming emotion.

Corrective Emotional Experience. Another way of transforming emotion is to have a new lived experience that changes an old feeling; this new experience with another provides a corrective emotional experience. Experiences furnishing interpersonal soothing disconfirm pathogenic beliefs or new "success experiences" can correct patterns set in earlier times. A client who faces shame in a therapeutic context but experiences acceptance rather than the expected disgust or denigration has the power to change the feeling of shame. Corrective emotional experiences in EFT occur predominantly in the therapeutic relationship, although success experience in the world also is encouraged.

Corrective interpersonal emotional experiences generally occur throughout the therapeutic process when the client experiences the therapist as someone who is attuned to and validates the client's inner world. Therapy offers new opportunities for affect regulation with a helpful other, new self-experience through being in contact with the other and being mirrored, and new experiences that promote activation of alternate adaptive emotion schemes, which can potentiate new emergent self-organizations. Overall, the genuine relationship between client and therapist—and the constancy of that relationship—is a corrective emotional experience. In addition, specific new emotional experiences with the therapist that supply an undoing of specific patterns of interpersonal experience provide the other form of corrective experience.

When to Activate and When to Regulate. In addition to these principles, in treatment, when emotions should be activated and regulated should be considered, as well as what emotions are to be regulated and how that will be done. Underregulated emotions that require down-regulation generally are either secondary emotions, such as despair and hopelessness, or primary maladaptive emotions, such as the shame of being worthless or the anxiety of basic insecurity and panic, that currently cannot be connected to adaptive cognition because they are so overwhelming. When distress is so high that the emotion no longer informs adaptive thought and action, the emotion needs to be regulated (Greenberg, 2015). Maladaptive emotions of core shame and feelings of shaky vulnerability benefit from regulation to create a working distance from them rather than one's becoming overwhelmed by them. In some cases, however, suppressing feelings can produce a rebound effect or a "bottle it up and then blow up" syndrome. Disengagement in many situations is not helpful. In other cases, people can effectively disengage from emotion; this disengagement can facilitate learning and memory. Too much emotion at too high an intensity, though, can be countertherapeutic. A crucial clinical judgment is to know when to distract and down-regulate and when to facilitate emotion approach and intensification.

How to Access New Emotions. With the emphasis on changing emotion with emotion, this question arises: How does the therapist facilitate the activation of new emotions? The following are a few methods; these and others have been elaborated elsewhere (Greenberg, 2015).

Empathic attunement to affect is continuously helping clients to access new feelings. Different types of empathy, ranging from purely understanding empathic responses to validating and evocative responses, to exploratory and conjectural responses, help clients access and symbolize their emotions range. *Empathic exploration,* the fundamental mode of intervention in EFT, is a response focused on differentiating the leading edge of the client's experience—that which is most alive or poignant or implicit— to help it unfold. When a therapist's response is structured such that it ends with a focus on what seems most alive in a client's statement, the client's attention is, in turn, focused on this aspect of his or her experience, so the client is more likely to differentiate this leading edge of his or her experience. By sensitively attending, moment by moment, to what is most poignant in clients' spoken and nonspoken, nonverbal narrative, the therapist, through verbal empathic exploration, can help capture clients' experiences even more richly than the clients' descriptions. Thus, clients are helped to symbolize previously implicit experience consciously in awareness. Drawing attention to implicit process (e.g., "I'm not sure, but there was this sadness") and making it explicit open the possibility of exploring the origins or function of that process and adapting the internal and external conditions in such a way that the emotion can be allowed and attended to fully. For example, the therapist might say, "I am not sure whether I am right, but just now, when you talked about your husband and how he is not there for you, I sensed that some sadness came up, and then it seemed like you held your breath, and it was gone. Is that right?" Client and therapist might then explore together what is preventing the client from staying with the sadness. *Empathic conjecture* goes beyond exploration in guessing at what the client is feeling: It is a guess the therapist offers without implying that the guess is correct. It is an inquiry rather than an interpretation.

When clients have difficulty finding words for their experience, a therapist's conjectures can help them check these against their bodily felt experience to see if there is a fit and to correct the offered symbolization of their experience, when necessary. For example a client might say, "When I realized she had left the party and not even told me she was leaving, I felt so bad." The therapist replies, ". . . so bad . . . somehow abandoned . . .?" The client then says, "But also like I just wasn't important to her. . . ." When clients do not have words for what they feel and are silent, therapists try to "speak the unspoken" for them, offering words and talking into the silence (Gendlin, 1996). This might be the case when a client is in a highly aroused state and is silently crying, for example. The therapist would offer empathic conjectures, perhaps saying, "It is so painful . . . so sad to lose this love and support." If the client agrees either verbally or by through a congruent nonverbal expression, such as nodding or intensified crying, the therapist would assumes that he or she is on the right track and continue helping the client symbolize and differentiate his or her experience.

In addition to empathy, therapists can help clients access new subdominant emotions occurring in the present by shifting attention to emotions that the client currently is expressing but that are just on the periphery of a client's awareness. This shift helps clients become reorganized by the newly attended emotion. Therapists also guide clients' attention by asking them to focus on their bodily felt sensation, pay attention to them, follow them, and symbolize them in words or images (Gendlin, 1996).

Therapeutic work also involves suggesting experiments: The therapist offers, "Try this" followed by, "What do you experience?" Experiments in EFT are designed to promote facilitating access to experiencing by articulating primary emotions and needs; accepting and transforming painful, unresolved emotions; and explicating implicit feelings and meanings. Important experiments involve using enactment and imagery to evoke emotions, remembering a time an emotion was felt, changing how the client views things, or even the therapist's expressing an emotion for the client. Once accessed, these new emotional resources begin to undo the psychoaffective motor program that previously had determined the person's mode of processing. New emotional states enable people to challenge the validity of perceptions of self/other connected to maladaptive emotion, thus weakening the hold those perceptions have on them.

A key means of activating a new emotion is focusing on what is needed (Greenberg, 2015). The essence of this process is this: When clients' core maladaptive emotions of fear, shame, or sadness are accessed, core needs for connection and validation are mobilized. If clients can be helped to feel deserving of the previously unmet need, a more adaptive emotion related to their needs not being met is generated. When clients can validate that they deserved to be loved or valued, the emotion system automatically appraises that needs were not met and generates either anger at having been unfairly treated or sadness and having missed the opportunity of having one's needs met. These new adaptive feelings become a new response to the old situation and act to undo the more maladaptive feelings. The result is an implicit refutation of the sense that the person does not deserve love, respect, and connection. The opposition of the two experiences "I am not worthy or lovable" and "I deserve to be loved or respected," supported by adaptive anger or sadness in response to the same evoking situation, produces a reorganization that undoes the maladaptive state and leads to a new self-organization. These new feelings are felt in the original situation but not expressed or are felt now as an adaptive response to the old situation. For example, accessing implicit adaptive anger at violation by a perpetrator can help change maladaptive fear in a trauma survivor. When the tendency to run away in fear is transformed by anger's tendency to thrust forward, a new relational position of holding the abuser accountable for wrongdoing is formed. Accessing adaptive needs acts automatically as disconfirmation of maladaptive feelings, and beliefs and new experience change old experience. EFT thus involves a combination of following and leading; however, following takes precedence over leading. More distressed and more avoidant clients often benefit from additional process guidance and emotion coaching, including a form of emotional reparenting that involves soothing and compassion. Clients with a greater internal locus of control or more reactant styles, or those clients who are more fragile, however, benefit from more responsive following and less guiding.

Case Formulation

Formulation in EFT occurs mainly through therapists' keeping their fingers on a client's emotional pulse. They listen for the most painful emotion that seems key to the client's suffering. A therapist's main concern is following the client's process: identifying core pain and responding to markers of current emotional concerns, rather than trying to formulate a picture of the person's enduring personality, character dynamics, or a core relational pattern. Process is privileged over content, and it is the client's pain that guides the process to the client's central concerns.

The first phase of formulation involves observing the client's emotional processing styles; the observations will guide how to work with emotion. As clients unfold their stories, their therapists pay particular attention to the emotional tone, listening for whether the client's emotions are over- or underregulated or whether the client has an internal or external processing style. The second phase of formulation involves the cocreation, with the client, of a focus that is identified by following the core painful emotion in the client's narrative. This phase involves a formulating the client's core painful emotion scheme. From following the pain compass, the therapist and client come to mutually understand the client's core painful feeling. Having formulated the client's painful emotions, the therapist continues to the third stage of the formulation process: to make more process-oriented formulations over time. Now, the focus is on moment-by-moment formulations of what is occurring in the moment and formulations on micromarkers of current client states to guide intervention (Goldman & Greenberg, 2015).

Marker-Guided Intervention

The course of treatment is directed by the perceptual skill of identifying problem *markers*, which are indicators of opportunities for intervention, and by executive skills that guide intervention. Marker-guided intervention is a defining feature of the EFT approach. Research has demonstrated that clients enter specific problematic emotional processing states that are identifiable through in-session statements and behaviors that mark underlying affective problems. These markers afford opportunities for particular types of effective intervention (Greenberg et al., 1993; Rice & Greenberg, 1984). Client markers indicate not only the client state and the type of intervention to use but also the client's current readiness to work on that problem. Emotion-focused therapists are trained to identify markers of different types of problematic emotional processing problems and to intervene in specific ways that best suit those problems (Elliott, Watson, Goldman, & Greenberg, 2004). Each of the tasks has been studied intensively and extensively, and those studies have specified the key components of a path to resolution and the specific form that resolution takes (Greenberg, 2017; Greenberg & Malcolm, 2002; Greenberg & Webster, 1982; Watson, 1996). Models of the process of change act as maps to guide therapist intervention. The following eight empirically investigated markers, interventions, and resolution processes have been studied:

1. *Problematic reactions* (Rice & Greenberg, 1984) are opportunities for a process of intervention that involves vivid evocation of experience to promote reexperiencing of the situation so that the person arrives at the implicit meaning of the situation that makes sense of the reaction. These reactions are expressed through puzzlement about emotional or behavioral responses to particular situations: For example, when a client says, "On the way to therapy, I saw a little puppy dog with long droopy ears, and I suddenly felt so sad, and I don't know why."

2. *Unclear felt sense* (Gendlin, 1996) is when a person is on the surface of, or is feeling confused and unable to get a clear sense of, his or her experience; for example, "I just have this feeling, but I don't know what it is." An unclear felt sense calls for focusing (Gendlin, 1996) in which the therapist guides clients to approach the embodied aspects of his or her experience with attention and with curiosity and willingness to experience those aspects and put words to their bodily felt sensation.

3. *Self-critical splits* (Greenberg, 2017), when one aspect of the self is critical or coercive toward another aspect, offer an opportunity for two-chair work. Two parts of the self are put into dialogue, and resolution occurs by a softening of the critical voice and an integration of sides.

4. *Self-interruptive splits* (Greenberg, 2017) arise when one part blocks or interrupts emotional experience and expression; for example, "I can feel the tears coming up, but I just tighten and suck them back in. No way am I going to cry." In the intervention, clients experience themselves as an agent in the process of shutting down and then challenge the interruptive part of the self with a need for self-expression.

5. *Unfinished business* (Greenberg, 2017; Perls, Hefferline, & Goodman, 1951) is a marker involving the statement of a lingering unresolved feeling toward a significant other and is an opportunity for an empty-chair intervention. This dialogue activates the client's internal view of the significant other and helps that client express and make sense of his or her emotional reactions to the other. Shifts occur in the in views of the other and the self.

6. *Vulnerability* (Greenberg et al., 1993) is a marker that indicates the emergence of a deep sense of fragility, depletion, weakness, self-related shame, or helplessness. What is most helpful is empathic affirmation in which the therapist is fully present and accepts and validates whatever the client is experiencing, thus allowing the client to be where he or she is. Doing so helps the client go into the experience and hit rock bottom before beginning spontaneously to turn upward toward hope.

7. *Anguish* or *emotional suffering* (Greenberg, 2015) is an opportunity for self-soothing and self-compassion dialogues with the goal of evoking compassion for the self. Typically, the anguish occurs in the face of powerful interpersonal needs (e.g., for love, for validation) that were not met by others. Intervention involves asking the client to imagine the self as an adult reentering an evoked scene of deprivation or invalidation. The therapist then provides a reparative response or a dialogue, asking the client if he or she, as an adult, could soothe his or her wounded inner child.

8. *Marker-guided homework*, either awareness or change-related homework, is given by the therapist to the client to foster experiencing outside of session. Homework involves practice of something that has occurred already in the session rather than seen as the site of change (Ellison & Greenberg, 2007; Greenberg & Warwar, 2006). For example, if, in a session, a client in a two-chair dialogue becomes aware of his or her critical voice, the therapist gives awareness homework so the client can practice awareness during the week and be aware of this voice and its effects. If, however, a change occurs in a session and the critical voice softens into a more self-compassionate voice, the therapist asks the client to practice being softer and more compassionate during the week to consolidate this change.

EFT is a process-guiding approach and marker-guided differential intervention is a key way that therapists guide clients in different forms of processing. Markers are opportunities for particular kinds of intervention that best facilitate different types of emotional processing most suited for different problems. For example, reevoking the situation and reexperiencing are helpful for resolving problematic reactions, whereas dialoguing with the critic is helpful for self-criticism, and expressing unresolved feelings to significant others in an empty chair is helpful in resolving unfinished business. In addition to the preceding four guiding principles—emotion assessment, principles of emotional change, case formulation, and marker-guided intervention—a variety of important skills is required in working with emotion.

General Methods and Skills

This section focuses on therapeutic methods and skills used to evoke emotion in the service of awareness and transformation. Methods include a variety of empathic responses that guide attentional focus and stimulate emotion. The focus first is on the perceptual skills that therapists need and then the microskills of intervention.

Perceptual Skills

Perceptual skills are needed to enable moment-by-moment attunement to emotion. As clients present their narratives, therapists need to implicitly ask themselves, What experience is most poignant or painful in the story? This question needs to guide listening, especially initially. Those stories that are emotionally tinged with feeling and move the therapist in some way are reflected back to the client, deepened, and further explored to identify core painful emotions. As clients talk, therapists listen for, from among the many things clients are saying, something that stands out with more force or concern behind it, something that captures the therapist's interest and pulls for attention. What makes it stand out might be a change in vocal quality, a sigh, or a change in breath, or maybe a stronger emotional intensity in the body, facial expression, or physical posture. There may be stronger emotional expression in the form of cries of distress or explosions of anger, or there may be confusion or puzzlement combined with a sudden more diffuse or vague presentation. All are indications of poignancy, and the therapist may feel a twinge in his or her chest or an anticipatory holding of the breath that indicates internally that the client is describing something important or meaningful (Greenberg, 2017).

Emotion-focused therapists adopt the notion of a *pain compass* that guides therapy sessions by directing the therapist to the client's chronic enduring pain (Greenberg, 2015; Greenberg & Paivio, 1997). Emotional pain is a strong cue that something for the client is feeling broken or shattered (Greenberg & Bolger, 2001). Therapists need to hear people's pain using a variety of sense mediums, including seeing, listening, and sensing. The goal of the treatment is to resolve this painful issue.

Therapists also need to be attentive to clients' emotional processing styles to help them determine the client's emotional accessibility and immediate amenability to emotion-focused treatment, and whether more specific work is needed to increase emotional accessibility. A variety of features and dimensions of manner of processing are to be considered in this process. First, when there is an activated client emotional expression, the therapist and client together need to determine whether the emotional expression is primary, secondary, or instrumental. For emotional processing to be productive, primary emotions need to be accessed. Thus, the emotion-focused therapist must know how to determine what type of emotion is being expressed: primary adaptive and maladaptive, and secondary and instrumental emotions (see the section The Two Paths to Adaptive Emotion later in this chapter).

In general, when working with emotion, therapists need to observe certain factors to perceive emotion. They need to attend to nonverbal expression, including facial expression, tone of voice, and how things are said are observed. When adaptive emotion is expressed, there tends to be a natural body rhythm: The person's whole system appears coordinated and congruent. Therapists need to use their knowledge about universal emotional responses and knowledge of their own emotional responses to understand their clients' emotions.

In attending to how clients process emotion, therapists need to observe client vocal quality, degree of emotional arousal, levels of experiencing, and degree of productive processing of the particular emotion. The quality of the client's voice is a crucial guide. Client vocal quality has been divided into four mutually exclusive categories that describe a pattern of vocal features reflecting the speaker's momentary deployment of attention and energy (Rice & Kerr, 1986; Rice & Wagstaff, 1967). Each of the four categories—focused, external, limited, and emotional—describes a particular type of engagement. *Focused* voice indicates that the client has turned eyeballs inward, is tracking internal experience, and is attempting to symbolize that experience in words. *External* voice is indicated by an even rhythmic tone and of energy turned outward. It has a prerehearsed speechlike quality and indicates a lack of spontaneity; it also has a "talking at" or lecturing quality. It is unlikely that content is being freshly experienced. *Limited* voice is low energy and often will come out high pitched, indicating that affect is being strangulated and that perhaps it is difficult to trust. The clinical picture is one of wariness. *Emotional* voice is indicated by emotion breaking though in the voice as the client talks. The presence of focused and emotional voice has been found to predict positive outcome in experiential therapy (Rice & Kerr, 1986; Watson & Greenberg, 1996).

Emotional arousal as defined on the Emotional Arousal Scale (Warwar & Greenberg, 1999) depends on the degree of intensity in the voice and body and degree of restriction of expression. Research has shown that moderate levels of emotional arousal in combination with meaning-making, rather than pure high emotional arousal, predict positive outcome in experiential therapies (Carryer & Greenberg, 2010; Missirlian et al., 2005; Warwar & Greenberg, 1999). Client depth of experience (Klein, Mathieu, Gendlin, & Kiesler, 1969) differs from arousal because it describes the extent and quality of clients' exploration of their inner experience to achieve self-understanding and problem resolution. The Experiencing Scale has been studied extensively (Klein, Mathieu-Coughlan, & Kiesler, 1986) and related to positive outcome in therapy.

Therapists also need to assess whether a client's emotion is being processed productively. To be productive, primary emotions require a particular manner of processing, which EFT refers to as being *contactfully* or *mindfully* aware of the emotion. A system of measuring productive emotional processing has been found to strongly predict therapeutic outcome (Auszra et al., 2013). That system comprises seven elements: (a) attending, (b) symbolizing, (c) congruence, (d) regulating, (e) accepting, (f) agency, and (g) differentiating. At the most basic level for emotion to be processed productively, the client has to attend to an activated primary emotion to be aware of it. Once a physical or emotional reaction is attended to, it has to be symbolized (i.e., generally in words, but it could be in some other form, such as painting or movement) to be able to fully comprehend its meaning. For example, a client attending to his or her feeling says the following:

> *Client:* I don't know what I feel. It just feels bad.
>
> *Therapist* (says something like): I feel it was sort of a loss, maybe sad or disappointed [empathic exploratory response].
>
> *Client:* Yeah, really disappointed. In some way, it has dashed some of my hopes [symbolizing].

Next, for a feeling to be congruent, what the client says needs to match how the client feels. Feeling sad is matched with a sad face and voice, not a smile; feeling anger is expressed with some energy in the voice and an assertive posture rather than no vocal energy and a downcast look. Another important aspect of a productive emotional processing is acceptance of emotional experience, in particular, acceptance of unpleasant and painful emotional experience.

Emotional experiences also have to be sufficiently regulated for the processing to be productive. The therapist needs to help clients develop and maintain a working distance from the emotion (Gendlin, 1996) so that it is not overwhelming. This distancing enables clients to cognitively orient toward emotion as information, thus allowing for an integration of cognition and affect. Productive emotional processing also involves a client's experiencing him or herself as an active agent, rather than passive victim, of the emotion. That involves a client's taking responsibility for his or her emotional experience and acknowledging it as a personal experience rather than caused by some external agency. With agency, clients feel that they are having the emotion (e.g., "I feel sad"), rather than the emotion having them (e.g., "It takes me over").

To be productive and for emotion use and transformation to occur, a client's primary emotional expression has to be differentiating over time. Fundamentally, the client must not be stuck in the emotion; rather, the client must explore and differentiate new aspects of experience. The client's emotional process is highly fluid.

Intervention Skills

There are three types or levels of intervention. The first level involves *empathic symbolization* in which the therapist empathically explores what the client might have felt in a certain situation and helps puts these emotional experiences into words. An exploratory and conjecturing stance allows the client to accept or refute the inferred feeling state. The second level involves *guiding attention*. The therapist guides clients to intensify the awareness of bodily sensations or action tendencies that occur when significant experiences, scenes, memories, or feeling states are being referred to. The third level, *emotional experiencing*, is actively stimulated by bringing up emotional memories and self–other representations using chair dialogues and imagery. Active interventions by the therapist involve a guiding of the process, not the content, of the session.

The relationship plays a key role in accessing and influencing the type of emotion experienced and how it is processed. The therapist's close attention to and inquiry into feeling evokes emotion. Sometimes this type of attentive listening is an experience clients have never had before, so eye contact with the therapist can evoke feeling the emotional pain of aloneness while simultaneously experiencing a deep sense of connection with the therapist. For some clients, it is the feeling of closeness to and validation by the therapist in the therapy relationship that are most important in accessing emotion; for others, it is the therapist's directions or questions that evoke automatic emotional experience.

Different types of empathy have been delineated; they range from purely understanding empathic responses to validating and evocative responses, to exploratory and conjectural responses (Greenberg & Elliott, 1997; Rogers, 1957, 1959). By sensitively attending moment by moment to what is most poignant in clients' spoken and nonspoken (i.e., nonverbal) narrative, a therapist's verbal empathic exploration can help capture clients' experience even more richly than can clients' own descriptions. This empathic exploration helps the client symbolize previously implicit experience consciously in awareness. When a therapist's response ends with a focus on what seems most alive in a client's statement, the client's attention is focused on this aspect of his or her experience. The client then is encouraged to focus on and differentiate the leading edges of his or her experience. Exploratory empathy of this kind, however, needs to be balanced with empathic understanding to provide a framework of safety, acceptance, and validation.

The therapist also can help the client experience more control over the process of contacting emotions by, for example, focusing on and allowing the emotion in small amounts, and then guiding the client to move out of the emotion by regulating and possibly moving back in again. In other cases, clients might need a better rationale for how "feeling bad leads to feeling good" to help them be motivated to overcome their avoidance. Sometimes clients might simply find it difficult to hold their attention on an experience. In those cases, the therapist might facilitate approaching and attending to the emotion by suggesting that the client close his or her eyes and "pay attention to that place inside where you feel your feeling."

Following the use of empathy, the therapist encourages the client to bring his or her attention to the client's experiencing as it is bodily felt; the therapist then gently asks, "What's wrong?" and waits. There is also the point at which the client must understand that words can come from a feeling and have an experiential effect. It is important to sense a problem as a whole and let what is important come up from that bodily sensing. This focusing process represents the basic style of engagement with internal experience that is being encouraged.

The therapist's use of metaphor, connotative language, and rhythm and tempo of speech can trigger emotional experience. Metaphors like "it's just like having been used and then thrown on the dump heap" or "it's like having a knife just slashed through the beautiful tapestry of your relationship" can evoke a great sense of rejection or loss. Certain expressions simply hit a nerve. At other times, it is imagery or the activation of a memory that precipitates feeling an emotion. For example, a client's envisioning a critical mother in an empty chair in front of him or her often evokes a gut reaction or picturing a little "me" who is so different from all the other kids, and can evoke tears sadness for oneself. Asking clients to recall or recount memories of distressing experiences helps evoke the emotion they had at that time. For example, at one point in a therapy session, the therapist asked a man to recount his memory of being bullied at school; the incident involved a physical assault by another student. While remembering and describing the assault, the man suddenly felt like he was in the body of his child-self. He felt the intense and painful physical and emotional feelings of that time.

Often, it is a sequence or combination of the aforementioned responses that activates emotion. Consider the following: During a therapy session in which a client is speaking to her mother in an empty chair, the therapist facilitates the experience of emotion by using a number of interventions.

The therapist who, by keeping a finger on the client's emotional pulse, hears the sadness emerging from the client's anger:

> Client: Yes, very angry at you for torturing me. It pulls at me. It affects me very, very often. I wouldn't, perhaps not daily, but very often, [Therapist: Hmm.] and there's just, there's certain, there are also certain times in my life when it pulls on me like that, it comes to light when I really would like you to be around.

At this point, the empathically attuned therapist facilitates a focus on sadness and asks the client to express what she missed. Using the word *missed* often is a more powerful way of accessing sadness than saying, "Tell me what you are sad about" because *missed* catches the longing and is more evocative:

> Therapist: Hmm. Tell her what you want her around for. What you've wanted, what you've missed.
>
> Client: I miss being able to go home at Christmas.
>
> Therapist (reflects and validates): Hmm, I miss a home. . . .

After a minute or two continuing in this vein, the therapist deepens her experience using an evocative image of "a big hole on my life":

> Therapist: Hmm. So, I've missed having you to lean on [Client: Right.] There's a big hole in my life.
>
> Client: I've missed having you all of my life.

Now the therapist uses repetition and exaggeration, which underline or amplify what is said and also explicitly focus on hurt:

> Therapist: Can you say that again: "I've missed having you"? Can you tell her more about what you've missed, that this is where it hurts, how much you miss her?

The combination of empathic attunement, a focus on what was missed, an evocative image, and repetition, in combination with a soothing voice and facial expression, act to stimulate the nodes of an emotion scheme that now is activated. The client's emotions emerge for the first time:

> Client (cries): It's very difficult for me to describe how much I miss you, the sense of loss inside is (voice breaks).

The therapist then validates the feeling and encourages further expression:

> Therapist: Yes, this is incredibly painful, the loss. [Client cries.] Yeah, this is important tell her about your tears.

> *Client* (crying):   I cry very often [Therapist: Hmm.] for no apparent reason, and I do. I cry, and I'm very emotional, even at happy times [Therapist: Hmm.] because I think it doesn't make sense at the time, but I think now that I cry because I miss you.
>
> *Therapist:*   "I miss you." Can you say this again? "I want you. I've wanted you. I miss you."

These are the type of therapist microprocesses that lead to emotion activation.

As just illustrated, emotional experience is triggered by the therapist's direction to express feelings in chair dialogues. Expressing feelings in two-chair dialogues directly activates the raw feelings of the emotional experience. A therapist's empathic conjectures like "just a big hole inside" or "I sense there's a lot of sadness that you still feel" help clients attend to and feel their sadness. Such empathic conjectures are felt deep inside and have the effect of evoking feelings of sadness. They seem to push a button in clients, who begin to feel what they are saying.

Emotional Change Processes

It is helpful to understand that the two important paths to emotional change depend on whether the previously disclaimed emotion the client is helped to arrive at in therapy is (a) an adaptive emotion, such as grief or assertive anger, which can be used as a guide to change ones way of being; or (b) a maladaptive experience of feeling, say, shame-based worthless, fear-based anxious insecurity, or the sadness of lonely abandonment. Another important process is working with emotion dysregulation.

The Two Paths to Adaptive Emotion

The two paths to primary adaptive emotion are through secondary or past primary maladaptive emotion. The first path is simpler to work on therapeutically. It involves the two-step sequence of moving from secondary reactive to primary adaptive emotions, such as from secondary anxiety (e.g., panic, worry) to underlying adaptive anger at having been abandoned or humiliated. The client is facilitated to "re-own" the adaptive emotion, accept it, and experience it in the therapy, and not just talk about it or have insight about it, but have the visceral experience of weeping for what was lost or assert the right to not be violated. Informed and transformed by this emotion, the client then symbolizes this emotion, reflects on it to create new meaning, and decides how to act. When, however, primary emotions do not give good information or adaptive orientation to the current situation, they are maladaptive responses that need to be changed.

When working on the second path, therapists first help their clients arrive at the previously disclaimed painful, maladaptive emotion of fear of abandonment or shame of inadequacy by attuning empathically to affect or stimulation via chair dialogues or imagery. This work involves either a two-step sequence of moving from secondary reactive to primary maladaptive emotions, such as from secondary anxiety to underlying maladaptive shame, or a three-step sequence of moving from secondary emotion, such as depressive malaise to core maladaptive sense of shame-based worthlessness or the fear of basic insecurity, to adaptive emotion, such as sadness of grief, assertive anger, or self-compassion (Greenberg, 2015; Greenberg & Paivio, 1997) These processes have been shown to predict outcome in EFT (Herrmann et al., 2016; A. Pascual-Leone & Greenberg, 2007).

Working With Emotion Dysregulation

When emotions are overactivated in life or in the session and can no longer be connected to cognition, some form of emotion regulation is required. Emotions need to be regulated in the session to reenable meaning creating, whereas regulation skills need to be developed to use outside the session to help people cope (i.e., deliberate regulation). Generally, it is either symptomatic secondary emotions, such as despair, hopelessness, or anxiety, or primary maladaptive emotions, such as overwhelming and traumatic fear or panic, that need regulation. People seek therapy to rid themselves of these emotions so that they may better cope in their lives. For some psychological disorders involving self-harm, trauma, and borderline functioning, it is the dysregulation of emotion that is the problem leading to these dysfunctional behaviors (Linehan, 1993). This requires is self-soothing in which the aim is to help people down-regulate their emotional arousal.

An important early step in regulation is to be able to represent the emotion to oneself. One has to label what one is feeling before one can regulate it. The person can then use distraction and distress tolerance skills (Linehan, 1993) Tolerating distress includes having a mindfulness of breath and mindful awareness of emotion. The ability to regulate breathing and to observe one's emotions, and let them come and go, are important processes that help regulate emotional distress. These processes involve self-soothing to help clients cope.

The development of automatic self-soothing for the purpose of transforming underlying emotions is different. This form of transformational self-soothing involves the activation of unresolved emotional suffering—the anguish of painful emotions that in the past never received the soothing needed—and the reduction of the experienced threat of isolation or disintegration by providing a new soothing experience in the present. Once a painful emotion schematic memory has been evoked, soothing of emotion can be provided both by individuals themselves, reflexively; by an internal agency; or by another person. Note the difference with coping self-soothing, which is a deliberate skill used to addresses symptomatic dysregulation that one needs to overcome, whereas transformational soothing focuses on bringing soothing to past unresolved painful emotions to resolve the past threat and to ultimately develop automatic soothing.

The first step in helping develop automatic emotion regulation is to provide a safe, calming, validating, empathic environment. Soothing comes interpersonally in the form of empathic attunement to one's affect and through acceptance and validation by another person. Being able to soothe the self develops initially by internalizing the soothing functions of the protective other (Sroufe, 1996; Stern, 1985) and, over time, helps clients develop implicit self-soothing, the ability to regulate feelings automatically without deliberate effort. Internal security develops by feeling that one exists in the mind and heart of the other, thus one is able to soothe the self. By activating compassion and comforting self-talk in two-chair dialogues involving caring for a wounded self, EFT therapists help clients develop self-compassion and their abilities to self-soothe.

EMOTION IN INTERPERSONAL RELATIONSHIPS

An emotion-focused approach applied to interpersonal conflict views negative interactional cycles combined with unexpressed underlying vulnerable feelings as a major source of couple distress. A couple's interactions are understood as occurring along the dimensions of affiliation and influence (Benjamin, 1996), and as developing into negative cycles when automatic, amygdala-based, emergency emotions are activated by threats to identity and security, and partners begin to express secondary defensive, rather than primary vulnerable, emotions. Conflict is seen as resulting from the escalating interactions that rigidify into negative interactional cycles in misguided attempts to get emotions soothed and needs met. Generally, negative interactional cycles are viewed as being driven by secondary reactive emotions, such as anger and disinterest, which obscure more rapid-acting and core emotions (e.g., fear, sadness, shame) that arise from core attachment and identity needs not being met. All are exacerbated by each partner's inability to soothe his or her own emotions.

As revealed in therapy, needs that seem to have developed and of the greatest psychological concern to most people in couple relationships are attachment, identity validation, and affection/liking (Greenberg & Goldman, 2008). The needs to be securely attached, to be valued by others, to experience mastery, and to have affection and novelty are critical to healthy development (Bowlby, 1969; White, 1959). These emotions provide the calmness, sense of value, pride and joy, and interest and excitement necessary for organisms to thrive. These emotions develop from the more fundamental processes of affect regulation and meaning creation that work in the service of survival. Relationships, however, are central to getting these needs met, and partners experience great distress when they are not.

The best way for couples in distress to free themselves from their mutual suffering is by revealing to each other the vulnerable attachment- and identity-related emotions and needs underlying their distress, being responsive to each other's feelings, and being able to self-soothe when the partner is unavailable (Greenberg & Goldman, 2008; Greenberg & Johnson, 1988). Vulnerability disarms and evokes compassion. Revealing anger at a loved one sets boundaries and, although seemingly assertive, is risky by making one feel vulnerable to abandonment. Revealing vulnerable attachment- and identity-related emotions and needs underlying inter-actional positions then is seen as an ideal means of changing negative interactional cycles. In more distressed individuals who become easily emotionally dysregulated, the ability to self-soothe also may need to come into focus. The fundamental task of therapy is to identify negative cycles related to threats to security and identity; to engender positive inter-actional cycles by having partners reveal previously unexpressed primary, adaptive attachment- and identity-oriented emotions and needs; and to respond to them by finding new ways of dealing with them.

Emotion-focused couple therapy (EFT-C) focuses on the expression of underlying vulnerable emotions to change negative interactions. Research has described its processes of change and shown that EFT-C is effective (Greenberg & Goldman, 2008; Johnson, Hunsley, Greenberg, & Schindler, 1999). McKinnon and Greenberg (2013) validated that it is specifically the expression of emotional vulnerability that predicts positive changes; couples favor sessions in which vulnerable emotions are expressed. Partners' affiliative responses add to the predictive power; however, it is the expression of vulnerability that is key.

EMOTION AND THE THERAPEUTIC RELATIONSHIP

EFT is built on a genuinely valuing, affect-regulating empathic relationship in which the therapist is fully present, highly attuned, and sensitively responsive to the client's moment-by-moment emotional experience. The therapist constantly keeps his or her finger on the client's emotional pulse. The therapist is respectful, accepting, and congruent in his or her communication to the clients. The relationship is curative in and of itself in that the therapist's empathy and acceptance promote the breaking of the isolation and validation of painful emotion, and promote a strengthening of the self and greater self-acceptance. The relationship with the therapist provides a powerful buffer to the client's distress by coregulating affect. A relationship with an attuned, responsive, mirroring therapist offers, over time, interpersonal regulation of affect that becomes internalized into self-soothing and the capacity to regulate inner states (Schore, 2002; Stern, 1985). When an empathic connection is made with the therapist, affect processing centers in the brain are affected, and new possibilities open up for the client. This type of relationship creates an optimal therapeutic environment that contributes to affect regulation and helps the client feel safe enough to fully engage in the process of self-exploration and new learning. As well as being curative, the therapeutic relationship promotes the therapeutic work of exploration and transformation of emotion and the creation of new meaning.

In therapy, emotion-focused therapists need to work with two main categories of therapist emotion. The first is their own fear of emotion combined with overprotective feelings that prevent them from going into clients' painful feelings or deflecting clients when the clients' feelings are too much for the therapist to bear. The other is therapists' personal reactions to clients themselves, ranging from their own so-called countertransference feelings, such as pain being evoked in response to clients' pain, feelings of anger at clients, or feelings of shame, boredom, or sexual attraction. I do not view these feelings in terms of concepts of transference; rather, I see them as being present to interpersonal reactions in the real relationship between people based on who they are and what is occurring between them. Geller and Greenberg (2012) suggested that therapists' ability to be fully present and engaged helps them be aware of and manage their own emotions, and helps clients feel safe and secure in the therapeutic relationship.

Therapeutic presence involves therapists' being fully in the moment on a multitude of levels: physically, emotionally, cognitively, spiritually, and relationally (Geller & Greenberg, 2002, 2012; Geller, Greenberg, & Watson, 2010). When a therapist is fully in the moment with a client, his or her receptive presence sends a message to the client that the client is going to be heard, met, felt, and understood, and this elicits a feeling of safety in the client. When clients feel met and felt by their therapists, their brain establishes a state of neuroception of safety (Porges, 1998, 2007, 2011). *Neuroception* is a neural process that constantly and automatically evaluates risk and triggers adaptive physiological responses that respond to features of safety, danger, or life threat. Porges (2011) showed that dysregulation can be stabilized through warm facial expression, open body posture, vocal tone, and prosody (i.e., rhythm of speech). When safety is perceived in these channels, heart rate slows down and states of calmness that regulate the facial muscles are supported: There is a face–heart connection through which vocal prosody and facial expression convey an individual's present physiological state to others. In the presence of someone with whom an individual feels safe, defenses become inhibited as physiology calms, and defensive strategies are replaced with gestures associated with feeling safe, such as spontaneous interactions that reduce psychological and physical distance.

Presence has another important role in helping therapists manage their emotional experience in therapy. Although presence is not a specific emotion, it is a way of being that speaks to the way a therapist feels in a session and, therefore, is highly relevant to how therapists manage feelings. If feelings rise up in the therapist, presence implies being aware of them and using them in a facilitative manner. Greenberg and Geller (2001) outlined principles of *congruence*, which involves being aware of what one feels and being transparent. Being therapeutically congruent relies on three factors: first, on therapist attitudes of respect and the ability to be nonjudgmental; and second, on certain processes, such as the ability to facilitate and disciplined genuineness; and third, on comprehensiveness. Disciplined genuineness requires that therapists be aware of their deepest level of experience to ensure that what is expressed is a core or primary, rather than a secondary, feeling. Furthermore, therapists need to be clear on their intention for sharing their experience—that it is to facilitate the client or the relationship, and is not for themselves—and they need, in this respect, to be sensitive to the timing of disclosure.

Another skill of congruence is comprehensiveness, which involves "saying all of it." The therapist not only expresses the central or focal aspect of what is being felt but also the metaexperience: what is felt about what is being felt and communicated. Saying that one feels irritated or bored is not saying all of it. Therapists need to communicate their concern and anxiety about this "saying all of it" potentially hurting their clients; they must express that they are communicating out of a wish to clarify and improve a connection, not destroy it.

A crucial aspect of being facilitatively genuine is the therapist's interpersonal stance in expressing difficult feelings. The different ways of dealing facilitatively with different classes of difficult feeling involve adopting a position of disclosing rather than enacting. Expressing a difficult feeling in a stance that is disclosing rather than enacting or expressing the feeling helps make it facilitative. Enactment means being angry, sad, or afraid, whereas disclosing means sharing that one feels a certain way without explicitly showing the feeling. Disclosure, implicitly or explicitly, involves and conveys a willingness to, or an interest in, exploring with the other what one is disclosing.

For example, when attacked or feeling angry, therapists do not attack their clients; rather, they disclose that they feel angry. They do not use blaming "you" language; rather, they take responsibility for their feelings and use "I" language that helps disclose the feeling. A therapist, for instance, might say, "I found myself feeling kind of annoyed that on a few occasions I have asked you to remove your shoes when it is wet or snowy outside, and yet it seems hard for you to do this." The disclosure needs to be comprehensive: saying "I am anxious about saying this" and "I am concerned about your feeling bad when I say this." Above all, therapists do not go into a one-upmanship, escalatory position in this communication; instead, they openly disclose feelings of fear, anger, or hurt in a vulnerable manner. When the therapist is experiencing nonaffiliative, rejecting feelings or loss of interest, the interactional skill involves being able to disclose these feelings in the context of communicating congruently that the therapist does not wish to feel that way. Or, the therapist discloses the feelings as a problem that is getting in the way and that he or she is trying to repair the distance so that he or she will be able to feel more understanding and closer to the client. The key in communicating what could be perceived as negative feelings is occupying an interactional position of disclosure and a congruent nondominant, affiliative manner of expression. It is not the content of the disclosure that is the central issue in being facilitative; rather, it is the interpersonal stance of disclosure in a facilitative way that is important.

CASE PRESENTATIONS

Two brief cases follow. The first is from a session that was recorded and can be viewed in the American Psychological Association video *Emotion-Focused Therapy for Depression* (American Psychological Association, 2007). The second vignette does not resemble any single case but is a composite designed to represent aspects of EFT case formulation and treatment.

Client A

A brief client–therapist interchange follows to concretize the central EFT process of first arriving at emotion, processing it productively, and then leaving it. The client is "Jennifer,"[1] a 29-year-old woman who had been

---

[1]For the purposes of this book, the client's name has been changed to protect her identity.

physically abused by her husband years ago. In the following dialogue, she discusses her current depressive experience:

Jennifer: Well, right now, I just feel like I'm kind of forcing myself to keep getting up and going to work.

Therapist: Pushing and pushing. Yeah. Yeah. I wonder if you can breathe, and, you know, maybe even let the tears come if you're willing, or . . .? It's like you're struggling on the brink of them, but they're important—tears. So, there's this struggle of pushing, and pushing. [Jennifer: Yeah.] Yeah.

Jennifer: And it just makes me tired. And I, I got my bachelor's degree. . . .

Therapist: If you could speak from the tears or actually let them speak, what would they be saying? "I feel . . ."?

Jennifer: Hopeless. I feel like I'm struggling, and. . . . [Arrives at a secondary symptomatic emotion; attends to and symbolizes]

Later in the session, she arrives at her core maladaptive feeling of shame at having allowed herself to be in an abusive relationship; that feeling underlies the depressive hopelessness. The therapist guides the client to her bodily felt experience:

Therapist: I imagine it must really bring an ache in your body. What's it feel like, the hurt inside?

Jennifer: It feels terrible. It feels like I just want to curl up and put a blanket over my head and just hide. [Begins to arrive at action tendency of core shame, and attends to, symbolizes, accepts, experiences agency, differentiates]

Arriving at her core pain makes it amenable to change. The client then expresses empowered anger, asserting that "I needed understanding and validation at the time"; she says to her own critical voice, "Stop blaming me." With the help of the therapist's validation of her need, she begins to feel deserving of the need to be understood and accepted rather than guilty. She asserts her need and then begins to feel more responsive to her pain; she feels forgiving and loving toward herself. These are the new primary adaptive emotions that transform her shame into self-acceptance and an inner calm and joy.

Client B

This example exemplifies a course of therapy over time in which case formulation, marker-guided intervention, and emotional change are exemplified. The client, "Monica," is a 39-year-woman who tearfully reports feeling down and depressed. She reports that she probably has been depressed most of her life but that the past year has been particularly bad. She has not been working and has fallen into a pattern of rarely leaving the house or answering the phone or the door. Her relationships with her family of origin are difficult and often painful.

In the first few sessions, the therapist listens, using empathic understanding responses, explorations, and formulations to communicate his understanding to the client. From the exploration of the first session, the therapist had a sense that throughout Monica's childhood and into her adult life, she frequently has experienced herself as alone and unsupported. She has internalized the critical voice of her parents and often judged herself to be a failure, and within the context of a physically and emotionally abusive past, she has often felt emotionally unsafe and abandoned. In terms of her emotional processing style, the therapist observed that the client was able to focus on her internal experience, particularly in response to therapist empathic responses. As the client reported, she tends to avoid (as many people do) painful and difficult emotions. There appears to be an identifiable emotional pattern: She moves into states of helpless and hopeless whenever she starts to feel her primary emotions of sadness or anger and when she experiences not being able to have her met needs for closeness and acceptance met.

The therapist provides a rationale that emotions need to be attended to because they provide information and that it is Monica's unresolved emotions that lead to her ruminative thoughts. Following the pain compass, the therapist helps the client articulate her chronic enduring pain of feeling unsupported and unaccepted by her family. Monica expresses intense emotions, feeling immediately overwhelmed by the thought that the support and acceptance will never happen, and that, ultimately, she does not deserve such support. She says,

> I tell myself a story over and over again to the point I believe it. I believe that it's so and that it can't be fixed. Or, I don't care. I don't want it to be fixed. . . . That I'm not loved, that I'm not as good as them. You know, my life is chaotic, and theirs [siblings] seems to be going, you know, their life seems so much easier.

In the first session, the therapist hears possible markers of unfinished business around feelings of being badly treated by her family, a self-critical split between a part of herself that labels her as a failure and not entitled to love, and another that part wants love and acceptance. In the second session, they engage in two-chair work on her self-criticism. In the third session, Monica recounts the history of the relationship with her father. She describes not having received any approval from him. In response, the therapist initiates an empty-chair dialogue to work on Monica's unfinished business with her father. In this dialogue with her father, she expresses her pain and hurt at her father's inability to make her feel loved:

> I guess I keep thinking that yeah, you will never be a parent, that you would pick up the phone and just ask me how I'm doing. It hurts me that you don't love me. . . . Yeah, I guess, you know.

She ends the session with a recognition that what she needed was acceptance. "I needed to be hugged once in a while as a child or told that I was OK," she says. "I think that's normal."

Monica harbors a great deal of resentment toward her father over his maltreatment of her as a child, but she tends to minimize it as "being slapped was just normal." She has internalized this as a feeling of worthlessness and as being unlovable. These underlying concerns lend themselves clearly to the emotional processing tasks of both the two-chair for internal conflict splits and the empty-chair for unresolved injuries with a significant other. In the fourth through ninth sessions, the client explores the critic who attempts to protect her through controlling and by shutting off needs, and the experiencing self who wants to be loved and accepted. She continues to define and speak from both voices and expresses a range of sadness, anger, and pain or hurt. The hopelessness that was so dominant in the early sessions decreases and, by the ninth session, is nonexistent. The voice that wants love and acceptance becomes stronger, and the critic softens to express acceptance of this part of her. At the same time, she is feeling much better, and activation of her negative feelings decreases.

By accessing pride and anger, and grieving her loss, her core shame is undone. Monica hereby begins to feel more deserving, and this feeling shifts her belief that her father's failure to love her was not because she was not worth loving. She says to him in the empty chair,

> I'm angry at you because you think you were a good father. You have said that you never hit us, and that's the biggest lie on earth, You beat the hell out of us constantly, you never showed any love, you never showed any affection, you never ever acknowledged we were ever there except for us to clean and do things around the house.

Having processed her anger and her sadness, and transformed her shame, Monica takes a more compassionate and understanding position with her father. In an empty-chair dialogue with her father in session 10, she says,

> I understand that you've gone through a lot of pain in your life and probably because of this pain, because of the things you've seen, you've withdrawn. You're afraid to maybe give love the way it should be given and to get too close to anybody because it means you might lose them. You know, and I can understand that now, whereas growing up, I couldn't understand.

At the end of the session when talking about the dialogue, Monica says, "I feel relief that I don't have this anger sitting on my chest anymore." The client goes on to describe how she can now accept that her father does not have more to give, which leads to feelings of pride and then joy for having overcome these feelings.

CONCLUSION

The most basic process for the client in EFT is developing awareness of emotion and discriminating which emotional responses are healthy and can be used as a guide, and which are maladaptive and need to be changed and or regulated. The way in which EFT works with emotion focuses on helping people "re-own" previously disowned feelings and unmet childhood needs, and helping them deal more adequately with the painful emotions. The goals are to activate the feelings, reclaim the need, and find ways of reexperiencing the past in the present by activating new emotions to change old ones. These processes lead to self-reorganization and reduction in behaviors related to avoidance of the painful feelings and needs, and/or to maladaptive ways to try to get needs met, or to dysregulating reactions to need frustration.

A key tenet of EFT is that to change, a person needs to experience emotion. However, people do not change their emotions simply by talking about them, understanding their origins, unlocking unconscious conflicts, or changing beliefs. Rather, people change by accepting and experiencing emotions, regulating them when they are overwhelming, opposing them with different emotions to transform them, and reflecting on them to create new narrative meanings.

REFERENCES

American Psychological Association (Producer). (2007). *Emotion-focused therapy for depression* [DVD]. Available from http://www.apa.org/pubs/videos/4310798.aspx

Angus, L. E., & Greenberg, L. S. (2011). *Working with narrative in emotion-focused therapy: Changing stories, healing lives.* Washington, DC: American Psychological Association. http://dx.doi.org/10.1037/12325-000

Auszra, L., Greenberg, L. S., & Herrmann, I. (2013). Client emotional productivity-optimal client in-session emotional processing in experiential therapy. *Psychotherapy Research, 23,* 732–746. http://dx.doi.org/10.1080/10503307.2013.816882

Bateson, G. (1999). *Steps to an ecology of mind: Collected essays in anthropology, psychiatry, evolution, and epistemology.* Chicago, IL: University of Chicago Press. http://dx.doi.org/10.7208/chicago/9780226924601.001.0001

Benjamin, L. S. (1996). An interpersonal theory of personality disorders. In J. F. Clarkin (Ed.), *Major theories of personality disorder* (pp. 141–220). New York, NY: Guilford Press.

Bohart, A. C., & Greenberg, L. S. (Eds.). (1997). *Empathy reconsidered: New directions in psychotherapy*. Washington, DC: American Psychological Association. http://dx.doi.org/10.1037/10226-000

Bowlby, J. (1969). *Attachment and loss: Volume 1. Attachment.* New York, NY: Basic Books.

Bowlby, J. (1988). *A secure base: Parent–child attachment and healthy human development.* New York, NY: Basic Books.

Buck, R. (2014). *Emotion: A biosocial synthesis.* Cambridge, England: Cambridge University Press. http://dx.doi.org/10.1017/CBO9781139049825

Carryer, J. R., & Greenberg, L. S. (2010). Optimal levels of emotional arousal in experiential therapy of depression. *Journal of Consulting and Clinical Psychology, 78,* 190–199. http://dx.doi.org/10.1037/a0018401

Damasio, A. R. (1994). *Descartes' error: Emotion, reason, and the human brain.* New York, NY: Putnam.

Damasio, A. R. (1999). *The feeling of what happens: Body and emotion in the making of consciousness.* New York, NY: Harcourt Brace.

Ekman, P. (1993). Facial expression and emotion. *American Psychologist, 48,* 384–392. http://dx.doi.org/10.1037/0003-066X.48.4.384

Ekman, P., & Davidson, R. (Eds.). (1994). *The nature of emotion: Fundamental questions.* New York, NY: Oxford University Press.

Elliott, R., Watson, J. C., Goldman, R. N., & Greenberg, L. S. (2004). *Learning emotion-focused therapy: The process-experiential approach to change.* Washington, DC: American Psychological Association. http://dx.doi.org/10.1037/10725-000

Ellison, J. A., & Greenberg, L. S. (2007). Homework in experiential emotion-focused therapy. In N. Kazantzis & L'Abate (Eds.), *Handbook of homework assignments in psychotherapy* (pp. 65–84). Boston, MA: Springer.

Foa, E. B., & Jaycox, L. H. (1999). Cognitive-behavioral theory and treatment of posttraumatic stress disorder. In D. Spiegel (Ed.), *Efficacy and cost-effectiveness of psychotherapy* (pp. 23–61). Washington, DC: American Psychiatric Association.

Fredrickson, B. L. (2001). The role of positive emotions in positive psychology: The broaden-and-build theory of positive emotions. *American Psychologist, 56,* 218–226. http://dx.doi.org/10.1037/0003-066X.56.3.218

Frijda, N. H. (1986). *The emotions.* Cambridge, England: Cambridge University Press.

Frijda, N. H. (2016). The evolutionary emergence of what we call "emotions." *Cognition and Emotion, 30,* 609–620. http://dx.doi.org/10.1080/02699931.2016.1145106

Gazzaniga, M. S. (1988). *Mind matters: How mind and brain interact to create our conscious lives.* Boston, MA: Houghton Mifflin.

Geller, S. M., & Greenberg, L. S. (2002). Therapeutic presence: Therapists' experience of presence in the psychotherapy encounter. *Person-Centered and Experiential Psychotherapies, 1,* 71–86. http://dx.doi.org/10.1080/14779757.2002.9688279

Geller, S. M., & Greenberg, L. S. (2012). *Therapeutic presence: A mindful approach to effective therapy.* Washington, DC: American Psychological Association.

Geller, S. M., Greenberg, L. S., & Watson, J. C. (2010). Therapist and client perceptions of therapeutic presence: The development of a measure. *Psychotherapy Research, 20,* 599–610. http://dx.doi.org/10.1080/10503307.2010.495957

Gendlin, E. T. (1996). *Focusing-oriented psychotherapy: A manual of the experiential method.* New York, NY: Guilford Press.

Goldman, R. N., & Greenberg, L. S. (2015). *Case formulation in emotion-focused therapy: Co-creating clinical maps for change.* Washington, DC: American Psychological Association. http://dx.doi.org/10.1037/14523-000

Goldman, R. N., Greenberg, L. S., & Pos, A. E. (2005). Depth of emotional experience and outcome. *Psychotherapy Research, 15,* 248–260. http://dx.doi.org/10.1080/10503300512331385188

Greenberg, L., & Pascual-Leone, J. (1995). A dialectical constructivist approach to experiential change. In R. A. Neimeyer & M. J. Mahoney (Eds.), *Constructivism in psychotherapy* (pp. 169–191). Washington, DC: American Psychological Association.

Greenberg, L. S. (2015). *Emotion-focused therapy: Coaching clients to work through their feelings* (2nd ed.). Washington, DC: American Psychological Association. http://dx.doi.org/10.1037/14692-000

Greenberg, L. S. (2017). *Emotion-focused therapy* (Rev. ed.). Washington, DC: American Psychological Association.

Greenberg, L. S., & Angus, L. E. (2004). The contributions of emotion processes to narrative change in psychotherapy: A dialectical constructivist approach. In L. E. Angus & J. McLeod (Eds.), *The handbook of narrative and psychotherapy: Practice, theory, and research* (pp. 330–349). Thousand Oaks, CA: Sage. http://dx.doi.org/10.4135/9781412973496.d25

Greenberg, L. S., & Bolger, E. (2001). An emotion-focused approach to the overregulation of emotion and emotional pain. *Journal of Clinical Psychology, 57,* 197–211. http://dx.doi.org/10.1002/1097-4679(200102)57:2<197::AID-JCLP6>3.0.CO;2-O

Greenberg, L. S., & Elliott, R. (1997). Varieties of empathic responding. In A. C. Bohart & L. S. Greenberg (Eds.), *Empathy reconsidered: New directions in psychotherapy* (pp. 167–186). Washington, DC: American Psychological Association.

Greenberg, L. S., & Geller, S. (2001). Congruence and therapeutic presence. In G. Wyatt (Ed.), *Rogers' therapeutic conditions: Evolution, theory and practice. Volume 1: Congruence* (pp. 131–149). Ross-on-Wye, England: PCCS Books.

Greenberg, L. S., & Goldman, R. N. (2008). *Emotion-focused couples therapy: The dynamics of emotion, love, and power.* Washington, DC: American Psychological Association.

Greenberg, L. S., & Johnson, S. M. (1988). *Emotionally focused therapy for couples.* New York, NY: Guilford Press.

Greenberg, L. S., & Malcolm, W. (2002). Resolving unfinished business: Relating process to outcome. *Journal of Consulting and Clinical Psychology, 70,* 406–416. http://dx.doi.org/10.1037/0022-006X.70.2.406

Greenberg, L. S., & Paivio, S. C. (1997). *Working with emotions in psychotherapy.* New York, NY: Guilford Press.

Greenberg, L. S., & Pascual-Leone, J. (2001). A dialectical constructivist view of the creation of personal meaning. *Journal of Constructivist Psychology, 14,* 165–186. http://dx.doi.org/10.1080/10720530151143539

Greenberg, L. S., Rice, L. N., & Elliott, R. K. (1993). *Facilitating emotional change: The moment-by-moment process.* New York, NY: Guilford Press.

Greenberg, L. S., & Safran, J. D. (1987). *Emotion in psychotherapy: Affect, cognition, and the process of change.* New York, NY: Guilford Press.

Greenberg, L. S., & Warwar, S. H. (2006). Homework in an emotion-focused approach to experiential therapy. *Journal of Psychotherapy Integration, 16,* 178–200. http://dx.doi.org/10.1037/1053-0479.16.2.178

Greenberg, L. S., & Watson, J. C. (2006). *Emotion-focused therapy for depression.* Washington, DC: American Psychological Association. http://dx.doi.org/10.1037/11286-000

Greenberg, L. S., & Webster, M. C. (1982). Resolving decisional conflict by Gestalt two-chair dialogue: Relating process to outcome. *Journal of Counseling Psychology, 29,* 468–477.

Guntrip, H. (1969). *Schizoid phenomena, object relations and the self.* New York, NY: International Universities Press.

Harlow, H. (1958). The nature of love. *American Psychologist, 13,* 673–685.

Herrmann, I. R., Greenberg, L. S., & Auszra, L. (2016). Emotion categories and patterns of change in experiential therapy for depression. *Psychotherapy Research, 26,* 178–195. http://dx.doi.org/10.1080/10503307.2014.958597

Izard, C. E. (1991). *The psychology of emotions.* New York, NY: Plenum Press.

Johnson, S. M., Hunsley, J., Greenberg, L., & Schindler, D. (1999). Emotionally focused couples therapy: Status and challenges. *Clinical Psychology: Science and Practice, 6,* 67–79. http://dx.doi.org/10.1093/clipsy.6.1.67

Kernberg, O. F. (1984). *Object-relations theory and clinical psychoanalysis.* Northvale, NJ: Rowman & Littlefield. (Original work published 1976)

Kircanski, K., Lieberman, M. D., & Craske, M. G. (2012). Feelings into words: Contributions of language to exposure therapy. *Psychological Science, 23,* 1086–1091. http://dx.doi.org/10.1177/0956797612443830

Klein, M. H., Mathieu-Coughlan, P., & Kiesler, D. J. (1986). The experiencing scales. In L. S. Greenberg & W. M. Pinsof (Eds.), *The psychotherapeutic process: A research handbook* (pp. 21–71). New York, NY: Guilford Press.

Klein, M. H., Mathieu, P. L., Gendlin, E. T., & Kiesler, D. J. (1969). *The Experiencing Scale: A research and training manual* (Vol. 1). Madison, WI: Wisconsin Psychiatric Institute.

Lane, R. D., Ryan, L., Nadel, L., & Greenberg, L. (2015). Memory reconsolidation, emotional arousal, and the process of change in psychotherapy: New insights from brain science. *Behavioral and Brain Sciences, 38,* E1. http://dx.doi.org/10.1017/S0140525X14000041

LeDoux, J. (2012). Rethinking the emotional brain. *Neuron, 73,* 653–676. http://dx.doi.org/10.1016/j.neuron.2012.02.004

Lieberman, M. D., Eisenberger, N. I., Crockett, M. J., Tom, S. M., Pfeifer, J. H., & Way, B. M. (2007). Putting feelings into words: Affect labeling disrupts amygdala activity in response to affective stimuli. *Psychological Science, 18,* 421–428. http://dx.doi.org/10.1111/j.1467-9280.2007.01916.x

Linehan, M. M. (1993). *Cognitive-behavioral treatment of borderline personality disorder.* New York, NY: Guilford Press.

Maslow, A. H. (1954). *Motivation and personality.* New York, NY: Harper & Row.

McKinnon, J. M., & Greenberg, L. S. (2013). Revealing underlying vulnerable emotion in couple therapy: Impact on session and final outcome. *Journal of Family Therapy, 35,* 303–319. https://dx.doi.org/10.1111/1467-6427.12015

Missirlian, T. M., Toukmanian, S. G., Warwar, S. H., & Greenberg, L. S. (2005). Emotional arousal, client perceptual processing, and the working alliance in experiential psychotherapy for depression. *Journal of Consulting and Clinical Psychology, 73,* 861–871. http://dx.doi.org/10.1037/0022-006X.73.5.861

Moscovitch, M., & Nadel, L. (1997). Memory consolidation, retrograde amnesia, and the hippocampal complex. *Current Opinions in Neurobiology, 7,* 217–227. http://dx.doi.org/10.1016/S0959-4388(97)80010-4

Nadel, L., & Bohbot, V. (2001). Consolidation of memory. *Hippocampus, 11,* 56–60. http://dx.doi.org/10.1002/1098-1063(2001)11:1<56::AID-HIPO1020>3.0.CO;2-O

Nader, K., Schafe, G. E., & LeDoux, J. E. (2000). Fear memories require protein synthesis in the amygdala for reconsolidation after retrieval. *Nature, 406,* 722–726. http://dx.doi.org/10.1038/35021052

Neisser, U. (1976). *Cognition and reality: Principles and implications of cognitive psychology.* New York, NY: Freeman/Times Books/Henry Holt.

Nolen-Hoeksema, S., & Watkins, E. R. (2011). A heuristic for transdiagnostic models of psychopathology: Explaining multifinality and divergent trajectories. *Perspectives on Psychological Science, 6,* 589–609. http://dx.doi.org/10.1177/1745691611419672

Paivio, S. C., Hall, I. E., Holowaty, K. A. M., Jellis, J. B., & Tran, N. (2001). Imaginal confrontation for resolving child abuse issues. *Psychotherapy Research, 11*, 433–453. http://dx.doi.org/10.1093/ptr/11.4.433

Paivio, S. C., & Nieuwenhuis, J. A. (2001). Efficacy of emotion focused therapy for adult survivors of child abuse: A preliminary study. *Journal of Traumatic Stress, 15*, 115–133. http://dx.doi.org/10.1023/A:1007891716593

Pascual-Leone, A., & Greenberg, L. S. (2007). Emotional processing in experiential therapy: Why "the only way out is through." *Journal of Consulting and Clinical Psychology, 75*, 875–887. http://dx.doi.org/10.1037/0022-006X.75.6.875

Pascual-Leone, J. (1987). Organismic processes for neo-Piagetian theories: A dialectical causal account of cognitive development. *International Journal of Psychology, 22*, 531–570. http://dx.doi.org/10.1080/00207598708246795

Pascual-Leone, J. (1991). Emotions, development, and psychotherapy: A dialectical-constructivist perspective. In J. D. Safran & L. S. Greenberg (Eds.), *Emotion, psychotherapy, and change* (pp. 302–335). New York, NY: Guilford Press.

Pascual-Leone, J., & Johnson, J. (1991). The psychological unit and its role in task analysis. A reinterpretation of object permanence. In M. Chandler & M. Chapman (Eds.), *Criteria for competence: Controversies in the assessment of children's abilities* (pp. 153–187). Hillsdale, NJ: Erlbaum.

Pascual-Leone, J., & Johnson, J. (2011). A developmental theory of mental attention: Its application to measurement and task analysis. In P. Barrouillet & V. Gaillard (Eds.), *Cognitive development and working memory: A dialogue between neo-Piagetian and cognitive approaches* (pp. 13–46). New York, NY: Psychology Press.

Pennebaker, J. W. (Ed.). (1995). *Emotion, disclosure, and health.* Washington, DC: American Psychological Association. http://dx.doi.org/10.1037/10182-000

Perls, F. S., Hefferline, R. F., & Goodman, P. (1951). *Gestalt therapy: Excitement and growth in the human personality.* New York, NY: Dell.

Piaget, J. (1954). *The construction of reality in the child.* New York, NY: Basic Books. http://dx.doi.org/10.1037/11168-000

Piaget, J. (1973). *Memory and intelligence.* New York, NY: Basic Books.

Porges, S. W. (1998). Love: An emergent property of the mammalian autonomic nervous system. *Psychoneuroendocrinology, 23*, 837–861. http://dx.doi.org/10.1016/S0306-4530(98)00057-2

Porges, S. W. (2007). The polyvagal perspective. *Biological Psychology, 74*, 116–143. http://dx.doi.org/10.1016/j.biopsycho.2006.06.009

Porges, S. W. (2011). *The polyvagal theory: Neurophysiological foundations of emotions, attachment, communication, and self-regulation.* New York, NY: Norton.

Rice, L. N., & Greenberg, L. S. (1984). *Patterns of change: Intensive analysis of psychotherapy process.* New York, NY: Guilford Press.

Rice, L. N., & Kerr, G. P. (1986). Measures of client and therapist vocal quality. In L. S. Greenberg & W. M. Pinsof (Eds.), *The psychotherapeutic process: A research handbook* (pp. 73–105). New York, NY: Guilford Press.

Rice, L. N., & Wagstaff, A. K. (1967). Client voice quality and expressive style as indexes of productive psychotherapy. *Journal of Consulting Psychology, 31,* 557–563. http://dx.doi.org/10.1037/h0025164

Rogers, C. R. (1957). The necessary and sufficient conditions of therapeutic personality change. *Journal of Consulting Psychology, 21,* 95–103. http://dx.doi.org/10.1037/h0045357

Rogers, C. R. (1959). A theory of therapy, personality, and interpersonal relationships, as developed in the client-centered framework. In S. Koch (Ed.), *Psychology: A study of a science. Vol. 3: Formulations of the person and the social context* (pp. 184–256). New York, NY: McGraw Hill.

Scherer, K. (2015). When and why are emotions disturbed? Suggestions based on theory and data from emotion research. *Emotion Review, 7,* 238–249. http://dx.doi.org/10.1177/1754073915575404

Schore, A. N. (1994). *Affect regulation and the origin of the self: The neurobiology of emotional development.* Hillsdale, NJ: Erlbaum.

Schore, A. N. (2002). Dysregulation of the right brain: A fundamental mechanism of traumatic attachment and the psychopathogenesis of posttraumatic stress disorder. *Australian & New Zealand Journal of Psychiatry, 36,* 9–30. http://dx.doi.org/10.1046/j.1440-1614.2002.00996.x

Schore, A. N. (2003). *Affect dysregulation & disorders of the self.* New York, NY: Norton.

Spinoza, B. (1967). *L'Éthique* (R. Caillois, Trans.). Paris, France: Gallimard. (Original work published 1677)

Sroufe, L. A. (1996). *Emotional development: The organization of emotional life in the early years.* New York, NY: Cambridge University Press. http://dx.doi.org/10.1017/CBO9780511527661

Stanton, A. L., Danoff-Burg, S., Cameron, C. L., Bishop, M., Collins, C. A., Kirk, S. B., . . . Twillman, R. (2000). Emotionally expressive coping predicts psychological and physical adjustment to breast cancer. *Journal of Consulting and Clinical Psychology, 68,* 875–882.

Stern, D. N. (1985). *The interpersonal world of the infant: A view from psychoanalysis and developmental psychology.* New York, NY: Basic Books.

Taylor, C. (1985). *Human agency and language.* New York, NY: Cambridge University Press.

van der Kolk, B. A. (2014). *The body keeps the score: Brain, mind, and body in the healing of trauma.* New York, NY: Viking.

von Foerster, H. (1995). *The cybernetics of cybernetics.* Minneapolis, MN: Future Systems.

Warwar, S., & Greenberg, L. S. (1999). *Client Emotional Arousal Scale–III*. Unpublished manuscript, York University, Toronto, Ontario, Canada.

Watkins, E. R. (2008). Constructive and unconstructive repetitive thought. *Psychological Bulletin, 134*, 163–206. http://dx.doi.org/10.1037/0033-2909.134.2.163

Watson, J. C. (1996). The relationship between vivid description, emotional arousal, and in-session resolution of problematic reactions. *Journal of Consulting and Clinical Psychology, 64*, 459–464. http://dx.doi.org/10.1037/0022-006X.64.3.459

Watson, J. C., & Greenberg, L. S. (1996). Pathways to change in the psychotherapy of depression: Relating process to session change and outcome. *Psychotherapy: Theory, Research, Practice, Training, 33*, 262–74. http://dx.doi.org/10.1037/0033-3204.33.2.262

Watzlawick, P., Weakland, J. H., & Fisch, R. (1974). *Change: Principles of problem formation and problem resolution*. New York, NY: Norton.

White, R. W. (1959). Motivation reconsidered: The concept of competence. *Psychological Review, 66*, 297–333. http://dx.doi.org/10.1037/h0040934

5

COMPARING APPROACHES

LESLIE S. GREENBERG, NORKA T. MALBERG,
AND MICHAEL A. TOMPKINS

In this concluding chapter, we discuss the ways in which the psychodynamic, cognitive behavior, and emotion-focused therapy approaches regard the role of emotion in therapy, in motivation for change, and in change methods. We begin by examining similarities in among the three approaches but first by identifying the level of analysis.

Goldfried (1980), in the spirit of promoting psychotherapy integration, suggested that similarities among approaches arise most prominently not at the level of technique or theory but at the level of clinical strategies or principles of change. For example, he proposed that feedback and new experience likely are common strategies across all approaches. Following a different path, in their survey of 50 publications on psychotherapy, Grencavage and Norcross (1990) identified 15 categories of methods and ranked them by frequency: *therapeutic alliance*, opportunity for *catharsis*, acquisition and practice of *new behaviors*, and clients' *positive expectancies*. In addition, they ranked

http://dx.doi.org/10.1037/0000130-005
Working With Emotion in Psychodynamic, Cognitive Behavior, and Emotion-Focused Psychotherapy,
by L. S. Greenberg, N. T. Malberg, and M. A. Tompkins

a series of change processes (excluding relational factors) and found that *catharsis* was the most commonly endorsed change process, *success and mastery* was moderately common, and *education and information transmission* was the least common. According to that study, most similarities occur at intermediate levels. The three approaches in this volume (i.e., Chapters 2, 3, and 4) certainly share a number of these intermediate-level change processes.

In addition to some of the general commonalities just outlined, the authors of Chapters 2, 3, and 4, in referring to how they work with emotion, endorse the following three, more emotion-specific, intermediate-level commonalities. Each approach aims to provide (a) corrective emotional experience; (b) emotional awareness or insight; and (c) exposure to, or a deeper experiencing of, emotion, and these can be seen as common, intermediate-level, emotion-specific factors. The three approaches also share the belief that emotion is an important aspect of change. In psychodynamic therapy (PDT), emotional insight is emphasized over intellectual insight; in cognitive behavior therapy (CBT), hot cognition is valued over cold cognition; and in emotion-focused therapy (EFT), depth of experiencing is valued over talking about experience. These emotion-specific common processes, however, are midlevel commonalities. To find out what these midlevel processes look like in practice and how they are facilitated in sessions, we need to look more closely at the higher and lower levels of description in each approach. It is at the higher level of theory of functioning and the lower level of technique that the differences among these approaches become more distinct.

To understand the similarities and differences among approaches, it is essential to first examine how each approach understands emotion functioning and the process of psychological change, and then compare the techniques used.

IS EMOTION THE PRIMARY TARGET OF CHANGE?

Is emotion seen as an independent variable that is worked on directly to produce change, which then leads to change in cognition, motivation, and behavior? Or is emotion the dependent variable in which emotional change is the result of change in cognition, motivation, and behavior? Another possibility to consider is how much emotion is seen as an accompanying or ancillary variable, such as a correlate of change. From this perspective, emotion signals that some other change process is occurring. Here, emotion is a signal that indicates another change process. We need to keep our eye on the following: Is intervention focused directly on emotion to produce a change in emotion, or is intervention focused on changing something else to produce change in emotion, or is the emotion a signal indicating that something else is changing? For example, is intervention directly changing fear, sadness, and shame, or is the intervention more focused on changing cognition, motivation, or behavior? Is it this change that leads to change in these emotions, or are these emotions a signal that cognition, motivation, or behavior are changing? A further question is what in the emotion is changing: Is it the degree of arousal, the degree of regulation, or is it that the emotion changes to a new emotion? What does emotional change lead to? Does it lead to change in motivation, cognition, behavior, or general well-being? In the sections that follow, we hope to provide answers to these and other questions.

MODELS OF EMOTION FUNCTIONING

All three approaches posit that activating emotion in therapy is helpful in promoting change. The approaches also assume that humans operate at a conscious and at an automatic or unconscious level, and see the relationship between the two levels as important.

In CBT and EFT, one information processing system is seen as rational, verbal, logical, and propositional without links to emotion. The second system is seen as a more holistic, nonlinguistic, automatic, and rapid information processing system with deep and extensive links to emotion. Although the psychodynamic approach does not disagree with this information processing view, it tends to apply a conflict model in which conscious and unconscious motivations are considered, as are the interactions among ego, id, and super-ego (i.e., internal wishes and needs, and ways of managing them and the pressures of the external world).

MENTAL STRUCTURE

The three approaches that are the focus of this volume posit that multilevel processing and an internal mental structure are involved in the generation of emotion. Psychodynamic theory talks in terms of internalized object relations, which are associated with affect; CBT refers to cognitive schemas or core beliefs and, more recently, to fundamental modes of processing, which result in emotion. EFT, on the other hand, refers to emotion schemes that when activated, produce emotion. The constructs within these three approaches are complex affective–cognitive structures that are hypothesized to influence mental life.

The constructs differ in the degree to which affect and relationship are represented in them. Emotion schemes view affect as the central organizing feature: Internalized object relations are most centrally relational but include affect as the thing that ties subjects and others together, whereas cognitive schemas are seen as free of affect. Beck (1996) theorized that a fundamental mode of processing lay beyond belief and activated belief, which are cognitive structures, but as a reactive process.

Automaticity and Unconscious

The three approaches also propose that emotion can be activated automatically by nondeliberate processes. Awareness of emotion has become a universal therapeutic principle embraced by all three approaches. The three also see emotion as information and as signaling something. EFT views emotion as signaling an unmet need and providing orienting action tendencies that aid in survival. In EFT, primary anxiety is seen as signaling a need for security and promoting protection seeking. Psychodynamic theory considers emotion, or at least anxiety, as signaling danger and a need for defense (i.e., ways of coping to maintain the internal balance). The danger can come from within (i.e., drives) or from the conflict between the external with the internal (e.g., desire vs. morals equals guilt). CBT sees cognition as moderating the expression of emotion; more specifically, that emotion marks core belief activation.

Adaptive or Maladaptive

All three approaches see emotion as serving either adaptive or maladaptive functions, although the approaches differentially emphasize the adaptiveness of emotion in therapeutic work. EFT sees emotion as a guide that emphasizes its basic adaptive and survival functions by informing people of what is important to their well-being. CBT and, to some degree, psychodynamic approaches, however, often place more of a focus on the maladaptive nature of emotional responses; they see emotions as needing regulation. For example, in CBT, the adaptiveness of an emotional response is influenced by the context in which it arises. Feeling anxious about driving through a neighborhood, for instance, depends on the objective safety of the neighborhood. That is, it makes sense to feel quite anxious when driving through an unsafe neighborhood. That same level of anxiety is disproportionate and therefore unhelpful if driving through a safe neighborhood. The goal of CBT is to assist clients to evaluate safety accurately so that anxious responses are proportionate to the objective safety of a particular context. In psychodynamic thinking, on the other hand, affect is seen as either experience to be defended against or as the ego's cognitive and motivational tool that provides information to the ego about psychic states. From this perspective, affect is regarded partly as an ego function (i.e., defensive and adaptive) and partly as a stimulus controlled by the ego.

Primacy

The three approaches recognize the important role of the physiological and emotional components in maintaining psychological disorders. Both the psychodynamic and EFT approaches see emotion as an internal state, a private experience that involves a bodily felt experience, and that this internal state can be consciously symbolized. CBT, however, tends to see the role of cognition as moderating emotional responses. All see a difference in a more intellectual form of self-understanding (i.e., beliefs, self-concept, or insight) and an experiential understanding: that these reflect different levels of information processing and that emotion becomes more modifiable when it is reactivated and experienced rather than just talked about. EFT and PDT tend to see emotion as a first response that precedes cognition and behavior, with a focus on emotion to change cognition and behavior. CBT, however, assumes that cognition and behavior moderate emotion; this approach tends to target cognition or behavior directly to influence emotion.

Development and Learning

Taking a more developmental perspective, PDT and EFT see emotion as central to attachment and identity formation, whereas CBT sees emotion more in terms of a learning process: as facilitating new learning in the service of new and more adaptive behaviors. In this regard, CBT does not emphasize attachment or identity formation; rather, it is a learning model whereby our emotional responses are moderated by a number of factors (e.g., attention, arousal, cognition). In terms of motivation, all three approaches see the person as being organized by a drive to survive, but the commonalities stop there because their views of motivation differ markedly.

PRIMACY OF EMOTION

Primary differences lie in the domain of the primacy of emotion about how central affect is in determining experience and change, as well as the nature of motivation. We look first at differences in how the three approaches view emotion. Whereas EFT sees emotion as the fundamental datum of human existence, the psychodynamic and CBT approaches often tend to see emotion as playing a somewhat less primary role.

Psychodynamic Therapy

Early psychoanalytic theory viewed affects as entirely drive derivatives, and anxiety represented a transformation of the instinctual drive energy of repressed contents. The first theory of anxiety, defense leads to anxiety, later changed to anxiety leads to defense. With that shift, affects could be regarded as responses of the ego rather than as being drive derivatives. The concept of anxiety as *signal affect* implied anticipation and symbolization. The concept of signal anxiety introduced new regulatory and communicative dimensions of affect. Repression was another important theoretical construct related to affect. The concept of *repression* involved a view that the mind has unconscious, preconscious, and conscious systems, and with it, the possibility of unconscious affects too.

With the development of object relations theory, affects became more explicitly linked to relationships. From that perspective, emotion is work within the here and now of the therapeutic relationship, and with the old versions of relationship emerging in the transference. People are defending not only against "causes" of feelings but also against the feelings themselves, which are both the cause of and the reaction to wishes. Wishes, as opposed to drives, are seen as entailing feelings, as well as self and object representations. Affects are viewed as developing together with the integration of internalized object relations into signals and monitors of activated drives. Emotions are seen as the holders both of memory in the mind and the body and of the developmental impact of early disturbed relationships with caregiving figures.

Cognitive Behavior Therapy

In CBT, emotion is moderated by cognition, and that cognition, emotion, and behavior influence each other such that emotion influences and is influenced by cognition and behavior. Maladaptive cognitions are hypothesized to contribute to the maintenance of emotional distress and problem behaviors, such as avoidance or withdrawal. The objective of cognitive restructuring is to shift key appraisals or cognitions in the service of moderating emotion. Beck (1996) introduced the concept of modes to address some of the criticisms and shortcomings of cognitive theory. He suggested as an addition to his model that there was a primary mode of processing underlying belief. Modes of processing included survival or threat processing, or self-expansive or joy processing. In this view, the processing of information results in an affective response; for example, processing threat information results in fear or anxiety. This appears to one of the authors (LSG) to be an affective level of processing; so, without being named as such, emotion crept back in as a fundamental concept underlying belief. If fully adopted, this concept would allow for a change in emphasis in practice; the therapist then could work on changing this primary mode of processing rather than on only changing beliefs. The CBT author (MAT), however, sees that the target for change in CBT is based on a choice the therapist makes, whether the target is emotion, cognition, or behavior. CBT targets the variables hypothesized to maintain emotional disorders. It seems to be a conceptual and practical choice. In targeting cognition, the cognitive behavior therapist does not assume that cognition is more or less important than emotion or behavior. Rather, cognition is a target for achieving change. CBT assumes that cognition moderates emotion and that behavior moderates emotion, and that emotion may moderate both. Emotion theory recognizes that several factors (e.g., cognition, attention, behavior) contribute to the subjective experience of emotion. EFT works directly with emotion to change it, whereas the psychodynamic therapist works with emotion as a part of relational patterns, and CBT works on thought to change emotion.

In psychodynamic thinking, disorder is seen as being maintained by arrested development, defensiveness, and the inability to mentalize internal experience (i.e., able neither to think about one's own thoughts and feelings from the outside nor imagine other's internal thoughts and feelings). In EFT, emotional disorder is seen predominantly as being maintained by preverbal emotion schemes that are activated automatically. In CBT, emotional disorders are maintained through a process of interpreting internal and external events through the lens of maladaptive beliefs. *Emotion avoidance*, the inability to confront, accept, and tolerate negative affect, is another factor hypothesized to maintain emotional disorders. Other factors include response persistence or a negative problem-solving set. To that end, many cognitive behavior strategies are in the service of increasing clients' willingness to approach and interact with their emotional responses rather than avoid (the persistent maladaptive response) these experiences. In this way, CBT recognizes that to succeed in life, it is necessary that emotional responses result in adaptive rather than maladaptive behaviors. For example, when treated unfairly, we feel angry and may assert our rights. However, asserting our rights in a thoughtful and appropriate manner may be difficult if we are too angry to control our impulses to strike out. That is, the goal of CBT is to assist individuals to regulate anxiety, anger, or mood in the service of goal-directed adaptive behavior.

Emotion-Focused Therapy

In EFT, emotion is viewed as fundamentally adaptive and as providing our basic mode of information processing. It rapidly and automatically appraises situations for their relevance to our well-being and produces action tendencies to meet needs. Emotions automatically evaluate immediate circumstances and consequences of action. Appraisal of an object or event strongly depends on the appraising individual's current concerns and his or her goals, sensitivities, interests, and values. It is not just an appraisal that activates an emotion but an appraisal in relation to a concern. Motivational tendencies therefore are part of every emotion, and emotion and motivation are closely linked. Similar to CBT, EFT sees the decision to engage in a particular behavior as closely linked to the expectation of the pleasantness or the relief associated with the motivated behavior.

Emotions produced by deliberative, orbital frontal cortex processes, such as thinking, are not nearly as important in function and dysfunction as the more primary emotions produced by the limbic system and other automatic processes. It is these nonlinguistic appraisals of relevance, goal congruence, novelty, danger, and control that are impenetrable to reason and, therefore, are hard to change by reason or deliberate will.

Emotion schemes that are organized, internal structures or networks are seen as being at the base of the adult emotional response system. They synthesize affective, motivational, cognitive, and behavioral elements into internal organizations that are activated rapidly out of awareness. Schemes are activated by cues that match the input features of the scheme or nodes of the network. Important life experiences that are significant by virtue of having previously activated emotional responses become coded into emotion schematic memory. Emotion schemes represent both the situation as construed and its emotional effect on the individual; they are response-producing internal organizations that synthesize a variety of levels and types of information, including sensorimotor stimuli, perception, motivation, action, and conceptual-level information. Once learned and organized into a schematic emotion memory system, emotion schemes, once activated, produce emotion automatically, as automatically as the in-wired biologically adaptive responses that they have integrated. They set the basic mode of processing that guides our life. In contrast to a cognitive schema, the emotion scheme is a network that produces action tendencies and experience as opposed to conceptual knowledge in language. Problems are seen as arising from a variety of sources: a lack emotion of emotion awareness, the disclaiming of emotional experience, and the perseveration of certain past emotional responses in the present through the activation of emotion schematic memory, as well as, on occasion, emotion dysregulation and faulty meaning creation.

Comparison

In psychodynamic thinking, affect appears as a correlate of other processes, such as being involved in transference, insight, or mentalization; overcoming defense; or being related to wish fulfillment or frustration. Generally, affect is not predominantly viewed as the independent variable that is focused on directly to produce change. What often is privileged are change in awareness of emotion and an understanding of things in a new way that result in increased self-observation during moments of strong emotional experience, integration of affects with each other, and integration or linking of emotion into one's narrative. Emotions are holders of memories; they are ways in which humans communicate what words cannot. Psychoanalysis seeks to integrate and link in a way that promotes affect regulation and increases capacity for mentalization and a sense of freedom in the context of both positive and negative emotion.

In CBT, cognition and behavior moderate emotion and emotional change. Modifying key misappraisals moderates emotional change. Modifying cognition is a practical choice, although not necessarily a theoretical choice. Cognitions are accessible factors hypothesized to moderate emotion, and strategies to modify cognitions can be taught and learned. Emotion is the dependent variable that is changed by changing cognition. When treating clients with emotional disorders, a key goal of CBT is to assist them to learn strategies to regulate their dysregulated emotional responses through examination of underlying cognitions that influence emotion or through altering behavior to learn something new and more adaptive that influences emotion (e.g., emotion-exposure and acceptance approaches).

In EFT, emotion is the independent variable and the direct target of change. It is worked with via acceptance and transformation. The first step of change that is facilitated is the acceptance and experiencing of the emotion. The next step is making sense of it, most often in language and narrative. Ultimately, though, what is sought after is a change in maladaptive emotion itself by another emotion. The result is a new feeling state and a new narrative.

MOTIVATION

With the recognition of the importance of emotion, all three approaches came to see motivational tendencies as a part of every emotion, so all agree that emotion and motivation are closely linked. The three traditions see that these emotionally based action tendencies and motivations can be adaptive and helpful at times but sometimes can be maladaptive and unhelpful. All three approaches also agree on a survival or life instinct—that this motivation guides behavior, but after that, there is not agreement on what the basic motivations are or even what *is* motivation.

A psychodynamic understanding of human motivation is fundamentally different from that of other approaches in that it considers conscious and unconscious motivations in the context of relationships. Survival in the context of relationships is fundamental for psychic growth and development; hence, psychodynamic thinking considers adaptive and maladaptive means by which people find ways of surviving and growing. CBT presents a different view of motivation: The basic motivation tendency seeks to attain reward and pleasure or to avoid punishment and misery; CBT also views expectation of reward or punishment as an important motivator of behavior. EFT and PDT differ from CBT: According to those two traditions, people are organized by a fundamental motivation to survive, and they thrive in the best way possible in the environment in which they find themselves. The organism is not determined by internal basic motivations but, rather, as a dynamic self-regulating system in a constant process of organizing adaptively at the boundary in an organism/environment field to survive and thrive.

Psychodynamic Therapy

Psychoanalytic theories over the years have developed varied complex views of motivation. As Malberg highlights in Chapter 2, Sandler came closest to revising psychoanalytic theory to be an affective theory by placing feeling states rather than psychic energy at the center of the psychoanalytic theory of motivation. Sandler also preferred to speak of wishes rather than drives, and of the relations between feelings and wishes rather than between feelings and drives. Rapport in ego psychology, however, moved in the other direction: It considered that a lack of internal balance (i.e., energy unbalance) and not feelings states motivated people. Kernberg (1988) later reclaimed affect by proposing a modification of drive theory that viewed affects as hierarchically more significant than drives. In that important shift, he saw affects as developing together with the integration of internalized object relations into signals and monitors of activated drives. Kernberg thereby retained the dual drive theory of Freud (i.e., Eros and Thanatos) but enveloped it in relational concepts. With the advent of object relations, which was followed more generally by attachment and interpersonal theory, the motivation to connect was a central one—a motivation that was innate in all humans from birth, and one that continued to be a major influence functioning from then onward.

Cognitive Behavior Therapy

The classical conditioning paradigm in behavior therapy bore some relationship to Freud's life motivations as both viewed the seeking of pleasure and the avoidance of pain as important to sustain life. Similarly, humanistic theory posited a life force, referred to alternately as the growth or actualizing tendency. Freud's death drive, however, is not shared by CBT or EFT, or by modern psychodynamic theory, given that it clearly has faded from prominence in modern object relational and interpersonal psychoanalysis. Early behaviorists viewed motivation as initiated and maintained through drive reduction, and this view had an affinity with Freud's view of drive reduction as a central motivation. In early behavioral theories, motivated behavior served to satisfy biological drives and later was elaborated to include learned associations between stimuli and rewarding or positive experiences. Motivation now was seen as more under stimulus control and no longer an internal drive. With the advent of more cognitive views, motivations also were understood as being driven by incentives. Ultimately, people are motivated by a combination of drive reduction and an incentive and expectation. For example, in Chapter 3, Tompkins explains that when people experience hunger, they have a strong need-driven motivation to eat, thereby reducing the hunger drive. However, after a full meal, the motivation to eat the baked apple pie is more incentive driven than need driven. He concludes that the more complex the behaviors, such as social behaviors, the more likely these behaviors are motivated by a number of need-driven and incentive-driven experiences.

Avoidance motivation also is a major concept in CBT. Every emotion has a motivational tendency, and these tendencies contribute to the adaptive value of the emotion itself. In the cases of anxiety, the motivational tendency is to avoid perceived threats or dangers, for example. However, these same motivational tendencies can maintain an emotional disorder, such as an anxiety disorder, when they become rigid and fixed despite evidence that there is no danger. The decision to engage in a particular behavior is closely linked to the expectation of the pleasantness or the relief associated with the motivated behavior. In this view, both external situations and internal experiences may be avoided. In CBT, experiential avoidance involves avoiding thoughts, feelings, memories, physical sensations, and other internal experiences that result in less adaptive day-to-day functioning. So, this is avoiding out of fear of emotion: either avoiding situations or behaving in ways to distract from negative emotion and thereby not feel it. In detaching people from feeling, experiential avoidance interferes with the function of emotional response, which is to inform us of our inner subjective experience. And because our inner experience is what informs our conscious choices, experiential avoidance has the effect of limiting options. It prevents people from acting on opportunities to pursue need satisfaction and living meaningfully. The closest concept to avoidance in psychodynamic theory is defense. People protect against their emotions to avoid the idea associated with them; they repress affect and are engaged in a struggle between the tendency to have consciousness and the wish not to have it, and between the capacity to tolerate emotion and the inclination to avoid it because of the pain feelings may bring. Here, emotions are being kept out of awareness rather than avoided.

EFT based on humanistic–experiential perspectives started with the notion that experience that is unacceptable to the self-concept is denied or distorted. So, what CBT calls experiential avoidance and psychoanalysis calls defending against emotion were seen in EFT as not experiencing or disowning. EFT now views people as blocking emotional awareness by actively interrupting emotional experience or disclaiming the action tendencies to protect themselves out of a fear of being overwhelmed by the emotion and disintegrating. The motivation to do this blocking in EFT, however, is understood as an attempt to cope and not fall apart rather than to avoid pain.

Emotion-Focused Therapy

Humanistic theory saw people as having an inherent tendency to grow and reach their full potential. According to Rogers (1951), individuals had an innate capacity to decide on their own best directions in life, provided circumstances were conducive to that, and this decision making was based on the organism's universal need to self-maintain, flourish, self-enhance, and self-protect. Eventually, he and other humanists named this theoretical construct the actualizing tendency (Maslow, 1962; Perls, 1969; Rogers, 1951). They believed that the behaviors of an organism can be counted on to be moving in the direction of maintaining, enhancing, and reproducing themselves. EFT, a neohumanistic theory, was similarly based on the notion of a survival and growth tendency but did not adopt the Maslowian view of an actualizing tendency: the motivation to become all we can be (Maslow, 1962). Rather, EFT sees adapting to the environment to survive and thrive as the only basic motivation; it also views emotion as the process that governs adaption by evaluating what is good or bad for the organism. In addition, rather than postulating a set of basic content motivations, such as attachment, mastery, or control, EFT understands psychological needs as arising from a process of construction from an interaction between basic inborn biases, preferences, and affective values of what is good and bad for us with lived experience. Motivation therefore is secondary to or is an aspect of emotion. EFT posits that organisms come into the world with a motivation to survive and thrive, and are accompanied by a set of basic affects that promote this aim. In addition, the organism is born with two general purpose mechanisms that help achieve this aim: the regulation of affect and the creation of meaning.

EMOTIONAL CHANGE METHODS

A growing body of evidence suggests that actively working to intensify a client's engagement with emotion in therapy can improve outcomes in a variety of psychotherapies (Greenberg, 2011; Whelton, 2004). In this section, we look at the methods of intervention, interaction, and techniques the different approaches use in working with emotion.

The relationship and alliance are considered important in providing the safety to disclose what is deeply personal and to become vulnerable. Collaboration is essential in all approaches to enable the dyad to work on emotionally difficult experiences. Furthermore, working with changing memories is an important method in all three traditions. Memory reconsolidation, a new approach to memory, recently was adopted by all approaches to help explain how affect is changed. Recent neuroscience (Nadel & Bohbot, 2001; Nader, Schafe, & LeDoux, 2000) has shown that every time a memory is retrieved, the underlying memory trace is labile and open to new input before it is reconsolidated as an updated memory. It is now believed that in therapy, problematic emotional memories can be changed through activation of the "old" emotional memory and introduction of new experience within the period of lability. So, emotional engagement reactivates old memories and makes them more labile and plastic, therefore open to new input and updating.

The different traditions all propose that their approach changes memory by providing new input, but they appear to differ in their view of that input in telling ways. In psychodynamic thinking, the new relationship with the therapist serves as a safe place to revisit the memories attached to the emotions. In this way, the therapist and client remember, revisit, and reexperience old memories, and attach them to new insights while experiencing and observing emotion. In CBT, the input is novel and unexpected information to inhibit or compete with previous learning, whereas in EFT, it is the introduction of a newly evoked emotional response to an old stimulus situation through in-session psychodrama enactments or imagery. In all, emotion activation plays a vital role, but how they explain change clearly illuminates the difference among the theories because each sees the process of memory reconsolidation in terms of their own core theories of change. Unsurprisingly, they view the introduction of new experience as occurring relationally cognitive or emotionally. Next, we elaborate on each perspective's approach to working with emotion.

Psychodynamic Therapy

Psychoanalysis believes that when emotion becomes symbolized in awareness and is conscious, it enters the mainstream of representations, granting the psyche a certain degree of stability. When this does not occur, it manifests itself in psychopathology. The earliest mechanism of change was probably the notion of transforming what is unconscious into what is conscious. That has remained an influential thread over the years not only in the psychodynamic approach but in the other approaches. Over time, that notion developed into a distinction between emotional and intellectual insight. For early psychoanalysts, when an emotion was verbalized and attached to a set of ideas, it helped people to metabolize and regulate what they were feeling.

In psychodynamic work, emotion generally is brought alive in the transference. What happens in the relationship between a therapist and a client in the transference allows for the revisiting, reexperiencing, and reorganizing of early emotional experience. In this view, no single process provides as potent a ground for the transformation of emotions as the repetition of earlier emotional experiences in the transference. This repetition provides crucial material for psychoanalytic interpretations, but the client does not merely recollect these experiences or have insight but relives them emotionally, transferring many past feelings onto the present relationship. Observing, acknowledging, and "working in the transference" remain a central aspect of the psychodynamic psychotherapist's methods. In addition, transference work requires the therapist's careful attention to his or her own emotional reactions and the capacity to acknowledge countertransference feelings, such as anger, boredom, rejection, and many other emotional experiences that inform what is going on in the therapeutic relationship. The transferential relationship and the belief in the unconscious thus are central to all psychodynamic endeavors to this day. Mentalization-based therapy (MBT), however, represents a significant modification of the more traditional psychodynamic technique. Its approach to working with emotion integrates developmental psychoanalysis and psychology, and neuroscience and attachment theory. From this perspective, the work with emotion is a central part of a scaffolding process of treatment in which affect regulation is a central aim. In MBT, emotion is activated in the relationship and then mentalized. In addition to mentalization, according to Kernberg (1988), maturity is indicated by the simultaneous awareness or integration of positive and negative emotions with regard to self and others, and an increasing ability to become aware of and to tolerate negative emotions.

In psychoanalysis, a focus on emotional insight is valued over intellectual insight, indicating that a new understanding needs to be accompanied by affect. This is done through the therapist's use of a combination of understanding, clarification, interpretation, and confrontation. One of the ways in which psychodynamic therapists support the client is by offering a hypothesis to clients about the way in which they cope with difficult feelings and thoughts via the use of defense mechanisms that help people to keep feelings, such as anxiety, at bay or under control. Once the hypothesis is given, the therapist checks for the emotional reaction in the client: verbal and nonverbal, conscious and unconscious. One classic guideline is to offer linking interpretations, working with the notion of the conflict. When interpretations focus on affect, it involves linking impulse or affect with anxiety and defense. In PDT, emotional insight is privileged over intellectual insight. Expression of emotions is the gateway to future construction of narrative meaning.

Most of these methods are fairly unique to a psychodynamic approach. Although EFT and CBT recognize the importance of the therapeutic relationship and the development of a working alliance, they do not explicitly use a concept of transference. They do not work with the transferential aspects of the relationship as a way of activating emotion or producing change in interpersonal patterns. Kernberg's (1988) notion of integrating positive and negative affects has been assimilated into EFT as an important process; however, it is not worked with in the transference, and there is no clear use of this concept in CBT. Mentalizing is a process that is probably all the approaches use, but it has a different meaning for each. CBT refers to distancing from emotion by monitoring and awareness. EFT refers to symbolizing emotion in awareness and making sense of emotion. In PDT, mentalizing is achieved by supporting new ways of interaction within the therapeutic relationship that promote affect regulation and, as a result, the capacity to mentalize even when recalling or reexperiencing traumatic memories or experiences. In EFT, symbolizing is achieved through empathic exploration and conjecture, and client discovery (e.g., "So that left you feeling so alone, I imagine you felt so unfairly treated and angry") in CBT, mainly through self-recording or mindfulness training, via the therapist's linking cognition to affect (e.g., "You seemed angry just then. What just went through your mind?") to enhance awareness in the moment of emotions, cognitions, and behaviors, and their interrelationships. In MBT, affect focused means grasping the affect in the immediacy of the moment—not so much in its relation to the content of the session but primarily as it relates to what currently is happening between client and therapist. MBT posits that a brief intervention identifying the current feeling between client and therapist, naming shifts in affects verbally and nonverbally, is likely to propel a session forward more effectively than interpretation of the content of the narrative. However, many affective storms and explicit required acts of love and care often are presented in this context. The MBT therapist observes them and reflects aloud in a curious and genuine tone that he or she feels the client can access and take in so that the client can achieve containment and an increasing sense of agency over his or her thoughts and feelings.

Cognitive Behavior Therapy

The cognitive behavior approach assumes a learning model. As such, the goal of CBT is to facilitate new learning in the service of new and more adaptive behaviors and emotional responses, which leads to significant differences in the methods to achieve change from PDT and EFT. The main methods are rational restructuring, psychoeducation, behavioral experiments (BEs), and exposure. Psychoeducation, BEs, and exposure are more relevant to direct work with emotion. In cognitive restructuring, clients learn to identify and then evaluate the cognitions that influence their emotional responses, thereby learning to shift a disproportionate emotional response to a proportionate emotional response. Although clients may not deeply believe something new, cognitive restructuring can assist them to be curious about what they believe to be true. The result can be a host of other strategies, such as BEs or exposure, that can provide new and deep learning.

Emotion also can be involved in enhancing new learning, skill acquisition, and adaptive functioning. The most effective skills are those that clients can use in the presence of high negative emotion. CBT assists clients to not only learn new skills but also to gain confidence that they can use these skills when feeling intense emotion. For example, it is important that clients are confident that they can speak assertively when feeling frustrated or irritated with others. Therefore, CBT is not limited to clients' learning skills to downshift their emotional responses when it makes sense to do so. CBT also assists clients to gain confidence that interpersonal skills, for example, will work even when feeling anxious, angry, or guilty. Therefore, cognitive behavior therapists always organize skill acquisition to include active practice of the skill in the face of strong negative emotion.

In CBT, clients with emotional disorders are taught strategies to manage their emotional responses to enhance their day-to-day functioning, so methods often focus on regulation of emotion either directly, through, for example, relaxation strategies, or indirectly through, for instance, cognitive restructuring strategies. Psychoeducation is a key strategy that provides clients with correct or accurate information to counter the misinformation hypothesized to maintain their maladaptive emotional and behavioral responses. For example, a client with a cat phobia who avoids information about cats may lack accurate and helpful information about feline behavior. CBT includes many techniques to assist clients to attenuate their emotional responses when it makes good sense to do so. For example, self-recording teaches clients about emotions themselves, for example, that emotions rise and fall rather than increase indefinitely, and that emotions are linked to cognitions and can be tolerated. In addition, through BEs, psychoeducation, or cognitive restructuring, clients can gain, explore, and test the beliefs they may have about emotional responses.

Other strategies to distance from emotion and thereby indirectly regulate the emotional responses involve attention regulation. Focused attention calms the mind by returning attention repeatedly to a single object, such as the breath. Open monitoring turns attention to what arises, such as a body sensation or an emotion that the client then labels. Third-wave cognitive behavior therapies emphasize contextual and experiential strategies to enhance the effectiveness of traditional cognitive behavior interventions. Examples include mindfulness meditation to enable clients to accept and tolerate emotions, and loving-kindness and compassion meditations that add an element of care, comfort, and soothing awareness.

In contrast to managing emotions to downregulate them, emotional engagement during BEs and emotional arousal during exposure are viewed as critical in producing deep and lasting change. Therapist use these strategies, along with imagery, role plays, or two-chair dialogues, to activate emotion. In addition, enactments have a more widespread effect on cognition, emotion, and behavior than purely verbal information. The new learning that may occur through the process of activating may result from encoding memory among several modalities (e.g., visual, auditory, kinesthetic) that result in emotionally or experientially acquired information.

Exposure procedures are seen as being most effective if there is an adequate level of arousal. Exposure generally involves setting up a hierarchy of exposure tasks, ranked from least to most anxiety evoking, that target the client's key internal and external fear cues. The client then moves through the exposure process, beginning with exposure tasks that evoke relatively low fear responses. The hierarchy provides the client with some perceived "control" over the exposure process and thereby increases the client's willingness to approach rather than avoid the feared situations. CBT strives to teach clients skills both to regulate maladaptive emotional responses and to fully experience some emotions when avoiding them creates problems for those clients.

CBT includes a variety of strategies to enhance the willingness or motivation of clients to act in ways that often are contrary to the way they feel. For example, cognitive restructuring can introduce novel information that piques curiosity and encourages clients to question their assumptions and beliefs in new ways, as when a client says, "I've never thought about it that way before." Graduated exposure in steps increases a client's willingness to approach rather than avoid the feared situation or the emotional response itself because the path forward is clear, determined, and in the client's control. The new learning derived through these processes motivates clients to engage in more adaptive responses to problem situations. It is seen as essential that clients learn the importance of responding counterintuitively to their motivational tendencies. In emotional disorders, responding intuitively to fear (i.e., avoiding), to anger (i.e., striking out), and to sadness (i.e., withdrawing) maintains the problem but does not solve it.

Emotion-Focused Therapy

EFT works to access underlying primary emotions by use of empathic attunement to affect, guided attention, and stimulation using psychodramatic enactment and imagery, and, if the emotion is overwhelming, to regulate it by getting a working distance from it. The distinction between primary and secondary, and adaptive and maladaptive is important in guiding intervention. The aim is to first arrive at primary emotion by moving beyond secondary, reactive emotion, which obscures the primary emotion. Once the primary emotion is arrived at, if it is an adaptive emotion, it is used to promote change via its action tendency and need. If it is a painful maladaptive emotion, it is transformed by activating opposing adaptive emotions. A key method of activating opposing emotions is by helping people feel they deserve to have had previously unacknowledged, unmet needs met. The dynamic self-organizing emotion system then automatically reacts with adaptive anger, sadness, or compassion at not having had the need met.

In EFT, change thus is produced by transformation not by exposure. Third-wave cognitive behavior therapies have tended to construe EFT as exposing people to emotion, but in EFT, transformation goes beyond exposure. Transformation is not a reduction in symptomatic emotion or extinction of unwanted responses; rather, it is change of an underlying emotion scheme through new opposing experience and the creation of new states. In addition, transformation is not the development of a new counteractive learning that overrides or suppresses the unwanted response but is a process of synthesizing the old with the new to form a totally novel response (Greenberg, 2015). EFT adopts a developmental view in which it is not simply conditioned learning or the meaning of the stimulus that needs to be changed by exposure and learning of more adaptive associations. Instead, transformation is seen as occurring by the synthesis of schemes that occurs through the coactivation of old painful emotion and new emotional experience to the same stimulus situation. Whereas exposure focuses on reducing symptomatic emotions, such as traumatic fear and phobias, EFT focuses on the experience and expression of new primary adaptive emotion to undo maladaptive emotion; it does not focus on the extinction or habituation of secondary emotion. The distinctions between primary/secondary and adaptive/maladaptive emotion are important differences between exposure and transformation. EFT promotes transformation using four processes: (a) acceptance, (b) making sense of, (c) changing emotion with emotion, and (d) the creation of new meaning. This is more than mere exposure and involves the creation of new feeling states rather than a decrease in symptomatic emotion.

Simply helping people accept painful primary maladaptive emotions is not enough. EFT moves beyond acceptance to promote transformation and making sense of emotion, which involves the construction of new narratives. Change ultimately involves the integration of reason and emotion through making sense of emotion rather than reducing emotion.

The first process of change is the two-step sequence of moving from secondary reactive symptomatic emotions to primary emotions, for example, from secondary anxiety to underlying adaptive anger or maladaptive shame. Another change process is the two-step sequence of moving from maladaptive emotions to adaptive emotions, for example, from maladaptive fear to adaptive empowering anger. That process is greatly facilitated by accessing a feeling of having deserved to have the unmet need in the emotion (in this case, the need for safety in the fear) met. In adaptive emotion, the need and action tendency provide meaning and orientation. In maladaptive emotions, it is a sense of entitlement to the unmet need and validation of that by the therapist that facilitates access to the adaptive emotions of assertive anger, or the sadness of grief, or compassion for the self for not having had the need met. This access to the need mobilizes a sense of agency in the person having approach action tendencies that undo the withdrawal action tendencies in the maladaptive feelings (often of shame and fear). It is the three-step sequence of moving from secondary emotion to core painful maladaptive, to adaptive emotion (Greenberg, 2002; Greenberg & Paivio, 1997) that is important and has been shown to lead to change in EFT (Herrmann, Greenberg, & Auszra, 2016; Pascual-Leone & Greenberg, 2007).

EFT works toward viscerally felt emotion to promote access to action tendency, and need activation and change is seen as occurring by way of transformation rather than by exposure, the understanding of patterns, learning through conditioning, skill training, or psychoeducation. EFT does not direct intervention toward the modification of the symptom; rather, the focus is on accessing emotion that underlies the symptom. And instead of understanding emotion, regulating it, or distancing from it, EFT accesses it for its information and action tendency. Once accepted and experienced, core feelings need to be processed according to the six EFT principles of emotional change (see the section Principles of Emotional Change in Chapter 4).

Comparison

How do the three approaches compare in their methods of working with emotion? There appears to be little similarity in actual methods at the level of technique. Psychoanalytic use of transference as a central method is not used in CBT or EFT. CBT's use of cognitive restructuring, BEs, or exposure is not used by psychoanalysis or EFT. EFT's use of activating new emotions to change old emotions by use of chair dialogues is not used by PDT or CBT. Chair dialogues have been incorporated in CBT but are viewed as a method to activate emotion in the service of developing new and more adaptive beliefs. All approaches use some form of psychoeducation, but not as explicitly as in CBT. The approaches probably are most different in their use of psychodynamic technique. EFT falls somewhere in between the other two approaches in terms of use of psychodynamic technique. BEs could be seen as bearing some similarity to transference enactments and empty chair dialogues with significant others in that all promote new experience; however, these methods clearly differ in significant ways and are based on different underlying ideas of how they promote change. There is commonality at the level of midlevel change principles, such as new experience and feedback, but difference at the specific lower level of action or technique.

All traditions consider approaching dreaded emotions—whether referred to as overcoming avoidance or defenses, or the disowning of emotion—to be useful. Furthermore, all view acceptance of emotion as curative. Verbal labeling of emotion—whether called awareness, mentalizing, symbolizing, or experiencing—similarly is seen as helpful. In addition, all three approaches use emotion regulation strategies, such as breathing, self-compassion, or self-soothing, or taking an observer's distance on one's emotions, although emotion regulation is spelled out more explicitly in both CBT and EFT.

A big potential area of overlap is activation of emotion and emotional arousal, which frequently is seen as synonymous with exposure. However, this apparent commonality bears closer inspection. In CBT, exposure involves repeatedly facing a feared object or situation to develop new learning that clients can use to inhibit the old and maladaptive learning. In PDT, emotion arousal is viewed predominantly as occurring in the transference and as embedding insight more deeply into a newly formed narrative, whereas in EFT, arousal is viewed as making the emotion open to transformation by the input of new emotion. In CBT, activation of core beliefs results in emotional arousal and, in this aroused state, new information is acquired that then forms new beliefs. Once formed, the new beliefs dampen arousal by inhibiting old maladaptive learning. These views all bear some similarity, but the type of arousal from relational experience with the psychodynamic therapist, such as fear of abandonment or criticism, is rather different from the type of arousal referred to in CBT, such as phobias or trauma. The type of arousal in EFT bears some similarity to PDT, but it occurs not predominantly in the relationship with the therapist but with imaginal dialogues with primary attachment figures in an empty chair. The EFT notion of transformation through emotion arousal is different from CBT's view. In CBT, the new information is new cognitive information that the belief was not rational or adaptive; in EFT, though, it is a new emotion. The more recent view in CBT that change in exposure involves new learning that can inhibit old learning (Craske et al., 2008) rather than habituation has some of the same elements of a new developmental emotional experience in psychodynamic work and changing emotion with emotion in EFT. Again, though, there are differences at a more process level. In psychodynamic work is exploration of new emotions in the context of new interpersonal experience; in CBT, new cognitive learning; and in EFT, new emotional experience.

Imagery probably is used in all approaches to help access emotion and promote change. In psychoanalysis, imagery is presumably most used to explore the unconscious, particularly in the exploration of dreams and day dreams.

CBT uses imagery in structured ways to expose people to feared situations and also possibly as imaginal experiments to promote reentry into painful memories. EFT similarly uses imagery to imaginatively reenter past situations and in chair dialogues, which themselves involve a combination of enactment and imagery.

Neither psychodynamic work nor EFT uses extra therapy experiences to create new expectation challenging experiences, although EFT uses homework to increase awareness and/or practice new emotional experiences that already have occurred in the session. CBT encourages the use of strategies that counter emotional avoidance, such as to approach a feared object or situation, or to engage in pleasant activities to counter the loss of motivation that accompanies depression. Neither psychodynamic nor EFT attempts to override intuitive emotional responses with deliberate will and would almost view it as countertherapeutic and as enhancing coping but not promoting deeper level change.

Both CBT and psychodynamic work focus on the maladaptive nature of emotion and its potential disruptiveness, particularly when clients cannot regulate their emotional responses to be effective in their lives. Both approaches emphasize the management of problematic emotions that overwhelm clients or lead to disorganization. EFT, on the other hand, does not focus centrally on dysregulated emotion as the site of change but views dysregulated emotion as being a reaction to, and obscuring, underlying emotions that generate the dysregulation; it focuses on accessing these underlying emotions. Psychoanalysis also focuses on underlying factors but tends to not explicitly conceive of these underlying causes as emotion.

As a quick way of comparing approaches to working with emotion, each author commented on what an emotion signaled to them in a common in-session situation and provided an example of a short response to the emotion. Of course, a therapist's way of responding would vary according to type of client, context, stage of therapy, and other factors.

The situation was taken to be one with an average client who is dealing with general depression and anxiety in the middle of therapy. The situation is one in which a client's eyes fill with tears of sadness as she talks about a past event, and her voice begins to tremble slightly.

In Chapter 2, Malberg suggests that emotion might signal to the therapist a communication regarding an interaction between the client and the therapist, one that might represent the return of a repressed memory attached to a specific feeling or a way of coping with conflictual or painful thoughts or feelings. In this context, a psychodynamic therapist might invite the client to pay attention to the affective shifts in the session. For example: "I noticed that when I began to ask you more about the situation with your sister, you became tearful and your voice became softer." The psychodynamic therapist tries to stay with the new emerging feeling and pace his or her next intervention while trying to link it to the process taking place in the session or to information shared in the past. For example: "The way you seemed to be feeling right now reminds me of your description of your reaction to your dad's anger when you were little." The first intervention focuses on the here and now of what psychodynamic psychotherapist call the transference; it also invites the client to self-observe and stay with the feeling. By inviting the client to stay with the feeling, the therapist intends to create a space in which emotion and memory can be linked and observed. With this intervention, the psychodynamic therapist attempts to achieve a balance between the cognitive and the affective in the client. The psychodynamic psychotherapist also listens to and names the defensive use of emotion. For example: "We were talking about the difficulties with your daughter, yet you keep letting me know how relaxed and happy you are. I feel a bit confused. I wonder if talking about this feels too painful at times." In summary, the psychodynamic psychotherapist addresses emotion implicitly by trying to "meet the client where they are" with the therapist's tone of voice, the speed of his or her speech, and other nonverbal ways of connecting around emotion The therapist explicitly listens to emotion as a communication about the here and now of the therapeutic relationship (e.g., "It seems like my comment made you a bit defensive") and the past (i.e., holder of memory).

In Chapter 3, Tompkins offers that in CBT sessions, emotion signals to the cognitive therapist a clinically relevant thought or belief on which the therapist then focuses. A watchful cognitive therapist might ask, "I see that you're feeling something right now. What went through your head just before you thought that?" In CBT, emotion signals cognition and, typically, a relevant cognition to target for change. Often these cognitions are automatic thoughts, such as "Nothing will ever change for me" and "What if this time I have a serious illness?" First, the CBT therapist links cognition to emotion and then emotion to behavior: "So, when you thought, 'Nothing will ever change for me,' you felt sad and then pulled the covers over your head." Once the therapist makes this link, the therapist might invite the client to examine the thought through collaborative empiricism, the process of gathering evidence to confirm or disconfirm a prediction, assumption, or interpretation.

In Chapter 4, Greenberg sees emotions as providing information about whether something is good or bad for a person—whether one's survival or well-being needs have been met or not. He suggests that an EFT therapist might respond in a compassionate voice: "Yeah, so painful, so sad. Can you just stay with this feeling, pay attention to what's it like in your body?" Then, assuming that the client remains silent and focuses inward for a while, the therapist, after a few moments, would say "What are the tears saying? Can you give them some words?" The intention is first to validate and convey empathy; second, to guide attention to the bodily felt sense; and, third, to help the client symbolize the feeling in words. The client may then say something like, "Just such a loss" or "It just leaves me feeling so abandoned." The therapist will then possibly conjecture about feeling empty inside or feeling so alone to pick up on the idiosyncratic meaning for the client. These conjectures help the client make explicit the implicit evaluation in the emotion and ultimately to get to the unmet need. Once the unmet need in the painful emotion is accessed, new emotions emerge and help transform the old painful maladaptive emotion.

The preceding snapshots of how different therapists might deal with the emergence in a session of the type of emotion depicted earlier highlight that the therapists of different orientations, consistent with their theories, respond somewhat differently. All take emotions as important, but how they work with them differs. PDT treats emotion as signaling a relational reaction and links the emotion to the process taking place in the session while listening for the unconscious processes. CBT sees emotion as a response to cognition and links the emotion to cognition. EFT sees emotion as containing information and needs, and rather than linking the emotion to something else, focuses directly on emotional experience as an intelligent language that is saying something important.

CONCLUSION

What is helpful in therapy is having another person, or a part of the self, who can listen to one's emotional state and help manage it. Psychotherapy of all persuasions seek to provide an environment of safety in which expression, witnessing, and processing of difficult emotion take place. Different forms of empathy, a variety of types of interpretation, and different methods of adaptive reasoning are used by all approached, to differing degrees, in working with emotion. In this chapter, we have attempted to compare how the different approaches think about and actually work with emotion in therapy, over and above the use of the more generic common factor skills.

In this endeavor, we have seen that similarities and differences exist in how different approaches view emotion and emotional change, as well as the different methods they might use to achieve change. In some instances, emotion is seen as the independent variable that can be worked with directly and changed. This probably is the oldest method in which catharsis has been considered as leading to change. However, that view fell out of favor and became seen as mere catharsis and as ventilation. With the proverbial swing of the pendulum, it returned later; now, emotional arousal and expression has become a newly recognized, possibly underlying, factor of all psychopathology and change. Emotion also can be viewed as the dependent variable that is changed by changing other processes. That certainly was the major initial offering of a cognitive therapy approach: that rational change can produce emotional change. Then, there is the view of emotion as a correlate of change as a necessary accompaniment of the processes of understanding, the construction of new narratives, or a change in beliefs or insight. All approaches, in part, hold this view of emotion as a correlate of change; PDT probably holds it most strongly, seeing emotion as a correlate of such processes as insight, mentalizing, increased self-observation, and transference.

One of the added complexities of comparing approaches to therapeutic change is being clear on what type of change is being focused on. Two important types of change seem to run throughout the chapters. Is the change a change in coping in which some form of relationship or coping skills are provided to help people feel better and provide symptom relief? Or, is the change aimed at more underlying structural change in personality, which is thought to be the cause of the symptom? In line with this emotional development that occurs by more automatic, unconscious synthesis, processes can be contrasted with conscious learning that involves the acquisition of knowledge or skills through skill training or psychoeducation. Learning of this type also focuses on the strengthening of correct responses and the weakening of incorrect responses, as well as the addition of new information to memory. Development involves a different type of change in which a person's basic modes of processing changes, so symptomatic reactions change without being modified directly. This difference reflects the age-old debate in psychotherapy that compares insight versus behavior change, which, in many ways, is now being repeated here in the domain of emotion. Coping and transformation are different, but both seem important. Questions to consider in this regard, regardless of approach, are these: When do I help people with coping skills? When do I go for transformation? More specifically, the questions become: When do I regulate emotion and activate it? When do I accept it and when do I change it? These questions require further investigation. In addition, it is not only what therapists do when working with emotion but when they do it. Further study and clarification of these emotion-focused questions, by the direct study of emotion in psychotherapy, will ultimately lead to a greater understanding and improved therapeutic effectiveness in working with emotion.

REFERENCES

Beck, A. T. (1996). Beyond belief: A theory of modes, personality, and psychopathology. In P. M. Salkovskis (Ed.), *Frontiers of cognitive therapy* (pp. 1–25). New York, NY: Guilford Press.

Craske, M. G., Kircanski, K., Zelikowsky, M., Mystkowski, J., Chowdhury, N., & Baker, A. (2008). Optimizing inhibitory learning during exposure therapy. *Behaviour Research and Therapy, 46*, 5–27. http://dx.doi.org/10.1016/j.brat.2007.10.003

Goldfried, M. R. (1980). Toward the delineation of therapeutic change principles. *American Psychologist, 35*, 991–999. http://dx.doi.org/10.1037/0003-066X.35.11.991

Greenberg, L. S. (2002). Integrating an emotion-focused approach to treatment into psychotherapy integration. *Journal of Psychotherapy Integration, 12*, 154–189. http://dx.doi.org/10.1037/1053-0479.12.2.154

Greenberg, L. S. (2011). *Emotion-focused therapy.* Washington, DC: American Psychological Association.

Greenberg, L. S. (2015). *Emotion-focused therapy: Coaching clients to work through their feelings* (2nd ed.). Washington, DC: American Psychological Association. http://dx.doi.org/10.1037/14692-000

Greenberg, L. S., & Paivio, S. C. (1997). *Working with emotions in psychotherapy.* New York, NY: Guilford Press.

Grencavage, L. M., & Norcross, J. C. (1990). Where are the commonalities among the therapeutic common factors? *Professional Psychology, Research and Practice, 21*, 372–378. http://dx.doi.org/10.1037/0735-7028.21.5.372

Herrmann, I. R., Greenberg, L. S., & Auszra, L. (2016). Emotion categories and patterns of change in experiential therapy for depression. *Psychotherapy Research, 26*, 178–195. http://dx.doi.org/10.1080/10503307.2014.958597

Kernberg, O. F. (1988). Psychic structure and structural change: An ego psychology-object relations theory viewpoint. *Journal of the American Psychoanalytic Association, 36S*(Suppl.), 315–337.

Maslow, A. H. (1962). *Toward a psychology of being.* Princeton, NJ: Van Nostrand.

Nadel, L., & Bohbot, V. (2001). Consolidation of memory. *Hippocampus, 11*, 56–60. http://dx.doi.org/10.1002/1098-1063(2001)11:1<56::AID-HIPO1020>3.0.CO;2-O

Nader, K., Schafe, G. E., & LeDoux, J. E. (2000). Fear memories require protein synthesis in the amygdala for reconsolidation after retrieval. *Nature, 406*, 722–726. http://dx.doi.org/10.1038/35021052

Pascual-Leone, A., & Greenberg, L. S. (2007). Emotional processing in experiential therapy: Why "the only way out is through." *Journal of Consulting and Clinical Psychology, 75*, 875–887. http://dx.doi.org/10.1037/0022-006X.75.6.875

Perls, F. S. (1969). *Gestalt therapy verbatim.* Lafayette, CA: Real People Press.

Rogers, C. R. (1951). *Client-centered therapy: Its current practice, implications, and theory.* Boston, MA: Houghton Mifflin.

Whelton, W. J. (2004). Emotional processes in psychotherapy: Evidence across therapeutic modalities. *Clinical Psychology & Psychotherapy, 11*, 58–71. http://dx.doi.org/10.1002/cpp.392

INDEX

ABOUT THE AUTHORS

Leslie S. Greenberg, PhD, is Distinguished Research Professor Emeritus of Psychology at York University in Toronto, Canada. He conducts a private practice for individuals and couples, and trains people in emotion-focused approaches. Dr. Greenberg coauthored the following books: with Jeremy D. Safran, *Emotion in Psychotherapy: Affect, Cognition, and the Process of Change* (1987); with Susan M. Johnson, *Emotionally Focused Therapy for Couples* (1988); with Rhonda N. Goldman, *Emotion-Focused Couples Therapy: The Dynamics of Emotion, Love, and Power* (2008); and with Shari M. Geller, *Therapeutic Presence: A Mindful Approach to Effective Therapy* (2012). He authored *Emotion-Focused Therapy* (2011, 2017) and *Emotion-Focused Therapy: Coaching Clients to Work Through Their Feelings* (2002, 2015). More recently, he coauthored with Rhonda N. Goldman *Case Formulation in Emotion-Focused Therapy: Co-Creating Clinical Maps for Change* (2015); and with Jeanne C. Watson, *Emotion-Focused Therapy of Generalized Anxiety* (2017). He has received the Senior Distinguished Research Career Award of the Society for Psychotherapy Research, Carl Rogers Award of the American Psychological Association (APA), and Award for Distinguished Professional Contributions to Applied Research of APA. He also received the Canadian Psychological Association Award for Distinguished Contributions to

197

Psychology as a Profession. Dr. Greenberg is a past president of the Society for Psychotherapy Research.

Norka T. Malberg, PsyD, is an assistant clinical professor at the Yale Child Study Center, Yale School of Medicine, in New Haven, Connecticut, where she also is in private practice as a child, adolescent, and adult psychoanalyst. Dr. Malberg is a member of the Western New England Psychoanalytic Society and the Contemporary Freudian Society. She also is coeditor of the Lines of Development book series by Routledge, for which she coedited the first book, *The Anna Freud Tradition* in 2012. She is on the editorial board of *The Psychoanalytic Study of the Child* and the *Journal of Infant, Child, and Adolescent Psychotherapy*. Dr. Malberg is the coeditor of the Children and Adolescent sections of the *Psychodynamic Diagnostic Manual—2nd Edition (PDM-2)*. In 2017, she coauthored *Mentalization-Based Treatment for Children: A Time-Limited Approach*. Recently, she was featured as guest master clinician illustrating mentalization-based therapy techniques in the American Psychological Association's Systems of Psychotherapy Video Series. Originally from San Juan, Puerto Rico, Dr. Malberg lectures and publishes on a variety of topics from a developmental psychoanalytic perspective in the United States, Europe, and Latin America. She actively works as consultant to community-based service organizations regarding applications of psychodynamic theory and technique to outreach settings.

Michael A. Tompkins, PhD, ABPP, is codirector of the San Francisco Bay Area Center for Cognitive Therapy, and assistant clinical professor of psychology at the University of California at Berkeley. He also is board certified in behavioral and cognitive psychology. He is a diplomate of the Academy of Cognitive Therapy and an adjunct faculty member of the Beck Institute for Cognitive Behavior Therapy in Bala Cynwyd, Pennsylvania. Dr. Tompkins is the author or coauthor of articles and chapters on cognitive behavior therapy and related topics. He has written nine books, including *Essential Components of Cognitive Behavior Therapy for Depression* (2001); *Using Homework in Psychotherapy: Strategies, Guidelines, and Forms* (2004; and *My Anxious Mind: A Teen's Guide to Managing Anxiety and Panic* (2009). Dr. Tompkins is a distinguished clinical instructor at the University of California at Berkeley, and, in 2013, received the Lifetime Achievement Award from the Mental Health Association of San Francisco for his contributions to the understanding of hoarding. He serves on the advisory board of the American Psychological Association's Magination Press, which publishes psychology-based books on topics of concern to children and teenagers. He also provides evidence-based treatments for adults, adolescents, and children.